SSSP

Springer
Series in
Social
Psychology

SSSP

Jerald Greenberg
Robert Folger

Controversial Issues in Social Research Methods

Springer-Verlag New York Berlin Heidelberg
London Paris Tokyo

Jerald Greenberg
Faculty of Management
    and Human Resources
The Ohio State University
Columbus, Ohio 43210-1399
USA

Robert Folger
A.B. Freeman School of Business
Tulane University
New Orleans, Louisiana 70118-5669
USA

Library of Congress Cataloging-in-Publication Data
Greenberg, Jerald.
    Controversial issues in social research methods.
    (Springer series in social psychology)
    Bibliography: p.
    Includes indexes.
    1. Social psychology—Research. I. Folger, Robert.
II. Title. III. Series.
HM251.67517 1988   302'.072   87-23237

Typeset by Best-set Typesetter Ltd., Hong Kong.
Printed and bound by R.R. Donnelley & Sons, Harrisonburg, Virginia.
Printed in the United States of America.

9 8 7 6 5 4 3 2 1

ISBN 0-387-96571-8 Springer-Verlag New York Berlin Heidelberg
ISBN 3-540-96571-8 Springer-Verlag Berlin Heidelberg New York

This book is dedicated to our families,
especially our wives—Carolyn and Pam—
and to our students,
who have gently taught us
that the quality of the answers we attain
is only as good as the questions we ask

Preface

It is often said that one of the key determinants of a book's worth is the extent to which it fulfills the reader's expectations. As such, we welcome this opportunity to help formulate the expectations of our readers, to express our view of what this book is and what it is not. We believe that fully appreciating this volume requires understanding its mission and how it differs from that of other books on research methodology.

We have *not* prepared a primer on research techniques. We offer no "how-to" guides for researchers—nothing on how to conduct interviews, how to design studies, or how to analyze data. We also have *not* prepared a partisan platform documenting "our way" of thinking about research. Very few, if any, attempts at proselytizing may be found in these pages. What we have done, we believe, is to bring together a number of recurring controversial issues about social psychological research—issues that have divided professionals, puzzled students, and filled the pages of our journals. Few scholars have missed reports arguing the sides of various methodological controversies, such as those surrounding the merits or shortcomings of field research in comparison to laboratory research, the use of role playing as an alternative for studies involving deception, or the value of informed consent procedures, to name only a few examples. Our aim in preparing this volume has been to organize and summarize the salient aspects of these and other important controversial issues.

The benefits of presenting various ideas about research methodology as controversies are many. For one, we believe that our direct, point-by-point comparisons of various aspects of controversial issues captures the excitement of the research craft that is usually missing from less dialectic presentations. From a more pedagogical perspective, we also believe that a true appreciation of the merits of any one approach to research can best be derived by comparing it to other approaches. The series of choices that fill the researcher's agenda can best be made by fully recognizing the relative strengths and weaknesses of the various alternatives. Only then will it be possible for researchers to appreciate the contribution of the research process in limiting and expanding the answers to their questions.

To realize these benefits, we have purposely avoided offering our opinions of *the* right answer. We hope our biases are more clearly revealed in the topics we selected to present than in the presentations themselves. In this regard we have tried to play the role of reporters of the research scene—delving into the issues, looking for all facets of all aspects of the controversies, but not offering our own opinions. This was difficult at times, and even the most nonpartisan of reporters cannot help but sometimes slant the presentation so that the conclusion is biased. Readers will, no doubt, occasionally be aware of such instances on our parts. In most places, however, the biases we present represent our report of the biases of the field. If all sides do not appear to be equally well represented, or if one position appears to be favored, this is probably an indication of our reading of the status of the field. Accurate reporting of biased opinions presented without prejudice, we believe, can be especially useful to those who wish to add their voices to the controversies in future generations. It was out of respect for this "chronicling" mission that we have purposely kept our own voices out of the cacophony.

We cannot have helped, of course, avoiding bias in our selection of the methodological controversies on which to report. Sharing this bias is simple; we have selected controversies relevant to the social psychological investigator. This is not to imply that our work would not be useful as well to social scientists in other disciplines, such as sociology, business, communications, and social work. Indeed, we believe it would. However, we feel that it was only by narrowing our focus that a maximally useful volume could be prepared. Social psychologists have written in great detail about their methods and appear to be in a state of uncertainty and transition with respect to them. As a result we believe that social psychology has offered us a very rich domain from which to sample, and we hope that our analyses may prove it to be an appreciative benefactor.

Our guiding philosophy in organizing each chapter was to present the material as logically and clearly as possible. The plan we imposed proved useful for guiding our presentation of the material. For each topic we (1) give a brief historical introduction, (2) provide an orienting description and definitions of the basic aspects of the topic, (3) present arguments surrounding the controversies, and (4) conclude by reviewing the current status of the controversy. Using this format as a template helped us to capture the flavor of each topic and the controversies each has spawned.

The ordering of chapters roughly parallels the ordering of issues as they are usually confronted by investigators. As such, we present issues germane to planning research strategy, conducting the research itself, and post-experimental issues. Although this ordering appears logical to us, we recognize that readers may prefer to reorder their forays into the topics we present, or to selectively pick and choose among them to suit their purposes. With this in mind, we have attempted to prepare a work whose individual chapters can be useful standing on their own. Although we have attempted to integrate the material to form a "whole" book, one that is greater than the sum of its parts, we have also organized, cross-referenced, headed, and indexed the parts so they can be readily extracted by the busy scholar.

The target audience for this book is composed of professional social psychological researchers and those who aspire to be among them. Accordingly, we believe this volume will ultimately prove useful as both a professional reference and an upper-level text. In so doing we have assumed that the reader is already familiar with the basic tools of social research methodology. Making this assumption allowed us to dive immediately into the rich and diverse material at hand without first having to provide an orientation to the more rudimentary prerequisites.

Chronicling methodological issues in even a narrowly defined area is no easy task. Fortunately, our efforts were not solitary; we were greatly aided by those whose efforts cut ours down to manageable proportions. First, we wish to thank our colleagues, whose patient comments on drafts of our manuscript provided invaluable assistance: Frank Dane, Justin L'Ecrivesse, and Bert Moore. We also wish to thank our past and present students for their assistance as research librarians: Erica Bliss, Mark McDonald, Bryant Morgan, Suzyn Ornstein, Kye Song, and Mark Winston. The typing and editing assistance of the following persons was also greatly appreciated: Roy Cromer, Clara Holmes, Ophelia Jackson, Loretta Venable, and Ann Wassel. Of course, we also wish to acknowledge the support of the editorial and production staff at Springer-Verlag for their fine professional work. Finally, our acknowledgments would not be complete without thanking our families for their support, encouragement, patience, and forbearance throughout this project.

Columbus, Ohio   Jerald Greenberg
New Orleans, Louisiana   Robert Folger

Contents

Chapter 1
The Scientific Status of Social Psychology

Modern social psychology is characterized by a fundamental commitment to the experimental method (Aronson, Brewer, & Carlsmith, 1985; Aronson & Carlsmith, 1968). However, faith in the experimental method, and confidence in the prospects for a "mainstream" social psychology grounded by it, have been subjected to tremors of doubt. Indeed, it is easy to identify a specific period—the 1960s—during which the legacy of experimental social psychology was first challenged in dramatic fashion. The repercussions of that challenge to orthodoxy constitute much of the subject matter of this book, and as a precursor, the nature of that challenge is reviewed in this chapter.

An overview of these effects can be achieved by placing them in historical context; that is, by contrasting the attitudes of social psychologists before this challenge with their attitudes in its aftermath. Elms (1975), for example, has offered the following description of the prechallenge attitudes.

> Social psychologists once knew who they were and where they were going. The field's major scientific problems were obvious, and means to solve them were readily available. Particularly during World War II and the two subsequent decades, the total number of social psychologists increased rapidly, exciting new research discoveries were often reported, and theoretical developments seemed to promise dramatic advances in the understanding of human behavior. (p. 967)

Elms then went on to contrast this period of exuberant enthusiasm with the state of the discipline as he saw it in 1975.

> The *Handbook's* second edition [Lindzey & Aronson, 1968, *Handbook of Social Psychology*] may now be seen as the high-water mark in social psychological sanquinity. During the past decade, beginning even before the revised *Handbook's* publication, many social psychologists appear to have lost not only their enthusiasm but also their sense of direction and their faith in the discipline's future. Whether they are experiencing an identity crisis, a paradigmatic crisis, or a crisis of confidence, most seem agreed that *a crisis is at hand*. (p. 967, emphasis added)

Now that more than a decade has passed since Elm's remarks, we feel that social psychologists should be in a good position to take stock regarding the crisis he described. We believe that the so-called "crisis" has given rise to a number of controversies. We do not attempt to propose resolutions in this volume; rather, our stock-taking consists off systematically reporting on the well-articulated positions that have emerged surrounding these controversies.

As others have suggested (e.g., Minton, 1984; Pepitone, 1976; Rosnow, 1981), these controversies have revolved around three general aspects of social psychological inquiry. One of these concerns the *moral health* of the discipline. Are established practices in social psychology on a sound ethical footing? Do we need further development of alternative methodologies that are more ethically palatible than those currently being most heavily used? (See Chapter 3.)

A second set of issues is somewhat more narrowly focused on *limitations of laboratory experiments* (see Chapter 4). As such, these issues might be considered the most purely methods-focused of the types of concerns that have been raised, although we believe that all three areas of concern have methodological implications. At issue, for example, is the extent to which the role of subject in an experiment introduces special forms of bias and what steps might be required to correct for such bias (see Chapter 6). Similar questions have also been raised concerning the role of experimenter (see Chapter 7).

A third set of issues emphasizes the broadest questions of all, those pertaining to the *philosophy of science* and fundamental presuppositions of the field. One form in which these questions have appeared is the focus of this chapter. This form has been aptly characterized by Minton (1984, p. 31).

> A common theme among these metatheoretical criticisms is the discipline's failure to deal with the political, ideological, and historical contexts of social behavior (e.g., Gergen, 1973; Moscovici, 1972; Sampson, 1978). Furthermore, these critics contend that the sociohistorical vacuum surrounding social psychology is due to the field's commitment to a positivistic conception of science in which facts and truths are viewed as abstract, general, and transhistorical. A paradigm shift is therefore advocated—a shift to a conception of social psychology in which facts and truths are embedded within concrete sociohistorical settings (see Gergen, 1982; Gergen & Morawski, 1980).

The thrust of this criticism has taken other forms as well, however, and these are the foci of other subsequent chapters. That is, the concern about context-specific knowledge and limited generalizability has also led to calls for social psychologists to move out of the lab and into the field (see Chapter 4). However, our interest in the present chapter concerns issues involving basic philosophical premises. Our focal question is: *In what sense, if any, can social psychology be considered a scientific discipline?*

Dimensions of the Controversy

A key charge leveled against social psychology is that the discipline has failed to produce socially relevant knowledge. As Minton (1984) has noted,

> It was not until the 1960s—a time of social upheaval when it seemed appro-
> priate that social psychology should have something to offer—that questions
> began to be raised about the relevance of social psychology to the real world.
> The current metatheoretical issues are being raised against the backdrop of a
> field that has not lived up to its earlier postwar promise. (p. 39)

We mention "root failings" such as this last one in particular because they seem to constitute a latent content underlying what might not otherwise be apparent in the manifest structure of the "dimensions of the controversy" that follows. These dimensions, as we outline them, derive from responses to positions advocated by Kenneth Gergen (e.g., 1973). Thus, whatever conclusions the reader will reach regarding various aspects of the controversy, we feel it is important to recognize Gergen's overarching goal of pushing social psychology to develop theoretical accounts and methodological approaches that have "the capacity to challenge the guiding assumptions of the culture, to raise fundamental questions regarding contemporary social life, to foster reconsideration of that which is 'taken for granted,' and thereby to furnish new alteratives for social action" (Gergen, 1978b, p. 1346).

The controversy we are considering in this chapter was initially sparked by Gergen's (1973) article on "Social Psychology as History." The best single source for a systematic statement of his position is in book-length form (Gergen, 1982), although other articles and chapters he has written provide comprehensive accounts for various aspects of that position (e.g., Gergen, 1976, 1977, 1978a, 1978b, 1979, 1980a, 1980b; Gergen & Bassechs, 1980; Gergen & Benack, 1984; Gergen & Gergen, 1983; Gergen & Morawski, 1980). Critics, defenders, and commentators on Gergen's position also have been numerous, as even a partial listing indicates (e.g., Buss, 1975; Forsyth, 1976; Greenwald, 1976b; Harris, 1976; Hendrick, 1976; Manis, 1975, 1976; Schlenker, 1974, 1976; Secord, 1976; M.B. Smith, 1976a; Thorngate, 1975, 1976).

Transhistorical Laws and Invariant Processes

Although we cannot do full justice to the richness of the arguments put forward by Gergen and this assembled multitude, we can begin by noting that virtually all of the writings just cited have touched on one central claim implied in the title of Gergen's original article—namely, the claim that "the study of social psychology is primarily an historical undertaking...[i.e., one providing only] a systematic account of contemporary affairs" (Gergen, 1973, p. 316). This proclaimed identification of social psychology with the discipline of history denies the possibility of developing explanations that would allow predictions in the contemporary historical epoch to be based on a accumulated evidence from events in preceding historical epochs. Rather, the "historical perishability of social knowledge" (Gergen, 1976, p. 373) is such that just as historians can only aspire to unique understandings of each historical event, so social psychologists must be content to enrich their understanding of the current scene without being able to establish scientific laws of social behavior.

In providing at this point only a brief overview for the basis of Gergen's claims, let us single out the role of "facts" as potential building blocks for the establishment of lawlike empirical generalizations. Since Gergen's account precludes such generalizations from the province of social psychology, it should come as no surprise that he is suspicious about the quality of the facts from which the discipline must attempt to do its work. Social psychology, Gergen (1973, p. 310) says, "deals with facts that are largely nonrepeatable and which fluctuate markedly over time."

> Principles of human interaction cannot readily be developed over time because the facts on which they are based do not generally remain stable. Knowledge cannot accumulate in the usual scientific sense because such knowledge does not generally transcend its historical boundaries. (p. 310)

The search for transhistorical laws, in other words, is futile. It should be abandoned in favor of alternative endeavors, such as attempts to sensitize decision makers about the multitude of factors operating to influence social behavior. Theory and research in social psychology, that is, should be viewed as "informing the inquirer of a number of possible occurrences, thus expanding his sensitivities and readying him for more rapid accommodation to environmental change...[providing] conceptual and methodological tools with which more discerning judgments can be made" (Gergen, 1973, p. 317).

If transhistorical social laws are impossible by virtue of the instability of social facts, then social psychology will inevitably be mistaken in making the assumption of underlying regularity that we have seen is crucial to inductive confirmation. Gergen's thesis to that effect, as well as his arguments and examples offered in support of that thesis (to be examined in more detail subsequently), quickly drew a response from several quarters.

One thrust of that response was to suggest that perhaps Gergen had looked for regularities in all the wrong places. Rather than looking for regularities manifested in people's behavior across different situations, for example, perhaps regularity could be inferred only be positing the existence of an underlying psychological process (whose operation would manifest itself in different forms of behavior under different circumstances). As Manis (1976, p. 431) put it, "processes that controlled social behavior might be relatively stable, although they might operate on an endless variety of social contents, to yield the instabilities that we often observe as we carry out our studies in varying times and places."

An alternative way of thinking about the search for transhistorical laws, therefore, is in terms of a commitment to conceptualizing invariant processes. Such psychological constructs are not themselves observable, but empirical research can be directed toward studying their (presumed) observable consequences. This approach has the effect of shifting attention from the role of facts to the role of theoretical abstractions, which we will later explore as another key issue in the Gergen debate.

Differences Between Natural Science and Social Science

A second dimension of the controversy has involved comparisons of the social science (social psychology being a useful exemplar) with the natural or physical sciences. The alleged absence of transhistorical laws and invariant processes in social psychology, for example, is compared infavorably to the stable phenomena with which the natural sciences deal and the durability of research findings in that realm: "In contrast to the mighty oaks of the natural sciences, one might describe the social sciences as a sprawling thicket...the sociobehavioral sciences seem to have no clear and dependable product" (Gergen, 1982, p. 3). But, in comprehensively examining possible differences between the natural and social sciences, Gergen's analysis pushes beyond the issue of regularity that we have identified as the first dimension of the controversy.

As evidenced at various points throughout his writings, Gergen (e.g., 1982) recognizes that regularities may be to some extent in the eye of the beholder. Thus, while he does expend some effort in trying to marshall evidence that such regularities are nonexistent in social psychology, he does not rest his case on that evidence alone. Rather, his broader treatment of the differences between natural and social science is intended to provide a variety of reasons *why* the search for regularities in the latter is such a much more difficult (and perhaps impossible) task.

There are essentially two types of fundamental differences between natural and social science that Gergen singles out for attention. One has to do with differences in the respective objects of study in the two areas and the other with differences in the respective consequences of that study. In the former case Gergen concentrates on differences between human beings and physical objects. In the latter case he focuses on the effects that result from reporting conclusions about human behavior, as opposed to the effects that result from reporting conclusions about the behavior of physical objects.

Humans as Objects of Study

How do humans differ from physical objects? One way of answering this question is to look at the kinds of categories used for classifying phenomena in each realm. To observe phenomena intelligently, one must make discriminations within the sensory field. The prospective scientist, that is, "must already harbor conceptions of what there is to be studied in order to carry out the task of systematic observation" (Gergen, 1978b, p. 1347). Gergen's contention is that even at this initial stage of the investigatory process, there is "far greater potential for such preconceptions to shape the phenomena for study in the social, as opposed to the natural sciences" (Gergen, 1978b, p. 1347).

Basically, Gergen argues that the preliminary orienting concepts available to the observer of natural phenomena are much more directly tied to rudimentary aspects of sense experience than are the orienting concepts available to the observer of social phenomena. In the former case, for example, such basic discriminations as that between light and dark (which help to define the contours of objects) give rise to "natural categories." Furthermore, as a result "the major proportion of theoretical terms in the natural sciences are tied rather closely to specific empirical operations or measurements" (Gergen, 1978b, p. 1350), and consensus among natural scientists regarding their observations is relatively nonproblematic.

Gergen sees far less consensus among social scientists and a much looser tie to operational definitions. Part of the reason is that "human social activity... appears in a state of near continuous motion, its forms are infinitely variable, and fresh patterns may emerge at any point" (Gergen, 1978b, p. 1348); thus this aspect of his argument recalls the assumption of instability in social behavior. Another reason is that the phenomena of real interest to social sciences are not physicalistic features of behavior that are more or less immediately given to the senses (e.g., descriptions of the position of someone's arm) but the social meanings attached to such behavior (e.g., that the arm is being used to hit someone as an act of aggression).

Another distinction between humans and objects is in terms of the inherent qualities of each (cf. our earlier discussion of dispositional properties). Essentially, Gergen (1973) argues that physical objects do have many strongly inherent properties, whereas humans do not. There is a sense in which human beings are physical objects (organisms), of course, and Gergen (1973) seems to grant that in this sense the study of physiological processes in experimental psychology at least approaches the character of natural science. But it does so only by limiting itself to biologically given features of the human organism, which Gergen considers of minor importance in determining the nature of social interaction. Human behavior of lower organisms, that is, and far more "dependent on acquired dispositions subject to gross modification over time" (Gergen, 1973, p. 318). It is in this sense that Gergen (1982, p. 15) describes the human organism as being much more "stimulus free" than physical objects whose dispositional qualities reflect constraints of natural law.

Although humans are thus described as possessing few if any qualities that inherently constrain social activity in rigid ways, people are said to share certain important conceptual capabilities that do influence their behavior (Gergen, 1982). The point is that even if one saw in them evidence for biologically given dispositional qualities, such evidence of their existence would be grounds for assuming variability in human behavior rather than the constancy that is presumably characteristic of physical objects (i.e., an indeterminacy of human reactions as opposed to the determinacy in reactions of physical objects to physical stimulation).

Similarly, Gergen (1973, 1982) posits the existence of certain commonly shared human values that disrupt attempts to generate lawlike empirical generalizations of the sort possible in the natural sciences. Chief among these are the frequently seen desires for "freedom against restraint" and for a sense of one's own "uniqueness," as well as the "frequent investment in maintaining unpredictability" (Gergen, 1982, pp. 19–20). Coupled with the preceding considerations, the prevalence of such values makes humans as objects of study fundamentally different indeed from the objects of study in the natural sciences.

Feedback to the Objects of Study

Gergen (1973, 1982) not only thinks that the objects of study are qualitatively different in the natural and social sciences; he also believes that in the process of transmitting information and conclusions drawn from such study, social scientists further alter the phenomena under investigation in ways that have no counterpart in the natural sciences. That is, the thrust of the previous arguments had been that objects in the two realms are fundamentally different in character to begin with, in ways that would be true even if no one had ever studied these objects. But in moving to a discussion about the consequences of research within each realm, Gergen adds the conclusion that *social scientists have opportunities unavailable to natural scientists for changing the very thing they are studying while they are in the midst of studying it.*

The basis for this conclusion, quite simply, is that human beings can learn about and be influenced by the knowledge social scientists acquire, whereas inanimate objects are obviously quite impervious to the things natural scientists say about them. The investigator in the natural sciences "cannot typically communicate his knowledge to the subjects of his study such that their behavioral dispositions are modified," but "in the social sciences such communication can have a vital impact on behavior" (Gergen, 1973, p. 313). Far from being a matter of trivial import, this divergence is seen as perhaps the most telling point of all. "The sociobehavioral scientist and the society thus constitute a feedback loop, and this fact does pose a radical difference between most sociobehavioral and natural sciences study" (Gergen, 1982, p. 22).

The significance of this communicative feedback loop lies in the potential for reciprocal causation it sets up. Although it is possible to argue that such a potential exists at every stage of the research process (Gergen, 1982), by far the most attention has been drawn to what Gergen (1973) termed "enlightenment effects" at the stage of prediction. *Enlightenment effects* as a broad term applies to any modification of behavior in light of social scientific knowledge. With respect to prediction, these effects operate via changes in subjects' or respondents' expectations. Once people learn about a hypothesized stimulus–response sequence, they have a new idea about what they are "supposed" to do next, and they may be influenced by these communicated expectations to confirm the prediction—but in this case, of course, the hypothesis possesses no independent validity (cf. Merton's, 1957, discussion of the "self-fulfilling prophecy").

Worse yet, as suggested by Gergen's characterization of humans in terms of their desire for autonomy, uniqueness, and unpredictability, enlightenment effects can occur in the opposite form as well. That is, knowledge of social science predictions might influence some people to act in a way that disconfirmed those predictions. This reversal could in turn lead social scientists to change their predictions (hence reciprocal causation), but there might be little to prevent the same process from occurring all over again.

Once the possibility of enlightenment effects has been granted, the distinction between natural and social science takes an additional significance that from Gergen's perspective strikes at the core of orthodoxy itself. That is, it challenges the allegedly objective, dispassionate, and value-free character of science. This impact is felt because enlightenment effects are said to do more than merely influence people's expectations and subsequent behavior; rather, the "enlightenment" of preferred theories and research findings serves to shape societal values in a direct way: "As its implications and applications are borne out, every theory becomes an ethical or ideological advocate" (Gergen, 1978b, p. 1354). Methods armed at dispassionate and objective description are doomed to failure, and "regardless of the traditional attempt to remain ethically neutral, the social theorist is inevitably favoring certain forms of social activity over others, certain strata of society as opposed to others, and certain values over their antitheses" (Gergen, 1978b, p. 1355).

Controversial Issues

Two central issues emerge from our consideration of the dimensions underlying the controversy. One of these has to do with the putative existence of stable (transhistorical) phenomena regarding human behavior. The other concerns differences between the domains of natural and social science. It will be convenient for us to examine each of these issues from a slightly different perspective. With respect to the stability issue, we identify arguments in the debate that seem to focus largely on empirical questions (i.e., what evidence of stability exists?). With respect to the domain issue, we consider arguments that, although inevitably interwined with the first issue, raise questions about the proper investigatory strategy itself (i.e., can the approach adopted in the natural sciences be fruitfully applied to the social sciences?).

How Stable Are Social Phenomena?

One thrust in many of Gergen's writings has been to document, or at least make a strong case for, the existence of social change. In his initial article (Gergen, 1973), for example, he pointed to changes over time in the reward value of social approval and to similar changes in factors affecting political activism. A subsequent piece expanded this theme by asking, "Where are the durables?" (Gergen, 1976, p. 377). As one example of the kind of general answer given to this query (viz., "nowhere"), Gergen (1976) cited repeated failures to replicate the "sleeper effect" (Hovland, Lumsdaine, & Sheffield, 1949). He also noted similar evidence of historically bound phenomena in various areas of psychology reviewed by Cronbach (1975), Ghiselli (1974),

Greenwald (1975a), and Atkinson (1974). The impermanence of even patterns of childhood development was later added to the list (Gergen, 1978b).

Schlenker (1974, 1976) has emerged as the main critic attempting to rebut these particular charges. One of Schlenker's (1974) counterclaims, for example, was that it is possible to discern a great many crosscultural similarities in human behavior (e.g., incest taboos). Likewise, evidence for regularities that have stood the test of time was said to be available in the writings of such philosophers and social commentators as Aristotle, Plato, Locke, Rousseau, and Hobbes. Schlenker also cited such phenomena as social facilitation effects (e.g., Zajonc, 1980) as illustrations that social psychology has developed universal and transhistorically valid generalizations.

Gergen (1982) has made specific rejoinders to each of these points and has also offered a more general critique of attempts to discern lawful patterns in human behavior. He does not consider any given finding in social psychology so incontrovertible as to be without controversy. Even evidence for transhistorical truth from ancient writings (e.g., Aristotle, Plato) is considered suspect on two grounds (Gergen, 1982). In the first place any similarity of current behavior patterns to those in ancient civilizations may merely reflect a common cultural heritage (e.g., historical origins of Western thought in Greece and Rome). Indeed, to the extent that these behaviors appear stable across time, this similarily may derive from our viewing behavior through a perspective provided by earlier thinkers. Hence the "evidence" is another indication that preconceptions shape observations, or that through the communicative feedback loop these preconceptions shape actual behavior. Second, given the infinite variety of human behavior, any claimed regularities may be coincidence. It will thus always be possible to find some similarities across time and cultures, but Gergen holds that the adequacy of such a circumstantial basis for presumed lawlike generalizations is yet to be proved.

Gergen's (1982) more general analysis challenges the very nature of any evidence for universal patterning in social behavior. Regarding correlational studies of hypotheses about crosscultural universality, for example, he states that "the precautionary qualifications surrounding any given finding in this area are so numerous that the claim to universals must be limited to a whisper" (p. 51). Likewise, in noting numerous methodological problems and failures to replicate among standardized experiments attempted in different cultures, Gergen finds evidence for universality highly limited and generally inconclusive.

Another possible route to discovering stability has been championed by Manis (1975, 1976). Manis' general argument is that regularities are to be found not in transhistorically stable patterns of behavior but at the level of universally applicable psychological processes. As, he puts it (Manis, 1976, p. 431), "the development of a major scientific theory quite commonly involves the construction (invention) of some hypothetical but unseen mechanism or process that lends coherence to an otherwise chaotic set of particulars." Thus, what Gergen sees as the arbitrariness of theoretical conceptions in imposing order in chaos, from Manis' perspective becomes the essence of science at its best. Manis (1976), in this vein, approvingly gives examples of process analysis as having been responsible for the utility of Mendel's and Darwin's work. Within psychology, models of transformational grammar were cited (Manis, 1975) as an illustration of the way that postulated cognitive processes introduce underlying stability to the variability of human communications.

Here again, however, stability seems to be in the eye of the beholder. Challenging Manis' conclusions, Thorngate (1975) argues that the evidence for process invariance is every bit as inconclusive as the evidence for transhistorical patterns of behavior. He lists, for example, a number of sources that attack the credibility of the work on transformational grammar (e.g., Anderson & Bower, 1973; Derwing, 1973; Dreyfus, 1972). He also points out that the cognitive processes underlying memory have also resisted an invariance analysis (e.g., Jenkins, 1974; Newell & Simon, 1972). Similarly, he suggests that the number of processes postulated to account for human judgments and decision making are too numerous to allow inferred stability.

Others have sought to locate process invariance at the physiological level. For example, Greenwald (1976b) illustrates this position in his comment that "As a psychologist, my faith in the lawfulness of human behavior rests on faith in the lawfulness of operations of the CNS [central nervous system]" (p. 391). Both Hendrick (1976) and Gergen (1973, 1982), however, suggest that even if invariable processes were identified at the physiological level, it would be impossible to reduce complete patterns of social behavior to an analysis at the level of such processes. In particular, Gergen (1982) identifies two kinds of difficulties facing reductionistic efforts. The first is pragmatic in nature. Even if complete understanding of human physiological mechanisms were achieved, predicting human behavior would still be dependent on additional knowledge about the relevant inputs to the physiological system; such inputs could not be totally controlled (except under some highly unethical arrangement whereby a child is isolated at birth), and the absence of comprehensive experimental control of incoming stimuli would necessitate impossibly accurate information about the entire life history of an individual. Second, there is an objection to the feasibility of reductionism in principle. That is, concepts relevant to understanding social interaction (e.g., status, obligation, shame) are not in principle reducible to descriptions of the determinants of bodily movements. Gergen's arguments to this effect take up one whole chapter of his 1982 book and thus cannot be examined in detail, but their thrust is to demonstrate the impossibility that "a language for describing human affairs [could] be reduced to the language of neurons" (p. 57).

How Should Social Phenomena Be Studied?

Questions regarding how one should approach the study of social phenomenon tend to be "social" in character. In particular, does that character involve properties that have no counterpart among the phenomena studied in the natural sciences? If so, is the implication that the social sciences must adopt a different method of analysis from the one employed in the natural sciences? We see these questions as involving attempts to provide a rational reconstruction of the scientific process, rather than as matters of empirical evidence. Conclusions about whether social science "measures up" to natural science depend on how one construes the yardstick. Ultimately, that is, these conclusions hinge on the credibility of various accounts about *what* natural science studies and *how* it goes about that study. We will consider each of these two points in turn.

Observed Phenomena

The members of a scientific discipline try to provide explanations for the observations they report, and presumably these attempts will be hindered if their observations are unreliable. With respect to the part played by observation in the social sciences, Gergen (1982) takes a very firm stand: "the sociobehavioral sciences are essentially nonempirical. . .[their theories are] neither engendered, stimulated, sustained, corroborated, nor falsified by observation" (p. 79). This statement is true, Gergen contends, because of the inherent unreliability of observations pertaining to social phenomena. Although we have touched on the basis for Gergen's conclusion in considering evidence for transhistorical laws and invariant processes, his contrast of natural and social science at the level of observation adds a new wrinkle to the arguments.

Gergen (1982) begins by asking how observation can be used to assess the truth or falsehood of some statement. The first step, he suggests, is to determine what the terms in the statement mean (i.e., to what observable properties do they refer?). *Meaning*, of course, is inevitably a function of social consensus and depends on "ostensive definition" and the development of a "denotative language" (Gergen, 1982, pp. 79–80) which involves naming by pointing. It is in this respect that the language (theories) of natural and social science are held to be fundamentally different, since the nature of the things to which members of each can point are different.

The differences are in terms of two dimensions: (1) the extent to which the phenomenon under observation has an *enduring* property and (2) the extent to which it is a *recurring* phenomenon. Obviously "a high degree of confusion in identification (if not its complete inhibition)" (Gergen, 1982, p. 81) would arise in the case of events at the nonenduring, nonrecurring extremes of these dimensions. And it is precisely here that Gergen locates the phenomena of interest of social psychologists:

> Of cardinal significance, it is clear that the vast share of human activity falls toward the latter end of the continua. Human activity furnishes the observer with a continuous and ever-changing array of experience. Eyes, facial muscles, limbs, voice, fingers, torso, and so on may all move simultaneously, and stability of pattern may be retained for only the briefest instant. Further, few patterns are recurrent. Seldom does an individual furnish others with precisely the same stimulus confluence over time. (Gergen, 1982, p. 81)

Phenomena to which natural scientists can point, in contrast, are presumed to be enduring and to recur frequently.

Schlenker (1974) has taken issue with this position because it "fails to take into account the essential uniqueness and non repeatability of all events, whether physical or social" (p. 8). No event, he points out, can be duplicated exactly down to the last detail. Godow (1976), a philosopher of science, maintains that "given the standard view of events as changes in an object at a time, Schlenker is surely right in urging that physical phenomena are non-repeatable in just the same way that social phenomena are" (p. 423).

As Hendrick (1976) has noted, however, any judgment about degrees of uniqueness is relative to such aspects of observation as the attribute dimension chosen for attention and the measurement scale used. In his view, "the question remains as to whether there is enough communality of social behaviors so that they may be partitioned into identifiable measurement classes" (Hendrick, 1976, p. 401). The issue of uniqueness has received relatively limited treatment beyond the kinds of comments we have described, but they are sufficient to show that thus far there is some lack of agreement about the possibility for consensus regarding observables.

Methods of Conceptualization and Investigation

According to Gergen, important differences between natural and social science exist not only at the level of observable phenomena, but also at the level of explanations (in terms of theories and laws regarding the phenomena) and predictions derived from explanatory accounts. We have referred to this level in the preceding heading as involving matters of conceptualization, that is, whether social science uses, or in principle would use, theories the same way natural science does. In terms of investigation, the question is whether research designed to test predictions from theories has similar prospects in the natural and social sciences.

Conceptualization. Our account of conceptualization issues begins with Schlenker's (1974) attempt to show that conceptual activity of comparable sorts goes on in both natural and social science. This attempt focuses on two aspects of such activity: (1) theoretical propositions, which are stated in abstract and conditional form, and (2) the systems to which these propositions apply. The *abstract* form of theoretical propositions refers to their being sufficiently general (i.e., stated at a high enough level of abstraction) as to encompass and subsume numerous specifics. This form allows specifics to be deduced or inserted as particular values of abstract variables. The *conditional* form of theoretical propositions refers to their being constructed as "if/then" statements; deductions, therefore, involve specifying the consequences that are entailed when relevant antecedent conditions have been met. The *systems* to which theoretical propositions apply are important to consider because such systems may vary in the degree to which they are "open" (subject to outside disturbances that preclude antecedent conditions from being met) rather than "closed" (isolated from these kinds of disturbances). On all these counts Schlenker (1974, 1976) argues that conceptual activity in the social sciences is (or should be, and is in principle capable of being) similar to that of the natural sciences.

Schlenker's statement about the need for abstract propositions is germane to Gergen's claim about the absence of evidence for transhistorical laws, insofar as Gergen's examples of unstable generalizations might be considered insufficiently abstract (i.e., contain too many references to specifics). Gergen's (1976) reply is that no abstraction is of any value unless it can be linked in some way to specifics. But this point is not a basis of disagreement, since Schlenker (1974) stipulated that abstract propositions must be stated so as to allow the deduction of specifics. Rather, the bone of contention is Gergen's further assertion that "Psychologists have found it virtually impossible to conduct critical tests [of deductions from their abstract propositions, in a way that would allow them]...to link general statements unambiguously to observables" (1976, p. 374).

Does this difficulty (or impossibility) serve to distinguish social science from natural science? On one account, at least, it does not. This account, originated by Duhem (1906/1954), has been put forcefully by Forsyth (1976). Without going into detail, we can say that Forsythe has demonstrated numerous reasons (e.g., the difficulty of disentangling methodological inadequacies from theory falsifications, the possibility of introducing ad hoc assumptions that can account for apparent disconfirmations) why philosophers now agree on the impossibility of an *experimentum crucis* to rule between competing theories or to confirm (or disconfirm) any single theory. These arguments, as Forsythe (1976) and Manis (1976) point out, apply to theories in the realms of both natural and social science with equal force.

The conditional (if/then) form of theoretical propositions contributes to a related line of defense for Schlenker's (1974, 1976, 1977) alleging the essential equivalence of natural and social science. Schlenker asserts that in either science, appropriate theoretical propositions only stipulate that certain consequences will follow *if* the relevant antecedent conditions have been met. Any replication failures that Gergen or others might cite as examples of historical instability, therefore, might represent merely instances in which the relevant antecedent conditions were not met. Since the proposition was only intended to hold true when those conditions had been met, the absence of the specified consequences does not thereby disprove the theory.

This line of defense has been taken up by Manis (1976), who added considerations pertaining to the elaboration and modification of theories. As Manis suggested, a failure to find the predicted consequences of a theoretical proposition is often the occasion for further specification of antecedent conditions (in both the natural and the social sciences). This necessary specification work may involve the search for previously unconsidered moderator variables and the revision of theory to incorporate higher order interactions of those variables with the originally specified set of antecedent conditions. Manis does not view this situation as cause for alarm, and he certainly does not see it as reason to differentiate between natural and social science in principle. He does seem to grant, however, that this elaboration process may require difficult work for social scientists as they attempt to discover what moderator variables may have been at work in producing changed patterns over time.

What Manis grants as a difficult task, Gergen (1982) considers impossible. Two types of reasons are given for this alleged impossibility. The first has to do with the presence of innumerable confounds in social conditions at different points in history:

> First, the solution assumes that one is able to locate the factor(s) responsible for the receding validity of the initial proposition. Yet, as time passes an indeterminant number of variously interrelated changes occur. Essentially, history may be viewed as the unfolding confluence of inextricably linked events. As both historians and social indicators researchers are well aware, there is no means of isolating independent alterations in social circumstances. Hence, how is one to locate the particular circumstances responsible for the emerging impotence of a theory? (p. 48)

It should be noted, however, that the impossibility ("no means") is here a matter of mere assertion, backed loosely by reference to conditions of which presumably authoritative sources are "well aware." This assertion is thus of a pragmatic character rather than representing a logical impossibility; indeed, elsewhere Gergen (1976, p. 377) referred to the elaboration approach as being "impracticable" rather than impossible. It does not preclude advances in social indicators research, for instance, that might mitigate the present difficulties. Furthermore, although it might remain impossible to ascertain conclusively which particular changing circumstances contributed the most to changing patterns, that does not rule out logically the possibility of an isolated (e.g., experimentally controlled) test regarding the effects of one factor or several factors suspected of having produced the change.

The second reason for Gergen's objection to the elaboration of if/then conditionals is that he considers this process necessarily post hoc and hence indefensible. That is, if any predictive failure is greeted by an after-the-fact revision of hypotheses, then no hypothesis is ever subject to the conclusive test of possible disconfirmation (Gergen, 1982). This statement, however, amounts to an affirmation of the Duhemian thesis, which was originally proposed in the context of the *natural* sciences. Indeed, it was after making this same point in an earlier article that Gergen (1976) alluded to the possibility of there being no essential difference between natural and social science in this respect.

The final issue of conceptualization concerns the nature of physical and social systems to which theoretical propositions (and predictions deduced from those propositions) are applied. A possible distinction between natural and social science is that theoretical propositions in the former are conceptualized vis-à-vis "closed" systems relatively isolated from outside disturbances, whereas the latter propositions necessarily apply to systems so "open" as to be continually affected by such disturbances. For example Hendrick (1976) points to an analysis offered by Scriven (1964, p. 172) concerning reasons for the success of classical physics at solving prediction problems in astronomy: "The good fortune of classical physics and the misfortune of psychology lie to a large extent in the kind of prediction problems which they inherit."

Schlenker (1974), however, had anticipated this point. His argument was that "few systems in [natural] science are for all practical purposes isolated systems as is the subject matter of astronomy" (p. 6). Indeed, bestowing all the natural sciences with the predictive precision of astronomy had been identified much earlier by Helmer and Rescher (1959) as a mistaken conclusion that "imputes to the so-called exact sciences a procedural rigor which is rarely present in fact" (p. 25).

It is the function of laboratory procedures in both the natural and social sciences, of course, to approximate idealized conditions by artificially creating relatively isolated systems, and hence Schlenker (1974) pointed to the necessity of the controlled experiment as a fundamental commonality of the two realms.

Even in terms of a highly controlled experiment, however, social psychologists sometimes aspire to a level of specificity and precision that is beyond their capabilities (Manis, 1976). Manis argues that such might be the case when social psychologists attempt to predict a specific behavior from a general measure of attitudes, rather than following the Fishbein and Ajzen (1974) recommendation of examining overall patterns (multiple, rather than single, acts) as the behavioral measurement criteria.

Two questions arise from this sort of analysis: (1) Do differences in the degree of specificity separate social psychology from the natural sciences? (2) To what level of specificity *should* social psychologists aspire? Answering the first question, Schlenker (1974) points to the impossibility of making specific predictions for leaves that are dropping on someone's lawn under windy conditions (despite the exactitude of physics regarding falling objects) (see also Helmer & Rescher, 1959). Hendrick (1976) echoes this sentiment, noting that the physical sciences are unable to provide absolute predictions about the location and time of earthquakes.

Nevertheless, Hendrick (1976) suggests that social psychology is in a unique position with respect to the second question. The predictions that people want from studies of social behavior (e.g., will a given marriage end in divorce?) are predictions about what will happen to a specific individual under particular circumstances; the demand is for what Scriven (1964) has termed *unconditional* predictions. Whether social psychologists should yield to this demand, on the other hand, is a matter open to debate. Certainly, it seems misguided to insist that specific prediction is required by the importance of the issues per se because, for example, the effect of earthquakes on people's lives can obviously be at least as momentous as failed marriages. And regardless of whether or not social psychologists can be accused of failing to meet their proper obligation to society, it is clear that the predominant approach in the discipline has not been to focus on predictions for specific individuals, but rather to make predictions at a statistically aggregated level of analysis (i.e., predictions about the average tendency among a group of individuals within a given experimental condition).

Hendrick (1976) (saying only that the openness of social sytems would constitute a problem *if* the goal of unconditional prediction were adopted) refers to another way that open systems in the social sciences might be more problematic than those in the natural sciences. Specifically, he claims that the former are move susceptible to problems involving the "relativity of causation" (Hendrick, 1976, p. 399). It is impossible to determine *the* cause of any social action because where the search terminates (what will count as a satisfactory causal explanation) depends on one's perspective. Thus "there is little hope of devising general explanatory theories which will account for social behavior within a nice deductive framework...[since] social causation, and thus explanation, is relative to the perspective of a given psychological system" (Hendrick, 1976, p. 399).

Investigation.   Recall that by *enlightenment effects*, Gergen (1973) meant the consequences of communicated social theories and research findings. The results of previous investigations regarding social behavior, for example, could inform the subjects of current investigations about what was expected of them, and their behavior might be influenced as a result. Thus, regardless of whether there are any problems of conceptualization that set the social sciences apart from the natural sciences (and our review suggests that differentiation along these lines is doubtful), the process of investigation itself might encounter unique problems in the former case. It is at this point that Godow (1976), who otherwise expressed scepticism about conceptual delineation of the two realms, found reasons for being sympathetic to Gergen's position:

> A physicist does not have to worry that a rock will learn about the laws of physics and then try to change its behavior; the physicist does not have to worry about affecting a rock's behavior by subtly communicating certain information to it; the physicist does not have to worry about a rock's trying to make sure that the experiment comes out "good" (or "bad"); the physicist does not have to worry about the rock's trying to exercise its freedom; the physicist does not have to worry about the attitudes or beliefs of a rock. (Godow, 1976, p. 424)

Godow concluded that these considerations make for "enormous methodological difficulties for the social psychologist that the physical scientist does not have to face" (p. 424). Finally, it seems, we have come upon one element that is indubitably unique to the social sciences—obviously rocks do not think.

Gergen (1982) identifies two ways whereby defenders of orthodoxy might try to deal directly with enlightenment effects: by trying to predict their impact and by trying to reduce or eliminate their impact. The first of these strategies—designed to develop a "science of enlightenment"—might "by careful documentation of enlightenment effects, and with the contribution of research on social influence, of psychological reactance, self-fulfilling prophecy, social expectancy, and so on" attempt desperately to "forge a series of objectively grounded principles systematically accounting for such reactions" (pp. 45–46). But this attempt would be one of sheer desperation, Gergen contends, and ultimate exasperation. Any such enlightenment principles from the new science could themselves become communicated to the public at large, and the cycle would begin all over again. The next stage might be a theory of reaction to enlightenment theories, but an inevitable problem of infinite regress is thereby created. Hence, Gergen deems this strategy unworkable in principle.

Schlenker (1974), on the other hand, finds this strategy defensible—at least in principle. That is, he sees no logical reason why an overarching, sufficiently abstract theory could not be generated so as to encompass both reactive and nonreactive behavior (rather than a series of theories about theories), thereby short-circuiting an otherwise neverending cyclical process. He is encouraged in this belief by what he considers to be a common occurrence whenever instances of suicidal predictions and self-fulfilling prophecies are noted, namely that they are subsequently "found to be *explainable*" (Schlenker, 1974, p. 10, emphasis added) within the context of some more abstract theoretical proposition.

We added the emphasis to this quote, because it is important not to confuse explanation with prediction. Although the essential equivalence of explanation and prediction (their logical symmetry) is asserted by the traditional hypothetico-deductive or "covering law" model of science (Hempel & Oppenheim, 1948) to which Schlenker apparently subscribes (see Godow, 1976, note 3), many philosophers have raised serious counterexamples indicating important asymmetries (e.g., Scheffler, 1963; Scriven, 1962). For example it might be very easy to *explain* why a man murdered his wife but virtually impossible to have *predicted* that event in advance (Scriven, 1959). Thus, one could grant the logical possibility of explanation (which is what Schlenker asserts) and yet still be sceptical about the prospects for usable predictions. Schlenker himself concedes that there would be a unique dilemma facing the social sciences "if subjects' behaviors seemed to follow no perceptible [predictable] pattern" (Schlenker, 1974, p. 10), but he denies that such patterns have not been discerned.

Evaluation of this first strategy, therefore, has reached a logical impasse. The vicious circle Gergen envisions might be broken if abstract explanations did provide the basis for predictions, but the predictability of human behavior is precisely one of the roots of controversy in the first place (cf. our discussions of the regularity issue). Nor does it help obviate this impasse by claiming, as Schlenker (1974) has, that Gergen himself is granting the existence of regularities in arguing for such human traits as the desire to be unpredictable. Gergen (1982) has countered this claim by asserting that such desires are mere tendencies, subject to waxing and waning influence: 'Firm predictions cannot be made with respect to the strength, prevalence, and effects of such disruptive dispositions over time" (p. 19).

The second strategy, that of trying to reduce or eliminate the impact of enlightenment effects rather than trying to eliminate them, could be pursued in several ways. Two of these Gergen dismisses rather easily: the possibility of restricting knowledge about social theory to a scientific elite, and the diminished potential for enlightenment when social theory is developed at a highly formalized (e.g., mathematical) level. The notion of an elite hiding its knowledge is certainly "repugnant" to the sensibilities of most social scientists (Gergen, 1973, p. 314). Mathematical formalization of theory, to the extent that it obscures and mystifies the meaning of theoretical terms, is in a sense a counterpart of the elitist approach. Furthermore, because formalized terms must be linked to more commonplace understandings (else how could they be used?) and because the implications of terms or policies based on their application (as when the elite is co-opted by government) can become known (e.g., public awareness of the consequences of IQ testing), these approaches are doomed to failure (Gergen, 1982).

The strategy of reducing or eliminating enlightenment impact, however, is not limited to these approaches. It is also possible to propose a methodological solution. As Schlenker (1974, p. 9) puts it, "the statement that a stone does not care what is done to it in a laboratory is [only] trivially correct. . . . [A solution to laboratory reactivity among humans] only requires changes in the specific techniques and methods employed by the social scientist in dealing with his subject matter." Indeed, Gergen himself admits that "both natural and social scientist can typically document their observations without unduly disturbing the phenomena under study" (1982, p. 22) in this sense.

It is instructive to consider why even Gergen accedes so readily on the issue of laboratory reactivity (although this issue will be examined more fully in Chapters 4 and 6) and hence why "many believe that such enlightenment effects are already at a minimum" (Gergen, 1982, p. 44). One reason is that a wide gap can exist between wanting to do something and being able to do it—as when audience members try to discover an illusionist's tricks but cannot. Social psychologists skilled in the art of laboratory deception may have become master illusionists, thereby finding ways of inducing predictability even from people who do not want their behavior predicted. A habitual way of responding might be elicited in a sufficiently involving laboratory situation, and as Schlenker (1974, p. 11) notes in this regard, "Habits are powerful controllers of action" (cf. Langer, 1975 on the "mindlessness" of much human behavior). When caught up in the press of involving situations, even the most knowledgeable student of principles of human behavior might thus remain subject to those principles. It is in this respect that Schlenker (1974) offers anecdotal evidence seemingly counter to the thrust of Gergen's views about enlightenment effects: "my personal unsystematic observations indicate to me that social psychologists' behaviors are remarkably similar to those of other 'less informed' mortals" (p. 10, n. 4).

Gergen's (1982) response has been twofold. On the one hand he finds it ironic that social scientists should thus take comfort in the lack of impact their findings have had. Surely, he reasons, this in itself suggests that they have been unable to discover anything very profound (perhaps because profound regularities do not exist). But this in no way precludes some future discovery of great public impact as a logically possibility: Gergen himself chides current researchers by pointing to the impact of social theorists in the past (e.g., Marx, Freud). Furthermore, as we have discussed here, the negated impact of enlightenment may occur not because of its absence, but despite its presence.

The other thrust of Gergen's (1982) rebuttal, however, is to reaffirm that enlightenment effects should not be construed as narrowly applicable only to laboratory phenomena. Perhaps as an unfortunate consequence of Gergen's earlier (1973) emphasis on suicidal predictions and self-fulfilling prophecies, some of his critics seem to have equated enlightenment with laboratory re-activity alone. But as other treatments (Gergen, 1976, 1982) make clear, Gergen has conceived the full range of enlightenment effects in much broader terms. In particular their total impact must take into account the "evaluative loading" of concepts, theories, and explanations in the social sciences.

In making charges against the orthodox "dispassionate observer" view of science, Gergen does more than merely join others (e.g., Scriven, 1974; C.P. Snow, 1962) who have pointed out that "all science is inherently valuational" (Gergen, 1982, p. 28, n. 23). To do this and no more would only serve to unify natural and social science, whereas Gergen presses the point to assert once again their incompatability. He does this by arguing that whereas all science adopts values taken from the culture (and even natural science may transmit back to the culture certain values), only in social science does this two-way flow affect the warp and woof of the very phenomena from which the scien-tific bystander is supposed to be objectively removed. In formulating concepts based implicitly on assumptions supportive of the existing power structure, for example, the social scientist not only draws from the culture but also works to shape it in certain ways (i.e., to maintain the status quo). These broader implications of the communicative feedback loop, if accepted as valid, are such that they could not be ameliorated methodologically by means of a deception experiment.

Current Status of the Controversy

We have examined a number of ways in which it has been argued that social phenomena cannot and should not be studied as natural science phenomena are studied. Claims regarding the uniqueness of social phenomena (viz., that they are inherently less stable than natural phenomena) are largely considered inconclusive because uniqueness must be judged with respect to some frame of reference, and there is lack of consensus regarding such a context.

In terms of methods for conceptualizing phenomena, it appears that Gergen has failed to make a convincing case that would preclude the social sciences from using the same methods as the natural sciences. In terms of methods for investigating phenomena, it is agreed that social scientists face certain problems involving reactivity that have no exact parallel in the natural sciences (the "rocks do not think" variety of problems). Were certain techniques (e.g., unobtrusive measures, deception experiments) to be successful in eliminating these problems, however, presumably social scientific investigations could proceed from that point forward in essentially the same manner as natural scientific investigations. Gergen seems to grant the success of these technical solutions, but he points to a larger context of the investigatory process, a context in which the two-way exchange of values between investigator and culture creates a potential for effects that are impossible in the natural sciences. Although here at last Gergen has made perhaps one of the best possible cases for the potential uniqueness of social science, it is clear that this is a potential capable of being realized to varying degrees. That is, while Gergen's argument suggests that social science concepts *can* have significant impact on society, it appears to be generally accepted in practice that they do not always do so.

To conclude, there can be little doubt that the questions raised about the scientific status of social psychology reviewed in this chapter have done much to inspire some needed scientific "spring cleaning" in the house of social psychology. But, to what avail? As E. E. Jones (1985) recently put it, "The crisis of social psychology has begun to take its place as a minor perturbation in the long history of the social sciences. The intellectual momentum of the field has *not* been radically affected by crisis proclamations..." (p. 100, emphasis added).

Although the so-called "crisis" seems to have passed, the current generation of social psychologists appear to have inherited a legacy of doubts and questions raised in the wake of the debates reviewed in this chapter. To a great extent these uncertainties have manifested themselves in the form of questions about the wisdom of blindly accepting the "tried and true" methodological techniques in the social psychologist's tool kit (many of which are addressed in the chapters to follow). Indeed, the inclusion of chapters on innovative quantitative methods (Kenny, 1985), systematic observations (Weick, 1985), and program evaluation (T.D. Cook, Leviton, & Shadish, 1985) in the third edition of the *Handbook of Social Psychology* (Lindzey & Aronson, 1985) may be seen as representing a movement toward a new scientific status for social psychology.

Chapter 2

Informed Consent

In 1946 the United Nations General Assembly adopted the Nuremberg Code in response to the atrocities of medical research conducted in the concentration camps of Nazi Germany. The first principle of this code—"The voluntary consent of the human subject is absolutely essential" (J. Katz, 1972, p. 305)—reflects an emphasis on human rights and personal freedom that remains one of today's most cherished values (Rokeach, 1973). Indeed, the belief that all people have the right to determine freely whether or not they wish to be involved in a research investigation is so basic that it is reflected in a variety of forms, including legal standards and regulations (e.g., Maloney, 1984), research agency guidelines (e.g., Quimby, McKensie, & Chapman, 1975), moral and philosophic discussions (e.g., Soble, 1978), and professional codes (e.g., "Committee," 1982). Respect for this right of self-determination manifests itself in the parlance of today's researchers as the principle of *informed consent*.

Diener and Crandall (1978) define informed consent as "the procedure in which individuals choose whether to participate in an investigation after being informed of the facts that would be likely to influence their decision" (p. 34). Accordingly, in order to give informed consent, potential participants must be accurately informed about the research in question and they must be free to decide on their willingness to participate in it. Although informed consent is a fundamental principle of medical research, it has been questioned from a practical perspective. For example, as we shall review in this chapter, issues have arisen concerning the most appropriate and feasible method for gaining informed consent, the need for informed consent in certain types of research, and the effects of informed consent procedures on research results, to name a few. Before examining the controversies that have arisen with respect to these and other related issues concerning informed consent, we will take a closer look at exactly what informed consent is.

What Is Informed Consent?

Although documented cases of human abuses and rights infringements in experiments date back as far as the 18th century (Annas, Glantz, & Katz, 1977), interest in the doctrine of informed consent peaked in the 1960s and 1970s (Lidz et al., 1984)—an era in which the values of individual autonomy and self-determination were quite strong (B. Barber, 1973). During this period we saw the adoption, in 1964, of the Declaration of Helsinki by the Eighteenth World Medical Assembly, which, in part, states as follows:

> In any research on human beings, each potential subject must be adequately informed of the aims, methods, anticipated benefits and potential hazards of the study and the discomfort it may entail. He or she should be informed that he or she is at liberty to abstain from participation in the study and that he or she is free to withdraw his or her consent to participation at any time. (Greenwald, Ryan, & Mulvihill, 1982, p. 232)

In the United States we also witnessed the widespread establishment of similar informed consent clauses in the guidelines of many federal agencies funding research—such as the United States Public Health Service (1969), the Department of Health, Education, and Welfare (1975), and the Food and Drug Administration (Maloney, 1984). Informed consent was so popular as a doctrine in the 1970s that by 1977, statutes dealing with informed consent were enacted in half the state legislatures (Ludlam, 1978).

Because informed consent regulations were inspired by the questionable practices of some medical researchers and clinicians and because it is within the biomedical field that the greatest potential for abuse to human welfare exists, we find that most of the literature on informed consent addresses issues of medical research (Annas, 1978; Lidz et al., 1984). Although some of the medically related research on informed consent is relevant to the concerns of social science researchers, some differences exist that influence the character of informed consent in social science research (Schwitzgebel, 1969). Given the orientation of this book toward social and behavioral research, as opposed to biomedical research, our presentation of the biomedically related aspects of informed consent is highly selective. As will become apparent, this restriction creates no shortage of controversial issues. Before reviewing these issues, however, we discuss two very fundamental matters necessary to understanding the essence of informed consent—its purposes and its basic elements.

Purposes of Informed Consent

As alluded to thus far, the principal purpose of obtaining informed consent from research participants is to allow them the opportunity to protect their own interests and to share the responsibility for their own welfare. Informed consent procedures further the right of self-determination, the right of those being investigated to determine if the research proposed to them is worthy of their participation (Diener & Crandall, 1978; Reynolds, 1979). In this manner, informed consent promotes respect for research subjects as unique individuals (J. Katz & Capron, 1975). It allows participants to make rational decisions about their own welfare (J. Katz, 1972).

Following from this, informed consent serves the purpose of stimulating investigators to create safeguards for those involved in their research (Diener & Crandall, 1978). Knowing that subjects must be told about the investigation sensitizes researchers to their ethical responsibilities toward their subjects. It minimizes fraud and deceit (Fletcher, 1973), discourages the possibility of using coercion (J. Katz & Capron, 1975), and as such, promotes self-scrutiny among investigators (J. Katz, 1972).

As a byproduct, informed consent procedures tend to create a positive image of the scientist. Open communication between the experimenter and his or her subjects promotes the image of the scientific investigation as a joint enterprise as opposed to a venture in which the subject is seen as being used as a human "guinea pig" (Diener & Crandall, 1978; Jerald Greenberg, 1987). These potentially more egalitarian relationships between investigator and participant (J. Katz, 1969) do a great deal to enhance the quality of the participant's experience and to nurture his or her support for and trust in the research enterprise (Gray, 1975).

A final purpose of informed consent—and to many, the most important—is to reduce the investigator's, and his or her institution's, legal liability (Levine, 1978; Reynolds, 1979). Indeed, although informed consent procedures do not absolve investigators from safeguarding the welfare of research subjects, the process of involving subjects in the decision to participate lessens the investigator's criminal and civil liabilities (Lebacquez & Levine, 1977).

These purposes, as noble as they may be, are often overlooked by investigators in the course of conducting their research. Indeed, informed consent procedures often tend to be regarded as bureaucratic obstacles to research (Gray, Cooke, & Tannenbaum, 1978). By experimenters expressing a casual attitude toward informed consent procedures, prospective subjects in their research frequently are discouraged from carefully considering all the information presented to them needed to make an informed decision (Lidz et al., 1984)—*if* that information is even comprehensible to them (Greenwald, 1982). So as not to undermine these purposes of informed consent, many have encouraged the inclusion of several basic elements into any informed consent system.

Elements of Informed Consent

There appears to be general agreement (e.g., Diener & Crandall, 1978; Lidz & Roth, 1983; Lidz et al., 1984; Reynolds, 1979) that in order for informed consent to be given, it is essential that subjects who are competent to make a decision must be provided with full information about the research in a form that is comprehensible to them and that they make a completely voluntary decision on this basis. Accordingly, four basic elements of informed consent may be identified: *competence*, *full information*, *comprehension*, and *voluntariness*. The importance of each of these elements to the purposes and ideals of informed consent are discussed following, along with consideration of the practical difficulties of incorporating these elements into informed consent procedures.

Competence

As Reynolds (1979) notes, a basic assumption of informed consent is that a decision is made by a responsible, rational, mature person. For this reason questions sometimes may be raised about an individual's capacity to make a decision. In determining who is competent, generally two criteria are used— the adequacy of their mental capacity, and the capacity for self-determination. On this basis, populations generally considered not capable of giving informed consent include young children, fetuses, comatose medical patients, and the mentally incompetent. More ambiguous with respect to the status of their competence are teenagers, institutionalized mental patients, and prisoners (Reynolds, 1979). In the case of research in which some immediate therapeutic benefit to the subject is expected, legal guardians are generally permitted to make decisions for noncompetent subjects. However, the use of noncompetent subjects in nontherapeutic research is generally prohibited (Annas et al., 1977).

Social scientists are especially familiar with the issues of competence that arise in the case of research involving young children (Melton, Koocher, & Saks, 1983) and mental patients (Annas et al., 1977). The legal protection afforded these groups is, in fact, derived from assumptions about their competence to make decisions (Maloney, 1984). In the case of children, federal law distinguishes between the *permission* a parent or guardian can grant his or her child to participate in research and that child's *assent* to participate, that is, the child's agreement to participate based on his or her limited understanding of the consequences (see Maloney, 1984, p. 315). Only when children have reached the age of 9 years do they appear capable of making informed decisions (Weithorn & Campbell, 1982), although proxy consent is still legally required until the age of majority is attained (Annas et al., 1977). As in the case of young children, research on mentally disabled persons is also regulated by a great deal of legislation and requires the permission of a legally authorized representative (Maloney, 1984).

Full Information

It has been argued that researchers should forego topics of investigation that cannot be studied without full disclosure (Murray, 1982). However, because researchers are attempting to learn about a phenomenon by doing research, it is not always possible for them to provide their subjects with *thorough* information (Belmont Report, 1978; Reynolds, 1979). Indeed, it has been argued (Ozar, 1983) that because the researcher's knowledge is not yet expert at the time of the investigation, the subject's decision to participate should be recognized as being of no less privileged status than the researcher's own decision on the matter. This does not mean, however, that informed consent procedures should be rejected as unrealistic (Laforet, 1976). Investigators may be able to tell prospective subjects enough of certain kinds of information that enable them to make an informed decision.

What information about an experiment is needed, then, for a competent individual to make an "informed" decision? Listings of many different types of potentially useful information have been prepared by various ethical commissions (Levine, 1975, 1978), professional societies ("Committee," 1982), and government agencies (Greenwald, 1982). Because the specific requirements for informed consent of various research funding agencies differ (for a useful summary comparison, see Reynolds, 1979, pp. 258–259) and are subject to change with the continuing passage of legislation (Maloney, 1984), it is not feasible to give here a complete listing of all the types of information that have been recommended. However, abstracting from these various sources, we may identify the most popularly cited types of information required for informed consent to be given. These include the following:

1. A description of any possible discomfort or risks
2. Notification of the completely voluntary nature of research participation—including the right to withdraw
3. A statement of the overall purpose and objectives of the research, including the benefits to be derived
4. An explanation of the procedures to be used (the things the subject would be expected to do)
5. Information regarding the procedures used to maintain the confidentiality of the data
6. An offer to answer any questions about the study

Research that puts subjects at risk of physical or psychological harm (typically, biomedical research, as opposed to social science research) requires the disclosure of additional information, such as the availability of alternative treatments and the provisions made by the researcher to handle complications (Lidz et al., 1984). However, because most social science research presents no more than *minimal risk*—risks of harm not greater than those ordinarily encountered in everyday life (Maloney, 1984)—these types of information need not concern us.

The problems with providing subjects with a formidable list of detailed facts to "inform" their decisions are obvious. For one, a great deal of that information may be unnecessary and can lead to more confused decisions rather than more informed decisions. A result of excessive disclosure is that subjects may be unwilling to participate because all the information scares them away (Epstein & Lasagna, 1969). Another possible problem is that some types of complete information, such as the basis for subject selection, actually may add to subjects' level of discomfort and distress—if, for example, the basis is the possession of some socially undesirable characteristic

("Committee," 1982). In this connection, Loftus and Fries (1979) have documented the possibility of iatrogenic harm to the subjects in a study in which informed subjects who took a placebo drug complained of negative effects. Finally, as we will discuss later in this chapter, some information provided in an attempt to be complete actually may influence the results of the study, jeopardizing its internal validity (Adair, Dushenko, & Lindsay, 1985; Belmont Report, 1978).

On what basis, then, should experimenters decide *what* information is necessary to give subjects to enable them to give informed consent? Some procedures that have been identified include soliciting the opinions of a committee of potential subjects (Levine, 1978) and groups of surrogate subjects (Fost, 1975). Diener and Crandall (1978) suggest that decisions about what information should be given to potential research participants should be made on the basis of "what a 'reasonble or prudent person' would want to know" (p. 43). It would be considered reasonable, for example, for someone to want to know about any potential harm they would face in the study, and subjects have an unconditional right to know of any such threat. In fact such risks must be disclosed according to federal regulations (Weinberger, 1975). However, in most—highly innocuous—social science research, flexibility in informing subjects about the research is called for. As Levine (1975) put it, "Each negotiation for informed consent must be adjusted to meet the requirements of the specific proposed activity, and more particularly, be sufficiently flexible to meet the needs of the individual prospective subject" (p. 72).

Comprehension

With the advent of legislation requiring investigators to give their subjects informed consent came the use of the *consent form*, a document on which the necessary information is disclosed in writing (Lidz & Roth, 1983). However, because subjects may not fully comprehend the information presented to them, a signed consent form does not ensure that truly "informed" consent was given (Greenwald, 1982). Commenting on the widespread nature of this problem, Gray, Cooke, and Tannenbaum (1978) noted that, "it is questionable whether many subjects would find most consent forms useful to them in making decisions regarding participation in research" (p. 1098). As Brady (1979) argues, a signed consent form does *not* ensure that consent was informed (see also, Stanley, Sieber, & Melton, 1987).

Elaborate descriptions of research, even in ordinary language, are often difficult for potential subjects to comprehend (Reynolds, 1979).[1] Compounding this problem, studies have shown that many consent forms in use are

---

[1]Special problems of comprehension arise in the case of ethnographic research in societies in which the language and cultural values of the people studied differ from that of the experimenter. For a discussion of the special problems attendant to such research, the reader is referred to Wax (1982).

written in language that is far from ordinary. Many consent forms are written at the advanced undergraduate level (Grunder, 1980) and use language found in medical journals (Morrow, 1980). In commenting on this problem, it was noted by one task force that, "overall, no more than 15 percent of the consent forms were in language as simple as is found in *Time Magazine*. In more than three-fourths of the consent forms, fewer than 20% of the technical or medical terms were explained in lay language" (National Commission, 1978). Moreover, comprehension has been found to be further limited by forms that are too long (Epstein & Lasagna, 1969) and administrative practices that do not permit prospective subjects sufficient time to read the forms (Golden & Johnston, 1970).[2]

One method advocated for avoiding this problem is to use only educated subjects (Reynolds, 1979). Because such a constraint on subject selection may be problematic for some research, other proposals for enhancing the comprehension of informed consent forms have been suggested. For example, research has shown that subjects' comprehension of procedures is enhanced by the use of discussions (Woodward, 1979) and repeated briefings (Brady, 1979). Although the consequences of lack of comprehension are likely to be more serious in medical research than in social science research, problems of comprehension are equally likely to arise. In this case, however, the difficulty is not as likely to be caused by the use of unfamiliar terms, as it is using familiar terms used in an unfamiliar way. Putting research into simple, direct language appears to be necessary—a challenge that faces today's scientists. Pilot testing procedures and questioning subjects about their understanding of informed consent procedures have been recommended as methods for ensuring the comprehensibility of informed consent information (Greenwald, 1982; Reynolds, 1979).

Voluntariness

After a full disclosure about a research investigation has been made a competent individual in a comprehensible manner, the doctrine of informed consent further requires that he or she be allowed to make a completely voluntary decision about participating.[3] Although the absence of coercion is

---

[2]Even if subjects understand the consent forms, they might not attend to all the information presented in them. Research has shown that in making decisions about their participation in research, subjects concentrate on the degree of stress they anticipate regardless of the benefits that may be expected to accrue from the research (Michaels & Oetting, 1979). This demonstrated self-protective mode of responding is interesting because it suggests that research subjects may not employ the same type of cost–benefit analysis that researchers are expected to incorporate into their ethical analyses of experiments ("Committee," 1982).

[3]As, C.P. Smith (1983) explains, being informed and being free of coercion are independent matters. Ideally, research participants should be both fully informed and

recognized as one of the most basic elements of informed consent ("Committee," 1982), it is one of the most difficult to assess and to attain (Lidz et al., 1984). The problem is that prospective research participants are in an inherently unequal power relationship with the authority figures—the researchers and their institutions—thereby introducing subtle pressure to consent to research, regardless of how truly "voluntary" participation is described as being. Once a consent form is presented to potential subjects, the casual demeanor of the researcher may encourage subjects to sign it, and once signed, the subject may feel committed to continue with the study despite the stated right to withdraw (Lidz et al., 1984; Tanke & Tanke, 1982).

Subjects in social science research who may be eager to please the experimenter—the "good subject" (see Chapter 6)—may begin by showing faith in the researcher's integrity by consenting to participate. Similarly, individuals who are physically ill may wish to be "good patients" by cooperating with requests by their physicians (who sometimes conveniently neglect to distinguish between treatment procedures and research procedures) (Lidz et al., 1984). At what price can student subjects withhold permission to participate in a research project that is supposed to be an "educational experience" for them and is required to fulfill a course requirement? Likewise, what ill persons would seek to deny the actions of physicians who they hope will cure them? There may be entire classes of people—prisoners, the poor, the disadvantaged—who, because of their particular vulnerabilities, may not view requests to participate as voluntary at all. Instead, they may view the researcher's request as a path to improving their situation (Reynolds, 1979).

To avoid such insidious coercion in research, it has been suggested that investigators refrain from using excessive inducements (Diener & Crandall, 1978; Reynolds, 1979). For example, prisoners who believe that they are enhancing their opportunities for parole by consenting to research may be facing such a strong inducement that their decision hardly may be considered voluntary (Annas et al., 1977; Reynolds, 1979; Schwitzgebel, 1968). In such cases, it has been recommended that the inducements for participating be minor "luxuries" (B. Freedman, 1975, p. 36) as opposed to more extreme intrinsic benefits. To help temper researchers' judgments about the voluntariness of their recruitment pleas, it has been recommended that investigators: (1) rely on the use of review panels (Levine, 1978; Veatch, 1978), (2) restrict research subjects to educated, upper middle-class persons because they are the "least captive" members of society (Reynolds, 1979), and (3) pretest their recruitment procedures to assess prospective subjects' honest reactions to

---

free of coercion. Sometimes, however, as in the case of prisoners or mental patients, they may be informed but not truly free to refuse. Other times, subjects are free to decide about participating, but are not given full information on which to base their decisions. This is the case with studies involving the use of deception (see Chapter 3). In the most extreme case, such as research conducted in Nazi concentration camps, subjects are neither informed about the study nor free to determine their own involvement in it.

them (Veatch, 1978). Of these three proposals the most practical and popular is the use of review panels. In fact one study has shown that it is not unusual for institutional review boards to devote as much as 75% of their discussions to issues of informed consent (Tanke & Tanke, 1982).[4]

Controversial Issues

Despite the widespread acceptance of the concept of informed consent among the scientific community (Diener & Crandall, 1978), the practice of obtaining consent has been the subject of considerable controversy. Our review of the controversies surrounding the use of informed consent will focus on three key issues: its necessity, the procedures for obtaining it, and its influence on research.

The Necessity of Informed Consent

Probably the most fundamental issue with respect to informed consent is its necessity. In this regard it should be noted that standards set by federal regulatory agencies requiring informed consent have changed in recent years. From 1974 to 1981 regulations by the Department of Health and Human Services (HHS; formerly the Department of Health, Education, and Welfare) required informed consent procedures to be followed in all research, but since 1981 these regulations were altered to allow for some exceptions (Maloney, 1984). Specifically, since 1981, the HHS empowered institutional review boards to exempt researchers from informed consent requirements in cases in which *all* of the following conditions are met:

1. The research exposes subjects to no more than minimal risk.
2. The absence of informed consent instructions will not adversely affect subjects' well-being.
3. It would be impractical for the research to be conducted without the waiver.
4. Pertinent information not provided in advance will be disclosed after participation.

The implications of this permission to waive informed consent are critical for many social psychologists, whose research, which typically poses no potential harm to subjects, relies on the use of deception (see Chapter 3). The ethical appropriateness of exempting innocuous deception studies from informed consent procedures has been supported by Diener and Crandall

---

[4]Established in response to federal laws passed in the mid-1970s (Evans, 1982; McCarthy, 1981), *institutional review boards* are local bodies charged with the responsibility for protecting the rights and welfare of human subjects involved in biomedical or behavioral research within the researcher's institution (for a detailed account of their background and operation, see Greenwald et al., 1982).

(1978): "Where active deceptions concern details of the study that do *not* affect subjects' welfare, rights, or freedom to withdraw, the deception may not jeopardize informed consent procedures" (p. 45). In deception studies, fully disclosing the nature of the experiment to subjects may invalidate the research (see Chapter 3). Although the HHS regulations do not encourage researchers to *misinform* prospective subjects, it permits them the opportunity to omit advance information that threatens to invalidate the research (Belmont Report, 1978). Of course, such information should be shared with subjects after the experiment is over, in debriefing sessions (see Chapter 8). Accordingly, it is not surprising that informed consent procedures were reported in only 9.6% of the empirical studies published in three major social psychological journals in 1983, compared to a reported debriefing rate of 39.7% (Adair et al., 1985).

More controversial is what subjects should be told about the possibility of deception and the use of incomplete information in the study. It has been recommended that subjects be told in advance that they will be informed of the complete purpose of the study only after it is over ("Committee," 1982; Diener & Crandall, 1978; Holmes & Bennett, 1974). However, Adair et al. (1985) argue that such a practice is problematic in that it may heighten subjects' sensitivity to demand characteristics (see Chapter 6). In pointing out methodological flaws in Holmes and Bennett's (1974) evidence showing that subjects who were forewarned about a possible deception did not behave differently from those who were uninformed, Adair et al. (1985) caution against the practice of holding subjects in a state of "suspended suspiciousness" (p. 60).

Even before HHS regulations permitted waivers of informed consent, Diener and Crandall (1978) argued against its automatic use in all social science research (a position more recently advocated by Adair et al., 1985). Their claim was based on the highly innocuous nature of social science research, in which, "there has never been a documented case of permanent harm" (p. 51). As M.B. Smith (1976b) whimsically put it, "surely temporary boredom is the most common harm" (p. 450). Research that does not threaten subjects' well-being, it is argued, does not warrant the use of informed consent. Indeed, HHS regulations recognize the value of waiving informed consent procedures in low-risk research (Maloney, 1984).

Extending this argument against the automatic use of informed consent procedures is the claim that they may tend to cause researchers to shift the responsibility for their actions to the subjects themselves—a caveat emptor orientation (Diener & Crandall, 1978). Using informed consent, of course, does not excuse other unethical practices; it is not an ethical panacea (Adair et al., 1985; Reynolds, 1979). Because informed consent is not sufficient to safeguard the rights of subjects, its use should not be required in all cases. Reynolds (1979) was most eloquent about this when he said:

> By itself, then, informed consent appears inadequate as a source of confidence that the rights and welfare of participants are protected in most research; investigators are assumed to retain responsibility for the partici-

pants regardless of what they sign, and are expected to take precautions for their welfare. (p. 113)

In cases in which informed consent is used with only a negligible increase in the protection of subjects' rights, the informed consent procedures may do more harm than good. Telling subjects all the unlikely things that could happen to them during the course of a research investigation may produce more discomfort than the research itself (Tanke & Tanke, 1982). Reynolds (1979) notes that informed consent procedures also can cost more than the research itself and that needlessly complicating the presentation of innocuous research trivializes the important ethical principles behind informed consent. In this regard, Diener and Crandall (1978) discuss the problems of obtaining informed consent in field studies, where its use may destroy the spontaneity of the setting. They assert that "When field studies do not significantly affect subjects' lives, informed consent becomes irksome and time-consuming for all parties and may be both ethically and methodologically undesirable" (p. 39). (A similar argument has been made with respect to the possibility of de-briefing participants in field studies; see Chapter 8.) Only when subjects' rights are jeopardized, or when they face the possibility of physical or mental risk to their well-being would informed consent be required. However, it would be considered ethically dubious for such a study to be conducted even *if* informed consent is given.

Procedures for Obtaining Informed Consent

As we have noted earlier in our discussion of the elements of informed con-sent, the procedures often used for obtaining consent do not always enable truly informed decisions to be made. Problems have been attributed to ex-perimenters rushing through important information during informational briefing sessions (Maloney, 1984), using language that is too difficult for sub-jects to understand (Grunder, 1980), and not clearly disclosing the voluntary nature of participation (Annas et al., 1977). The result is that many pro-spective subjects fail to have sufficient understanding about the study to give truly "informed" consent. Not surprisingly, then, some of the purposes and objectives of the doctrine of informed consent are not realized in actual practice (cf. Stanley et al., 1987).

As originally conceived, the doctrine of informed consent requires investi-gators to provide prospective subjects with information about the research *before* the investigation begins.[5] If this is to be done, we must consider how much information is to be given and the cost of providing that information.

---

[5]Some researchers (e.g., Milgram, 1974) have claimed that their subjects gave in-formed consent because those who participated in their research later reported not minding the experience. This practice, which Soble (1978) refers to as "ex post facto consent" (p. 42), may be problematic in that these self-reports may be ingenuine, merely attempts to self-justify their involvement.

Earlier in this chapter we provided a list of the types of advance information that are usually required. If the research does not place subjects at risk, then detailed accounts of experimental procedures may be withheld (Belmont Report, 1978; Diener & Crandall, 1978). This provision in the 1981 revision of the HHS regulations (Maloney, 1984) makes it possible for social psychologists to conduct innocuous deception studies without giving subjects so much advance information as to jeopardize invalidating their findings (Adair et al., 1985). In fact, research by Berscheid, Baron, Dermer, and Libman (1973) has shown that subjects are much less likely to grant consent when they are given complete procedural information than when they are given only more cursory rationale. Although some might argue that it is ethically unacceptable for subjects to be given less than total information about the research in which they will be participating (Murray, 1982), most social scientists consider it acceptable practice in minimal risk situations not to give a full advance disclosure (Reynolds, 1979; M.B. Smith, 1976b).

Diener and Crandall's (1978) claim that investigators should provide the information that a reasonable or prudent person would want to know leaves the decision about what information to provide directly in the hands of the experimenters themselves. The rationale is that investigators should try to anticipate whether or not subjects would consent to participate in their research if they were given full procedural information. The practice of "anticipating informed consent" (Berscheid et al., 1973) in this way leaves too much to the discretion of the investigator. To avoid the possibility of having scientific self-interest override the rights of subjects, the use of an advisory group—such as an institutional review board (Greenwald et al., 1982)—has been recommended (Levine, 1978). Berscheid et al. (1973) have argued that although such a procedure may be less vulnerable to self-interested judgments, the accuracy of such outside observers in being able to predict subjects' objections is questionable.

They propose an alternative way of anticipating informed consent by which the experimental procedure to be used is explained to a sample of subjects from the same population to be used in the study who are asked if they would agree to participate. Soble (1978) has referred to this as the technique of *presumptive consent*. Although this method is "an inexpensive and quick device for screening a variety of procedures" (Berscheid et al., 1973, p. 924), Soble (1978) argues that it is unacceptable because it questionably assumes that the actual subjects used would agree to participate. In addition it raises questions about how many anticipated refusals make an experimental procedure unacceptable. Baumrind (1971), for example, has argued for a 5% cutoff level, although Soble (1978) feels that this is too high and that no less than unanimous agreement about the acceptability of a procedure should be required before that procedure is considered acceptable.

The procedure for obtaining informed consent recommended by Soble (1978) calls for obtaining *prior general consent and proxy consent*. This technique requires investigators to tell subjects in advance that they may be deceived and asks subjects to designate a relative or friend to decide on their behalf if the procedure is acceptable. Soble (1978) admits that this proposal may prove to be impractical because it involves the use of a third party. Although the proxy may be assured of protecting the interests of the subject, the administrative difficulties of designating such a person and then explaining the procedure to him or her may make the proposal unworkable. Moreover, Adair et al. (1985) have argued that the use of procedures that lead subjects to anticipate deception heightens sensitivity to demand characteristics and is therefore potentially problematic (see Chapter 6).

Given the problems of these various techniques for obtaining informed consent, it is reasonable to ask what should be done. Unfortunately, as Adair et al. (1985) point out, we gain little guidance from existing research reports.[6] They note that journal editors typically do not encourage authors to describe their informed consent procedures, a practice that has resulted in the mentioning of the use of informed consent in only 8% of the 284 empirical studies reported in the 1979 issues of the *Journal of Personality and Social Psychology*.[7] The question of which informed consent procedures should be used, they argue, is an empirical one, an issue itself worthy of research. "Only then will we be in a position to identify the kinds of research in which consent procedures are necessary and workable. In some cases, consent procedures may be in need of elaboration, or may be unnecessary or undesirable" (Adair et al., 1985, p. 61).

The Impact of Informed Consent on Research Findings

One of the major reasons for researchers' resistance to adopting informed consent procedures is the belief that providing complete advance information about a research project may have adverse effects on the research itself (C.P. Smith, 1983). Although most investigators are unwilling to jeopardize the rights and well-being of their subjects, they are likewise concerned about the imposition of ethical safeguards that are so stringent that they may threaten the integrity of research activities (Belmont Report, 1978). If research is conducted to derive some common good, then obstacles to those research activi-

---

[6]For a notable exception, Sobal (1984) examined the types of information disclosed to potential survey respondents. The most popular disclosures were the identification of the research organization (85.9%), the name of the interviewer (82.1%), and the research topic (80.8%).

[7]Not surprisingly, given the medical nature of much psychiatric research, reports of informed consent procedures in psychiatric journal articles tend to be more common. In a review of the 1981 and 1982 issues of two psychiatric journals, Edlund, Craig, and Richardson (1985) noted that the mention of informed consent procedures was more frequent in experimental reports involving the use of drugs or other treatments (42.9%) than those that did not (16.9%). However, indications of the number of refusers and consenting subjects, as well as the characteristics of the refusers were very infrequent.

ties—as some view informed consent—may be viewed as costly (Soble, 1978). In this connection Suls and Rosnow (1981) captured the researcher's dilemma when they said, "the behavioral scientist is caught between the scylla of methodological precision and the charbydis of ethical concerns" (p. 61). Two sources of potential threats to research findings caused by informed consent have been documented—lowered survey response rates and differential responding to experimental manipulations.

Survey Response Rates

An obvious concern of researchers is that informed consent procedures may scare away some prospective subjects, leaving a biased sample of consenting participants. Unfortunately, the results of several investigations suggests that such a fear is not unwarranted (for a review of research relating response rates to survey introductions, see Sobal, 1984).

Consider, for example, a study by Lueptow, Mueller, Hammes, and Master (1977). These investigators compared the response rates of high school seniors who completed a survey assessing their educational and occupational orientations in 1964, when participation was required, and in 1975, when informed consent regulations made participation voluntary. The investigators found that although only 59.8% of the students completed the survey when participation was voluntary, this sample was *not* biased with respect to the major criterion measures of interest (intelligence and academic performance). However, not all studies have found that participants consenting to research following informed consent procedures represented unbiased samples. Notably, Spohn and Fitzpatrick (1980) reported that subjects who consented to treatment (consisting of withdrawal from antipsychotic medication) were not representative of those who did not participate. Not only were there significant differences with respect to a variety of demographic characteristics (e.g., the consenting subjects were younger and hospitalized for a shorter period), but these subjects responded differently from another group of subjects who were withdrawn from medication for other reasons. Specifically, there were important differences found with respect to proneness to relapse and other clinical criteria (see also Edlund, Craig, & Richardson, 1985). Apparently, informed consent procedures may differentially influence acceptance of experimental procedures, which in turn may alter responses to criterion measures.

In several studies Singer (1978a, 1978b, 1983) considered some specific elements of informed consent procedures that might influence survey response rates. For example in reporting the results of a large survey, she found that asking for a signature to document consent either before or after a survey lowered the response rate (to 64% and 65%, respectively) compared to those whose signatures were not requested (71% of whom consented). Singer also found that the assurance of confidentiality had a small impact on the response rate, although it was not qualified by the sensitivity of the questions. Not surprisingly, subjects believe their signature on a consent form may jeopardize the possibility of the confidentiality of their responses (Reynolds, 1979). Thus, although response rates may be enhanced by the assurance of confidentiality, the practice of having subjects sign consent forms may inadvertently counter this effect.

Impact on Experimental Manipulations

It has been established that subjects in laboratory experiments who are aware of what is being studied sometimes behave differently from those who are not aware (see Chapter 6). Consequently, investigators usually try to avoid having their subjects become aware of what is being studied (Lichtenstein, 1970). Informed consent procedures, however, appear to be a major contributor to subjects' awareness of experimental hypotheses and may be responsible for altering reactions to experimental variables (Adair et al., 1985).

Resnick and Schwartz (1973) conducted the first experiment to systematically manipulate the effects of informed consent information within a laboratory context. Specifically, they compared the verbal conditioning responses of a group of subjects who were fully informed of the anticipated effects of the procedure with those of a group who were not so informed. They found that only uninformed subjects showed the conditioning effect; fully informed subjects demonstrated no conditioning whatsoever. Interpreting these findings, Adair et al. (1985) speculate that, "Informed consent stimulated a search for alternative hypotheses that led subjects to respond contrary to expectation" (p. 60). We believe that the effects would be equally dramatic even if the findings were reversed. The mere finding of significant differences between informed and uninformed subjects, regardless of the direction of those differences, raises serious questions about the acceptability of informed consent procedures.

Several other experiments, mostly dealing with the effects of environmental stressors, have demonstrated that informed consent procedures can alter research results—even if information related to the hypothesis is not communicated. This was demonstrated in a series of studies by Gardner (1978) on the aftereffects of noise. Some of the studies were conducted before the implementation of informed consent procedures, and some were conducted afterward. Although the studies conducted before the informed consent procedures were applied replicated the negative aftereffects of noise found in earlier investigations (e.g., D.C. Glass & Singer, 1972), later studies failed to replicate these results. To eliminate the possible confounding effects of time, Gardner also conducted a cross-sectional study in which informed consent information was manipulated, and Gardner found here, too, that informed consent procedures ameliorated the negative aftereffects of noise.

An aspect of the informed consent procedure that appears to influence responding is the statement informing subjects that they can withdraw at any time. Dill, Gilden, Hill, and Hanselka (1982) explicitly manipulated subjects' freedom to withdraw from a study to determine its effects on reactions to noise. Apparently, the freedom to withdraw from the study lessened the aversive impact of the noise. The sense of control given subjects by informing them that they can withdraw at any time ameliorated the impact of the stressor. Similar ameliorative effects of another environmental stressor, high social density, have been demonstrated when informed consent instructions explicitly mentioned subjects' right to withdraw from the experiment (Robinson & Greenberg, 1980).

Current Status of the Controversy

There can be little doubt about the prevalence of concerns about informed consent as a mechanism for ensuring the rights and welfare of subjects in today's social science experiments. The great amount of time that institutional review boards devote to discussions of informed consent (Tanke & Tanke, 1982) and the impact of these discussions on research activities (Gray & Cooke, 1980) strongly indicates that considerations of a subject's consent to research are of major concern to the scientific community.

Clearly, in recent years scientists have become sensitive to weighing the rights of their prospective subjects against the benefits to be derived from their research activities. Although social science research has not been the subject of as much concern about possible human harm as biomedical research (Reynolds, 1979), indictments about possible ethical violations in human social experimentation have reached the level of public awareness (London, 1977). Rapidly advancing legal regulations also reflect the need to protect the rights of participants in research (Maloney, 1984). Despite questions raised about the ethical practices of some research activities—notably Milgram's (1963) work on obedience to authority (Baumrind, 1964)—most social science research is considered very safe, perhaps even boringly so (M.B. Smith, 1976). There can be little doubt that this state of affairs is, in great measure, the result of intense scrutiny over research activities by governmental agencies (Tedeschi & Rosenfeld, 1981). In an atmosphere of meticulous concern for the protection of human rights, it is not surprising that social scientists have taken to doing increasingly more innocuous types of research (Aronson et al., 1985).

Although we have not seen any questions raised about the need for protecting human rights and welfare, several researchers have challenged the ability of informed consent procedures to offer such protection. Given the difficulties that subjects may have understanding consent forms, as documented in this chapter, it is no wonder that the process of informed consent has been referred to variously as "a fairy tale" (J. Katz, 1977, p. 137), a "myth" (Beecher, 1966), and "fiction" (Laforet, 1976). Also, given the potentially adverse impact of informed consent procedures on the integrity of the research (Adair et al., 1985), it is not surprising that some investigators have viewed the informed consent process as a nuisance at best and an impediment to scientific progress at worst (Lidz et al., 1984).

There appears to be a consensus that informed consent is not always needed and that it is not always desirable in social science research. Informed consent regulations are considered more useful in studies placing subjects in danger than those that do not. When subjects face risk, it has been argued that informed consent procedures provide inadequate safeguards, and that when subjects face no risk, the procedures may be either unnecessary or inappropriate (Adair et al., 1985; Diener & Crandall, 1978). *Flexible* standards for determining the need for informed consent, rather than rigid rules, are recommended (Adair et al., 1985; Diener & Crandall, 1978; Reynolds, 1979) and have been realized in the form of loosening governmental regulations (Maloney, 1984) and pleas for continued research on effective consent procedures (Stanley et al., 1987).

In conclusion it appears to be the practice of obtaining informed consent rather than the principle behind the doctrine that causes concern. As Beecher (1962) put it:

> There is nothing wrong with the principle of consent. . . . The difficulty lies in achieving it, and the fallacy lies in uncritically accepting it as an easily attainable goal whereas it is often beyond our full grasp. Except in the simplest situation, it can only be approached, almost never fully attained. (p. 142)

Chapter 3
Role Playing Versus Deception

The controversy over role playing and deception can be traced back to the late 1960s when the then-popular topic of cognitive dissonance—which usually employed a research paradigm in which the use of deception was widespread (e.g., Festinger & Carlsmith, 1959)—confronted challenges on both conceptual and ethical grounds. Notably, in developing his self-perception theory, Daryl Bem (1967, 1972) conducted several experiments demonstrating that observers of a cognitive dissonance situation were able to successfully judge the attitudes of others who were described as actually being in that situation (see Bem, 1967). These studies employed a type of role playing Bem referred to as the "interpersonal simulation" method, a technique in which "an observer-subject is either given a description of one of the conditions of a dissonance experiment or actually permitted to observe one of these conditions and then asked to estimate the attitude of the subject whose behavior is either described or observed" (Bem, 1972, p. 23). Adherents of dissonance theory (e.g., Jones, Linder, Kiesler, Zanna, & Brehm, 1968) also challenged the use of this methodology on epistemological grounds that soon became controversial (see review by Bem, 1972, especially pp. 27–31). It is this controversy that appears to have sown the conceptual seeds of more general arguments about the value of role playing in social psychological experimentation.

Contemporaneous with Bem's conceptual challenge, Herbert Kelman (1967) issued an ethical challenge to dissonance researchers by questioning the morality of research paradigms involving the use of deception. Following in the shadows of critiques of the ethics of deception in Milgram's (1963) studies on obedience to authority (e.g., Baumrind, 1964), Kelman's remarks proved extremely influential in raising the scepter of righteous indignation against the unethical practice of deceiving experimental subjects. In addition to Kelman (1967), others soon began to propose role playing as a more ethical alternative to deception research (e.g., Darroch & Steiner 1970; M.S. Greenberg, 1967). The combined impact of these conceptual and ethical chal-

lenges to deception experiments represents the roots of a lively controversy
that has taken many forms in recent years.

This chapter examines the predominant issues in this debate over the use of
role playing as an alternative to deception. Before presenting that discussion,
however, we will attempt to clarify our terms by describing what is meant by
role-playing and deception methodologies.

Dimensions of Deception and Role Playing

The terms role playing and deception do not each refer to a single experimental technique. As we will demonstrate, there are many different types of
role-playing experiments and many different forms of experimental deception. Describing these will not only provide a useful summary of the techniques in their own right, but will also provide a foundation for appreciating
the issues involved in the controversy.

Experimental Deception

Following Kidder (1981), we consider an experiment involving deception to
be one in which the research participants have been either: (1) uninformed
that an experiment was being conducted or (2) intentionally misled about the
nature of the study in which they are participating. The deception may be
either passive, such as by selectively sharing only part of the truth with participants, or active, by misinforming them.

We should note at this point that strictly speaking, deception is *not* a specific type of research methodology and that participants in any type of research
may be deceived (Cooper, 1976). As the term has been commonly used, however, experimental deception typically refers to studies involving the creation
of an experimental situation (in either the laboratory or field) in which subjects are confronted with carefully manipulated variables of interest to the
experimenter, who measures their reactions to them. Because either the
manipulation of the independent variables, the dependent measures, or the
experimental context itself may involve misinforming the participants, this
type of experimentation is commonly referred to as the deception technique.
We will follow this convention in making reference to deception research in
this volume.[1]

The use of deception in experimentation has been quite widespread (Gross
& Fleming 1982; McNamara & Woods, 1977; Menges, 1973). Seeman (1969),
for example, has noted that the number of experiments reported in the *Jour-*

---

[1]J. Cooper (1976) prefers to call this type of research "involved participation." However, because role-playing research can also be made quite involving, we will adhere to
the conventional terminology.

nal of Personality and the *Journal of Abnormal and Social Psychology* in which some types of deception was employed more than doubled from 18.47% in 1948 to 38.17% in 1963. Updating these data, Krupat (1977) reported that deception was used in 65% of the laboratory studies published in the 1975 issues of the *Journal of Experimental Social Psychology* (*JESP*) and the *Journal of Personality and Social Psychology* (*JPSP*). As recently as 1983, Adair et al. (1985) found that deception was used in 49.7% of all the empirical studies published in *JPSP* and 81.2% of those appearing in *JESP*.[2] These figures make it clear that deception is a well-established and popular element of contemporary social psychological research.

Three distinct types of experimental deception have been identified (Kidder, 1981; Kidder & Judd, 1986). These include deception designed to conceal: (1) the true purpose of the experiment from the subjects, (2) the actual purpose of the participants' own actions, and (3) the experiences that researchers have planned for the subjects during the course of the study.

Deception to Conceal the True Purpose of the Experiment

The most common form of experimental deception deceives subjects with respect to what the study is about (Gross & Fleming, 1982, reported this type of deception in 81.5% of the deception studies published in social psychology journals from 1959 to 1979.) The assumption behind this practice is that subjects' knowledge about what the experimenter is interested in might lead them to bias their responses—to behave in a manner that is not natural and spontaneous (Aronson et al., 1985).

There are several good examples of such studies in the literature. One that may be used to illustrate this type of deception is Rosenthal and Jacobsen's (1966) important research on expectation effects. In this experiment randomly selected students were misidentified to their teachers (who were uninformed about the purpose of the study) as being intellectually gifted, so as to determine the effects of this labelling on students' subsequent IQ test scores. (As predicted, students labeled as gifted showed greater increases in IQ relative to equally able children who were not labeled as such.) Further examples include the classic studies of conformity conducted by Asch (1956) and Sherif (1937), whose subjects were led to believe that they were participating in research on perceptual judgments. In an experiment by West, Gunn, and Chernicky (1975, Study 1), subjects were led to believe they were being asked to participate in a burglary and did not know that they were un-

---

[2]As might be expected, the prevalence of deceptive practices differs as a function of content area of the research; in some areas a firm tradition of deception exists, while in others, the practice is scarce. Surveying 1,188 articles published in four leading social psychology journals from 1959 to 1979, Gross and Fleming (1982) found incidents of deception ranging from 96.7% in the area of compliance/conformity to 0% in the realm of cross-cultural research.

witting participants in a study designed by investigators interested in compliance and actor–observer differences in attribution. Latané and Darley's (1970) subjects, who revealed so much about the lack of bystander responsiveness in emergencies, were led to believe they were participating in various group discussions on topics of interest to the experimenter. Finally, in his research on obedience to authority, Milgram (1963, 1974) led subjects to believe they were participating in a study of human learning. What these vastly different studies have in common is that the participants in all of them were misled or uninformed about the true purpose of the experiment.

Deception to Conceal the True Purpose of Behavior

A related type of deception employed in some studies involves misleading subjects about the true purpose of their actions. These deceptions involve the introduction of "cover stories" designed to misdirect subjects' beliefs about *why* they are being made to behave as they are. For example, Elms and Janis (1965) led subjects to write counter-attitudinal statements about studying in the Soviet Union by having the request come from persons alleged to be representatives of the U.S. State Department or the Soviet Embassy who solicited their arguments to help prepare a pamphlet. We can also include in this category the classic study on cognitive dissonance by Festinger and Carlsmith (1959). Their subjects expressed their attitudes about an experimental task under the pretext of informing a waiting participant about the task they just completed. In both cases subjects' behavior was elicited under disguised purposes.

Kidder (1981) also includes in this category of deception those studies in which subjects are led to believe they are interacting with another subject, but are actually being fed information from an experimenter or a confederate. Many of the studies in the field of bargaining and negotiation (for a review, see J.Z. Rubin & Brown, 1975) fall into this category—particularly those employing the "prisoner's dilemma" game. In these studies subjects believe that the purpose of their actions is to earn money, while in reality, their behavior is designed to assess reactions in a variety of independent variables within a negotiation–bargaining context.

Deception to Conceal Forthcoming Experimental Experiences

Finally, deception is also used to keep subjects ignorant of events the experimenter has planned for them during the course of the experiment. The subjects in the experiment by Festinger and Carlsmith (1959) described above experienced this type of deception. Their subjects were not informed in advance that they would have to talk to another person (the waiting accomplice) about their attitudes toward the task. Kelman (1967) has referred to this as "second-order deception"; it not only involves misinforming subjects about the study and the true purpose of their actions but also makes deception the entire basis for the subject–experimenter relationship.

Another example of research using this category of deception is the classic "Robber's Cave" experiments conducted by Sherif and his associates (Sherif, Harvey, White, Hood, & Sherif, 1961). The success of this field study in being able to control levels of intergroup conflict and cooperation required the participants' naivete about changes (common threats) that were forthcoming in their summer camp.

Role-Playing Methodologies

Because the concept of role playing has been applied to a wide variety of contexts in the social sciences, it is important not only to converge upon various aspects of the term as we use it here but also to discriminate between these and other uses of the term. Specifically, we do *not* address the concept of role playing as it has been used in conjunction with simulating international conflict (Guetzkow, Alger, Brody, Noel, & Snyder, 1963), social skills training (Trower, Bryant, & Argyle, 1977), the social learning process (Bandura, 1969, 1986), or as a psychotherapeutic technique (A.P. Goldstein & Simonson, 1971). Instead, we refer to role playing as a specific class of experimental techniques.

In their classic chapter on social psychological experimentation in the Second Edition of the *Handbook of Social Psychology*, Aronson and Carlsmith (1968) describe the role playing study as an "'as-if' experiment in which the subject is asked to behave as if he were a particular person in a particular situation" (p. 26). Although this definition is essentially accurate, it fails to capture the wide variety of role playing studies that have actually been performed. To better describe role playing experiments, we categorize them along several dimensions.

Level of Active Involvement

The one dimension shared by all conceptualizations of role playing is the subjects' level of activity and involvement in the experimental situation (e.g., Ginsburg, 1979; V.L. Hamilton, 1976; Hendrick, 1977; Mixon, 1971, 1976). (Indeed, Hamilton, 1976, has gone so far as to subsume other dimensions of role playing under involvement, considering them subsidiary contributors to this one overriding continuum.) At the low end of this dimension we would find role-playing studies that have been referred to as "nonactive" (Mixon, 1976), or those in which subjects are required to "imagine" being in a certain situation (Hendrick, 1977; Mixon, 1971). The dependent measures in such experiments are usually verbal utterances or their paper-and-pencil equivalent rather than overt behaviors (Ginsburg, 1979; V.L. Hamilton, 1976).

A classic example of a role-playing study low on the active involvement dimension is Mixon's (1972) role playing replication of Milgram's (1963, 1974) obedience studies. Mixon's subjects were asked to imagine that the office in which they were seated was actually a well-equipped laboratory, that they were the teacher, and that the experimenter was both the learner and the authority figure. A simple line drawing of the shock generator was provided, and subjects were asked to pretend that a regular chair was actually used to deliver the shocks. Subjects were to report whether or not they would administer the shocks at various levels of intensity. We will discuss Mixon's findings later in this chapter, but for now, suffice it to say that this study represents a good example of nonactive role playing. A second example is represented by the research of Rosenberg and Abelson (1960). These experimenters had subjects play the role of department store-owners who held certain attitudes toward various objects (sales volume, modern art, and the manager of their rug department) in order to see how the imbalanced structures were resolved. Instead of actually having or being given the attitudes, subjects were merely required to assume that they held a particular attitude, an approach that required a relatively low level of involvement on their part.

In contrast many theorists have favored a more active, involving type of role playing (e.g., Alexander & Scriven, 1977; R.M. Baron, 1977; Krupat, 1977; Movahedi, 1977). This involves, at the very least, measuring overt, behavioral actions (Ginsburg, 1979; V.L. Hamilton, 1976), typically with some use of props to enhance realism (Sarbin & Allen, 1968). Sometimes it can involve analyzing complex patterns of behavior in very realistic naturalistic settings. As such, active role playing, as some have noted (e.g., V.L. Hamilton, 1976; Krupat, 1977), is essentially a *simulation* of a social situation.

An interesting example of an active, involved type of role playing is provided by a study by Clore and Jeffery (1972), which R.M. Baron (1977) referred to as an example of an "ecologically-oriented use of role playing" (p. 508). Subjects in this study were required to negotiate by wheel chair a predetermined course around a university campus to determine its effects on attitudes toward handicapped persons. An even more complex and highly involving study is Zimbardo's classic research in which college students played the role of prisoners and guards in a simulated prison (Haney, Banks, & Zimbardo, 1973). Although the participants in this research knew that the situation confronting them was simulated rather than genuine, it is argued that such situations can be extremely involving and elicit very "real" reactions from participants (Mixon, 1976). In this regard, one need merely recall the very involving experiences created by the "illusion" of reality in an emotionally moving play, or even a game of Monopoly.

Role Being Played

Theorists have also distinguished between role playing studies in which subjects are typecast as themselves as opposed to some specific or general other person (V.L. Hamilton, 1976; Hendrick, 1977; Mixon, 1971). It has been noted in this regard (Hendrick, 1977; Movahedi, 1977) that the use of the term *role playing* is sometimes inconsistent with its true sociological meaning: the enactment of behaviors appropriate to *one's own* roles in a given situation

(Coutu, 1951; R.H. Turner, 1956). Although it is usually assumed in most experiments that subjects are acting as themselves, and playing the self-role, Hendrick (1977) has argued that this might not be what subjects are actually doing, especially when they are anxious about being in an experiment. Accordingly, Hendrick recommends that experimenters clearly specify to their subjects the role they are expected to play. When this requires subjects to act as they think someone other than themselves would—a "generalized other" (Hendrick, 1977), or "everyman" (Mixon, 1971)—Hendrick (1977) asserts that they would be *playing at* a role rather than "role playing" per se.

An ingenious example of subjects "playing at" a role can be seen in a study by Mann and Janis (1968) in which college women who were heavy smokers played the role of cancer victims. These subjects acted out scenes with the experimenter (playing the part of the physician), who discussed their illness with them—showing them a chest x-ray, and informing them of their impending pain, hospitalization, and early death. (They found that 18 months later, these subjects reported smoking significantly fewer cigarettes than control subjects who did not engage in the role playing). Participants in the Mann and Janis study were asked to assume a role of another that was highly relevant to them and was made very involving. In some other studies role-playing subjects are merely required to predict their *own* behavior in an experimental situation described to them (e.g., Darroch & Steiner, 1970; Mixon, 1972; West et al., 1975; Willis & Willis 1970).

Although these enactments of, or reports about, others' behavior can tell us a good deal about the way others' roles are perceived (Hendrick, 1977), it has been cautioned that reports about others' roles require the players to be adequately informed about the character being played (Ginsburg, 1979). This would seem to apply to cases in which the character played is another with specific role requirements. Consider, for example, the series of studies by Rosen and Jerdee (1973, 1974) in which college students were asked to assume the role of personnel consultants. In this research one may wonder whether college students are sufficiently familiar with the job of personnel consultants to put themselves in that role.

Degree of Response Specificity

We may also categorize role-playing studies in terms of the degree to which role-playing subjects are free to improvise their behavior or are required to behave in highly specified, "scripted" ways (V.L. Hamilton, 1976; Hendrick, 1977). Mixon's (1972) subjects, for example, had to respond in a highly specified manner in reporting their obedience to the experimenter's demands to deliver electric shock. Zimbardo's (cited in Haney et al., 1973) prisoners and guards, on the other hand, were free to respond in an unspecified manner. These same studies also provide examples of carefully prepared (Mixon) versus loosely described (Zimbardo) scripts used by the experimenter in describing the role-playing situation to the subjects (see Ginsburg, 1979).

Hypothetical Versus Empirical Role Playing

Finally, a distinction between hypothetical and empirical role playing noted by Spencer (1978) deserves mention. Hypothetical role playing refers to role playing carried out without any independent verification or monitoring of the role-playing response. In contrast, the empirical role-playing procedure requires the experimenter to (1) carefully describe the role to be played by the subjects and (2) monitor the subjects' behavior so as to verify their acceptance of the role—independent of reference to the dependent variable.

Most role-playing studies fall into Spencer's (1978) "hypothetical" category, and these can have certain characteristic problems. In general the experimenter does not have the capacity to tell whether or not subjects were able to "get into" the role assigned them. Such a problem may result from the subjects' lack of relevant experience on which to draw (see Darroch & Steiner, 1970; Ginsburg, 1979, especially p. 137), as when college students played the role of personnel consultants in Rosen and Jerdee's (1973, 1974) studies—a role about which they may have little knowledge. Subjects may also fail to accept their roles because they lack the cognitive capacity to make sense out of a complex set of abstractions presented to them. This may be the case in some cognitive balancing research (e.g., Rosenberg and Abelson 1960) in which subjects are asked to assume that they hold various complex patterns of attitudes. To the extent that such problems may exist, Spencer recommends that role-playing procedures be used that allow the experimenter to identify (and discard the data from) subjects who appear to have not accepted their prescribed roles (a similar recommendation has been made by Krupat, 1977). Such procedures are essentially manipulation checks (see Chapter 9).

The advantage of empirical role playing, Spencer (1978) claims, is that it minimizes the threat of lowered internal validity posed by hypothetical role playing. This is because it allows the experimenter to determine the extent to which subjects successfully adopted the desired role. Although empirical role playing studies are less prevalent in the literature, Spencer points to a few good examples. Because of "the overt nature of the role enactment" (p. 267), he considers Zimbardo's (cited in Haney et al., 1973) prison simulation research an example of the empirical role playing approach.[3] Another illustration is provided by Holmes and Bennett (1974), who had subjects imagine they would be receiving painful electric shock, and monitored their feelings through self-report measures of affect as well as their actual pulse and respiration rates. Because subjects only responded to role-played stress through their self-reports, but not the physiological indices, Spencer concluded that Holmes and Bennett's subjects failed to adopt the prescribed

---

[3]Although the internal validity of this research has been questioned (e.g., Banuazizi & Movahedi, 1975), Spencer (1978) contends that internal validity problems are no more inherent in role-playing research than in other types of experimentation.

role.[4] He furthermore concludes that independent monitoring of the role-playing effects precluded the temptation to assume that the role playing successfully induced stress—a potential problem in hypothetical role-playing studies in which subjects are asked to imagine that they are in stressful situations (e.g., Dabbs & Helmreich, 1972).

Controversial Issues

Now that the dimensions of deception and role playing have been described, we can elucidate the various issues in the controversy over their use. There appear to be five aspects of the debate that have generated the most attention. These concern (1) methodological problems, (2) epistemological characteristics of the data, (3) empirical comparisons between the methods, (4) ethical problems, and (5) public image considerations. After describing the issues germane to each of these areas of controversy, we summarize the positions taken by advocates of each approach.

Methodological Biases

Theorists who have challenged the use of deception on methodological grounds have expressed concern over the apparent tendency for deception to be used without question. The practice of using deception as the "single experimental method" (Mixon, 1974, p. 74), or as the "standard operating procedure in the social psychologist's laboratory" (Kelman, 1967, p. 3), has led to some concern over potential methodological problems.

Initially, several theorists noted the possibility that the continued use of deception could lead to word getting around that social psychological researchers cannot be trusted, thereby threatening the validity of studies whose success is based on the naivete of its participants (Aronson & Carlsmith, 1968). Martin Orne (1962) and Chris Argyris (1968), for example, feared that college students have come to *expect* experimenters to deceive them. Similarly, Brown (1965) wondered whether or not our subjects will ever believe in us. Kelman (1967) posed the very practical question of how much longer it will be possible for us to find naive subjects. In fact, some have noted that it is the experimenter who is really naive if he or she believes that the use of deception has been an effective tool for imposing experimental control

---

[4]We should note that Alexander and Scriven (1977) argue against the failure to find physiological reactions as evidence of the failure of the role-playing procedure. They contend that physiological reactions may not necessarily be associated with cognitive activities. We do not mean to argue for or against this issue. However, we do not feel that this debate over the meaning of Holmes and Bennett's (1974) data in any way diminishes Spencer's (1978) general point about the importance of independently assessing the success of role playing.

(Seeman, 1969). Probably the most pessimistic observation regarding the problems of hostile and mistrusting subject pools arising from the use of deception has come from Ring (1967), who remarked that "It would be ironic, indeed, if by their very style of research, social psychologists were to put themselves out of business" (p. 118).

Given these fears, the question is whether experimental subjects actually do expect some degree of deceit from experimenters. On the basis of both experimental and anecdotal evidence (see also Diener & Crandall, 1978; Krupat, 1977), the answer appears to be "yes"! For example, T.D. Cook et al. (1970) found that experimental subjects who had prior research experience believed the experimenter less than did those participating in their first experiment. Similarly, Shulman and Berman (1975) reported that subjects at four different universities characterized themselves as being suspicious of experimenters, Y.M. Epstein, Suedfeld, and Silverstein's (1973) subjects likewise expressed an expectation of being deceived during the course of an experiment. Likewise, Z. Rubin and Moore (1971) found that subjects' suspiciousness about experimental procedures covaried with the number of psychology courses that they had taken (cf. M.M. Page, 1969).

The belief that deception is a way of life in social psychological research appears to be so prevalent that sometimes college students come to think of many actual situations as possibly being psychology experiments. Consider, for example, an incident that occurred on the Scattle campus of the University of Washington in 1973. A male student accosted and shot another student as bypassers on their way to class failed to either offer assistance to the victim or to follow the assailant. When questioned by a campus reporter about why the onlookers were so unresponsive, some said they thought the incident was merely a psychology experiment (Gay, 1973)! In a more recent incident, Mac-Coun and Kerr (1987) found that three out of five subjects who witnessed a cohort having an actual grand mal epileptic seizure during the course of a laboratory study reported in postexperimental interviews that they thought the seizure was bogus. Certainly these incidents constitute intriguing evidence in support of the claim that college students harbor suspicions about the truthfulness of experimenters. What may be even more damaging is that subjects are frequently reluctant to admit to experimenters that they are knowledgeable about an experiment (Dane, 1975; Levy, 1967)—particularly when questioned verbally (Newberry, 1973) and may even break a pledge of secrecy to inform others (Wuebben, 1967).

Might subjects expecting to be deceived produce biased results? Many theorists have made a cogent case in the affirmative (e.g., Argyris, 1968; Forward, Canter, & Kirsch, 1976; Schultz, 1969). Their arguments center around the possibility that deceived subjects might bias the results in several ways, such as by being overly cooperative and doing what they think the experimenter wants (Orne, 1962) or by going so far as to intentionally sabotage the study by behaving counter to the assumed expectations of the experimenter (Masling, 1966). Even "professional subjects" (T.D. Cook et al.,

1970), who participate in many deception studies, might bias the results by not behaving naturally. In this connection, Silverman, Shulman, and Wiesenthal (1970) compared subjects who previously experienced deception and debriefing with those who had not. They found that "the deception experience sensitized subjects to possible ulterior purposes of experiments, increasing evaluation apprehension and their tendencies to present themselves as psychologically 'strong and stable'" (p. 209).

The biasing effects of suspecting deception have been demonstrated in at least two studies. In a conformity experiment Stricker, Messick, and Jackson (1967) found that subjects who were successfully deceived behaved similarly to those who suspected deception but failed to act on it, while those who acted on their suspicions did *not* replicate these results.[5] Further evidence comes from a study by Golding and Lichtenstein (1970) in which there was a deception about deception. These experimenters had accomplices surreptitiously inform naive subjects about the deception involved in the study—an investigation using Valins' (1966) false heartbeat feedback paradigm. Afterward, they assessed whether or not subjects admitted having prior knowledge of the experimental procedure. Interestingly, subjects who knew about the experiment in advance, but who failed to admit it to the experimenter responded similarly to the truly naive subjects. In contrast subjects who admitted knowing about the deception in advance responded very differently. Apparently, expecting to be deceived *can* lead experimental subjects to respond unspontaneously, in ways that bias the results.

Epistemological Characteristics of the Data

One of the most intensely debated issues in the role playing versus deception controversy concerns the nature of the knowledge derived from each approach. The early proponents of role playing argued that their method was superior to deception in accumulating valid knowledge. Consider, for example, the remark by Schultz (1969) that "Perhaps the best way of investigating the nature of man is to ask him" (p. 227). Even earlier, and more boldly, Brown (1962) flatly asserted that "a role playing subject will behave in a way that corresponds more closely to the life situation than a hoodwinked subject will" (p. 74). In response, J.L. Freeman (1969) remarked, "This is difficult to understand" (p. 110). He went on to argue that role-playing studies only tell us "what people think they would do, not necessarily what they would do" (p. 110). Such data, he contends, merely represent a consensus of opinions,

---

[5]In a study by Willis and Willis (1970), the results were *not* significantly affected by the inclusion of the large group of subjects (54.2%) who were suspicious. This finding has been interpreted as the result of subjects responding to the deception at face value—playing the role of the "faithful subject" (Fillenbaum, 1966)—and not acting on their suspicions (Alexander & Scriven, 1977; V.L. Hamilton, 1976). This itself, of course, can be a source of bias (see Chapter 6).

and should not be taken as the truth. McGuire (1969) similarly objected to what he referred to as "this 'public-opinion polling' approach of having quasi-subjects tell us how the experiment would probably come out had we done it" (p. 52).

What J.L. Freedman (1969) appears to have been reacting against is the very limited, nonactive type of role playing in which "the experimenter merely describe[s] a situation to a subject and ask[s] him how he would behave if he were in that situation" (p. 108). This type of experimentation was also criticized by Aronson and Carlsmith (1968) on the grounds that it lacks realism and therefore constitutes invalid data. Their argument is that experimental realism requires subjects' reactions to be natural and spontaneous. Such realism is often facilitated by deception involving the use of convincing cover stories that divert attention away from the true purposes of the study and in which subjects are led to believe that the stimulus conditions experienced and/or the consequences of their reactions are genuine. In this regard Aronson and Carlsmith (1968) have commented, "It is an apparent paradox that experimental *realism* can be achieved through *falsehood*, but it is nevertheless the case" (p. 26, italics in original).

With respect to reality, however, it has been strongly argued by Mixon (1971, 1976, 1977, 1979) that role-playing experiments can be made very realistic and involving for participants (see also Movahedi, 1977). The Stanford prison experiment (Haney et al., 1973) is frequently taken as an example of an extremely realistic and involving role-playing study. Thus, Aronson and Carlsmith's (1968) and J.L. Freedman's (1969) criticisms of the noninvolving role-playing procedures seem to be based on consideration of only nonactive role-playing procedures. Interestingly, J.L. Freedman (1969) envisions that it might be possible to create a more involving role-playing situation, but concludes that even this would result in subjects' "pretending rather than actually behaving" (p. 108).

Such role enactments, it has been argued, can provide an epistemologically superior view of human behavior (e.g., see Forward et al., 1976; Ginsburg, 1979; Mixon, 1976). Deception designs, some have argued, preclude unambiguous references being made about how subjects experience the experiment, leaving open the possibility that the experimenter and his or her subjects defined the experimental situation very differently (Alexander & Scriven, 1977; Baron, 1977; Mixon, 1979; Ginsburg, 1979). By asking subjects about their experiences (verbal role playing), role-playing researchers are supposedly in a better position to understand subjects' phenomenology (i.e., their private, sensory experiences)—what some claim to be the most important aspects of human behavior (V.L. Hamilton, 1976).

A related epistemological argument is that role playing provides a broader, more accurate view of human behavior. Unlike deception, role-playing studies do *not* attempt "to exclude or control out subject capacities for choice and self-presentation that are inherently a part of human behavior" (Forward et al., 1976, p. 602). Hence, role-playing data have been claimed to paint a more accurate and complete picture of the human experience. J. Cooper (1976) has referred to this argument as "a unique twist of logic" (p. 607). He counters that self-presentation is not *always* a focal concern and that making it such may be problematic if it obfuscates the behavior in question. As such, he concludes that role playing (what he calls "role-enactment") is far from being more inclusive, as claimed, and may actually interfere with subjects' reactions to the variables of interest.

Some critics of role playing (e.g., J. Cooper, 1976; Miller, 1972) have also claimed that subjects in role-playing studies may be faced with having to figure out whether to perform as they would like to, as they feel they should, as they believe the experimenter wants them to, or in a way that would make them look best (cf. Orne, 1962). However, proponents of role-playing recognize the value of these options in providing information about the "role/rule" structures in which the behavior is situated (Alexander & Scriven, 1977; Baron, 1977; Mixon, 1974, 1976, 1977). In other words role playing can reveal a great deal about the perceived roles and rules of the social system that regulate behavior (Harré & Second, 1972). By having subjects intentionally play the role of themselves, or some specific or generalized other, as Hendrick (1977) suggests, we can potentially learn a great deal about the way various social rules are perceived. Even if this might interfere with the expressed purpose of the experiment (as J. Cooper, 1976, would claim), it can be argued that subjects in deception studies have the same options. Hendrick (1977) contends, for example, that the apprehensive subject interacting with a domineering experimenter might take comfort in temporarily shifting from acting as the natural self to some other nonself-role in order to escape the threat to personal freedom imposed in the experimental situation.

A final epistemological argument that has been raised concerns the validity of self-reports about affect and behavior. Arguments on this topic have been most cogently expressed by A.G. Miller (1972), who voices concern over the status that should be given to verbal utterances in the absence of converging behavioral data in role-playing studies. To A.G. Miller's (1972) arguments based on the discrepancies between attitudes and behavior, we may also add Nisbett's (Nisbett & Ross, 1980; Nisbett & Wilson, 1977a) influential arguments about the inconclusiveness of self-reports about private feelings. Similarly, Harré and Second (1972) have asserted that there is no reason to expect that people can give accurate accounts of their behavior. Thus, anti-role-playing advocates claim that people's reports of their own behavior and feelings may be inaccurate and biased. Accordingly, they should not provide a basis for understanding human behavior. Yet, as Krupat (1977) has noted, such a position is somewhat hypocritical given that experimenters often accept as legitimate postexperimental self-reports of suspicion about deception. Why then, he asks, should such data be any less legitimate in the "real" experiment?

Empirical Comparisons Between Role-Playing and Deception Studies

An issue that draws on and extends the methodological and epistemological arguments discussed so far involves the comparability of the results of conceptually similar investigations using role-playing and deception techniques. Interest in making such comparisons can be traced back to 1954 when Vinacke recommended that experiments using deception be compared to those not using deception to see if analogous results are obtained. As we report here, many such studies have now been conducted. These include investigations in which role playing is compared to deception in (1) the same experimental design (e.g., Holmes & Bennett, 1974; Horowitz & Rothschild, 1970), (2) separate conceptual replications conducted by the same experimenters (e.g., J.H. Goldstein, Davis, & Herman, 1975; West et al., 1975), or (3) conceptual replications of well-known studies previously reported by other researchers (e.g., M.S., Greenberg, 1967; Mixon, 1972). Although there are undoubtedly more, we believe that the investigations reported in our discussion are representative of the variety of approaches and findings of such empirical comparisons. Our presentation is, of necessity, highly abstracted, and therefore may fail to capture some of the subtle points of criticism that have been the focus of some attention (e.g., see A.G. Miller, 1972). We will, however, attempt to survey what has been done so that the general issues raised in making such comparisons will be better understood.

Review of Comparison Studies

One of the first studies examining the comparability of role-playing and deception results was Martin Greenberg's (1967) attempted replication of Schacter's (1959) classic work on the effects of anxiety and birth order on affiliation. Greenberg described Schacter's procedure to his subjects and asked them to respond as if they were actually in that study. When anxiety was manipulated (by subjects' being told to expect severe or mild electric shocks), the predicted interaction between birth order and anxiety found by Schacter was *not* replicated. Similarly, Dabbs and Helmreich (1972) found that their subjects, who were asked to imagine being in car accidents and helicopter crashes, did not become more affiliative (and this was also not qualified by birth order). However, when Greenberg looked at perceived anxiety (self-rating of being high or low anxiety) he successfully replicated Schacter's finding that high anxiety leads to greater affiliation than low anxiety among first-born and only-child subjects.

    Like M.S. Greenberg (1967), Holmes and Bennett (1974) had subjects anticipate receiving electric shock, but they directly compared the reactions of those who believed they actually would be shocked to those who were asked to pretend they would be shocked (see also Houston & Holmes, 1975). Using more involving role-playing instructions than Greenberg, Holmes and Bennett measured subjects' arousal through self-reports and actual physiological measures. Interestingly, both role-playing and deception subjects reported being aroused. However, only deceived subjects showed any actual physiological reactions to the fear manipulation. While Holmes and Bennett view this as evidence of the ineffectiveness of role playing, others (e.g., Alexander & Scriven, 1977) have argued that imposition of this criterion is too harsh and that physiological reactions should not necessarily be expected to coincide with certain judgmental processes.

While Greenberg's (1967) study made anxiety the first topic researchers looked at in using role playing to replicate the findings of deception studies, the most popularly researched area of investigation in this regard has been social influence—studies of conformity, compliance, and obedience. Included in this group are studies that compared deception with role playing in situations in which subjects were given varying degrees of advance information about the actual purpose of the study. For example, using an Asch-type conformity paradigm, Horowitz and Rothschild (1970) compared the conformity behavior of subjects who were deceived, and therefore naive about the true purpose of the study, to that of subjects who played the role of such deceived subjects. Role-playing subjects were either given partial information about the study (the forewarned group) or were told virtually everything about the study (the prebriefed group). It was found that deceived and forewarned subjects were equally likely to conform to others' judgments, but prebriefed subjects were less conforming. It would appear that subjects (in the forewarned group) were successfully able to play the role of deceived subjects but not when they had complete information about the study (as in the prebriefed group).

Extending this analysis, Willis and Willis (1970) found that even completely prebriefed subjects were able to predict the behavior of deceived subjects, but only when these behaviors were obvious (such as the tendency to conform more to superior- than to inferior-status others). However, some of the more subtle effects demonstrated by deceived subjects were not replicated by role-playing subjects. In contrast to these findings, Mitchell (1975) found that conformity responses were unaffected by the degree of advance information provided role-playing subjects. (These results are consistent with those of Gallo, Smith, and Mumford, 1973, who found that their deceived subjects showed no differences in conformity as a function of their prior knowledge about deception.) Apparently, subjects appear capable of adopting the role of subjects who are deceived into experiencing the pressure to conform to others. However, subtle, nonobvious interactive effects may not be replicated.

Role playing of compliance behavior has been studied by West et al. (1975). In the first of two studies, subjects were approached by an experimenter posing as a private investigator, who presented them with elaborate plans for burglarizing a local advertising firm. Different rationales for the crime were provided. The percentage of subjects who complied with the experimenter's request to participate in the burglary given each rationale was compared to the estimates of the percentage of others who would participate in the burglary provided by another group of subjects. Although the per-cell rates of compliance were very different, the overall pattern of compliance across the various conditions was not significantly different for those who were deceived compared to those who estimated others' rates of compliance. (For a critical analysis of the role-playing procedure employed in this study, see Ginsburg, 1978.)

An even more dramatic demonstration of agreement between role playing and deception can be seen in Mixon's (1972) replication of Milgram's (1963) obedience research. Using very carefully worded descriptions of the experimental situation, Mixon was able to create conditions in which subjects were obedient to the experimenter's authority in degrees ranging from never to virtually always. Most interestingly, when the apparent consequences of being obedient were described as being ambiguous, as they were in Milgram's research, Mixon was successfully able to replicate the 65% rate of obedience obtained by Milgram.

Role playing has also been compared to deception in other areas of research, such as aggression. Nickel (1974), for example, observed that subjects retaliated against intentionally given low levels of aggression with equal force whether they were deceived or role playing. Similarly, the tendency for aggressive responses to escalate over time has been replicated by both deceived and role-playing subjects (Goldstein et al., 1975).

Finally, the comparability of role playing and deception results has been examined in attitude research. In their investigation, for example, Darroch and Steiner (1970) found that role-playing subjects were successfully able to predict the overall relationship between variables in a forced compliance paradigm. However, not all their role-playing and deception results were analogous. In a similar vein, Rozelle and Druckman (1971) found that deceived and role-playing subjects were equally unlikely to compromise their positions on various issues when their initial positions were extreme. However, like Willis and Willis (1970), these investigators also found that role-playing subjects were not able to replicate the more complicated pattern of interaction noted among deceived subjects.

Controversy Over Empirical Comparisons

Probably the main reason why researchers sought to compare the results of role-playing and deception studies is that role playing was offered as a more ethical *alternative* to deception studies (e.g., Darroch & Steiner, 1970; M.S. Greenberg, 1967; Kelman, 1967). As such, some have noted that it is understandable for deception studies to have been taken as the criterion against which to judge the effectiveness of role-playing studies (e.g., see R.M. Baron, 1977; Ginsburg, 1979). Consider A.G. Miller's (1972) admonition that "one would always have to perform the real experiment to know how much faith to place in the role playing surrogate" (p. 627).

Recently, however, some theorists have questioned both the need to make such comparisons and their meaningfulness. Mixon (1971) was among the first to argue against the comparability of these two methodologies, claiming that the hypothetico-deductive method used in most deception studies makes different assumptions about behavior than role-playing studies. Building on this foundation, Forward et al. (1976) have argued that since role-playing studies examine behavior under self-presentational control ("intentional" behavior) while deception studies do not (they examine "incidental" behavior), the results of both types of studies are not directly comparable (see also Movahedi, 1977). If such comparisons are made, Forward et al. (1976) argue that role playing—since it provides a broader view of behavior—should be the criterion against which to compare deception studies, instead of the other way around. Although this viewpoint appears to be in the minority (see criticism by J. Cooper, 1976), it appears to be part of a growing movement against accepting the criterial status of deception studies. In this vein theorists have noted that instead of simulating deception studies, role-playing investigators should attempt to simulate field research (Krupat, 1977), or, more generally, any natural social situation (Mixon, 1977).

Both Krupat (1977) and Hendrick (1977) have noted how proponents of deception have stacked the decks against role-playing studies. If the results of comparison studies are similar, it is argued, epistemologically, that this does not provide assurance that the underlying processes producing the results are equivalent: "Even if role playing produces data comparable in its topography to actual behavior, it is not precisely the same thing as the actual behavior in its antecedent and theoretical properties" (A.G. Miller, 1972, p. 634). If the results are different, it is argued that the role-playing studies provide an inadequate substitute (J. Cooper, 1976). However, as Krupat (1977) notes, differences in results are produced by any different methodologies—a finding that speaks to the inherent nature of different experimental methods in telling us different things about behavior.

On this note Ginsburg (1979) has cogently argued that deficiencies in the deception method make it an unsuitable standard against which to compare the results of role-playing studies. Citing various problems of validity (caused by lack of subject naivete, questionable assumptions about the perceived meaning of the experimental manipulations, and the like), Ginsburg (1979) concludes that deception experiments have no absolute claim to truth, and that their own inherent weaknesses preclude unambiguous inferences to be made about social behavior.

Ethical Issues

One of first criticisms of deception studies to be voiced was that they are ethically dubious—a concern that continues to be sounded (Baumrind, 1985). Concerns about the questionable morality of deceiving subjects have been expressed as far back as 1954 when Vinacke asked, "What, in short, is the proper balance between the interests of science and the thoughtful treatment of the persons who, innocently, supply the data?" (p. 155). For Seeman

(1969), the answer is that scientific knowledge is *never* worth the ethical costs of deception: "If knowledge in psychology is won at the cost of some essential humanness in one person's relationship to another, perhaps the price is too high" (p. 1028). Likewise, Baumrind (1985) also rejects as being too high scientific gains derived at the cost of deception. Others, such as Kelman (1967), agree that deceiving experimental subjects represents a potential threat to the preservation of basic human dignity but recognize that it *sometimes* may be justified in the pursuit of scientific knowledge (see also, R.A. Baron, 1981).

It is possible to identify two distinct, although not unrelated, aspects of the ethical problems of using deception in research. The first is simply that deceiving is lying and that lying in any form is wrong; it is a practice that runs counter to the standards of most contemporary religious and cultural systems (Diener & Crandall, 1978; Warwick, 1975) and that violates human rights (Baumrind, 1985; R. Goldstein, 1981). In this regard Kelman (1967) points to an intriguing contradiction: Outside of the experimental context, most of us would never think of lying and tricking others as we do in our experiments, but yet, in our experiments, we often forget that the relationship between subjects and experimenter is a real interhuman one that should be subject to the same rights of human dignity. How can experimenters morally justify such behavior? Kelman (1967) suggests that there appears to be a suspension of the normal moral standards in an experiment—a situation that is sometimes not real, and therefore, "the usual criteria for ethical interpersonal conduct become irrelevant" (p. 5).

Indeed, there is evidence for such a dual standard from several sources. After finding that his deceived subjects did not mind beng lied to, MacKinney (1955) observed that "being deceived as an experimental subject is more a problem when viewed in the abstract that when it actually happens to the subjects concerned" (p. 133). Similarly, deceived subjects in other experiments have also reported almost total acceptance of the deception to which they were subjected (Clark & Word, 1974; Ring, Wallston, & Corey, 1970). These findings are consistent with other evidence showing that college students—the usual victims of experimental deception—do not consider experimental deception evil or ethically unjustifiable (Y.M. Epstein et al., 1973; Gerdes; 1979; Rugg, 1975; Sullivan & Deiker, 1973). Interestingly, research subjects tend to be *less* bothered by the ethical problems of deception than are the institutional review boards designed to protect subjects (C.P. Smith & Bernard, 1982; C.P. Smith, Bernard, & Malinowski, 1980). However, Baumrind (1985) notes that the postexperimental questionnaires used to assess reactions to deception are "tacked on as an afterthought and generally lack psychometric sophistication" (p. 168). Her claim is that the validity of subjects' self-reports following deceptive experimental practices is suspect, and likely to be the result of processes such as differential compliance to the experimenter and identification with the aggressor (Baumrind, 1985).

In addition to the ethical violations of lying per se, a second ethical issue

surrounds the fact that deception experiments may lessen a subject's opportunity to freely decide in advance whether or not he or she wants to be subjected to the experiences to be encountered in the experiment. This is essentially
a matter of *informed consent*, that is, the research participant's right to make
a free choice about whether or not to participate in the research given accurate knowledge about the potential harm that may be encountered (for a
more detailed discussion, see Chapter 2). To the extent that subjects are
deceived about the risks to which they will be exposed during the course of an
experiment, this is a clear ethical violation in that informed consent is not
given (Diener & Crandall, 1978). In fact Dresser (1981) has referred to the
practice as "misinformed consent" (p. 3). Giving subjects enough experimental details in order to obtain informed, voluntary consent in compliance
with the American Psychological Association's ethical guidelines ("Committee," 1982), the U.S. Department of Health, Education, and Welfare's guidelines (DHEW, 1975), and other legal and moral codes (see Reynolds, 1979),
has been recognized as creating a source of experimental artifacts (Suls &
Rosnow, 1981). Indeed, there are already several examples of studies in
which strict adherence to ethical guidelines has severely biased the results
(e.g., Gardner, 1978; Resnick & Schwartz, 1973).

Finally, we should note that not all scientists share the concern over the
importance of informed consent in the context of the role playing versus
deception debate. For example Movahedi (1977) refers to the informed consent issue as "overstated and...the weakest argument in support of role
playing" (p. 491). Similarly, some have argued that deception is sometimes
used to make an experiment *more* ethical. This point is made by J. Cooper
(1976) with respect to Milgram's (1963, 1974) research on obedience, and by
Diener and Crandall (1978) with respect to studies on aggression using the
shock machine (e.g., see review by R.A. Baron, 1977). In both cases, subjects were deceived into believing they were administering electric shocks to
another person. It is argued, however, that this deception is *more* ethical
than actually administering shock to another person for the sake of avoiding
deception.

Public Image Considerations

We have already established that common knowledge about experimental
deception can contribute to methodological artifacts as the pool of naive
subjects grows smaller. A related problem is that deception on the part of
psychologists may contribute to their negative image in the eyes of the public.
Vinacke (1954) first raised these questions about deception when he asked,
"What sort of a reputation does a laboratory which relies heavily on deceit
have in the university and the community where it operates?" (p. 155), and
"What possible effects can there be on [the public's] attitude toward psychologists...?" (p. 155).

According to some (e.g., Kelman, 1967; Seeman, 1969), the widespread use of deception in psychological experimentation leads to public mistrust about psychologists that helps foster the image that they cannot be believed, a cost that undermines public support for the research enterprise (Baumrind, 1985). When debriefed, not only might deceived subjects come to doubt the veracity of the experimenter, but such a lack of confidence may generalize to other psychologists, thereby creating a public relations problem (Seeman, 1969). Such widespread mistrust of psychologists who use deception has been recognized as being responsible for the widespread legal and political intrusions into social research activities (e.g., "Committee," 1982)—a kind of monitoring for the public good (Mitchell, Kaul, & Pepinsky, 1977), a safeguard against experimental "snoopology" (Jung, 1975).

Finally, not only has it been argued that using deception can lead the public to hold a negative image of psychologists but also that the experimenters may feel badly about carrying out the deception (Diener & Crandall, 1978). A particularly poignant case in this regard involves an experiment by Walster (1965) in which female college students were asked out on a date by a handsome male graduate student posing as another subject. It most certainly was disappointing to the subjects to learn that this person's flattering interest in them was just a hoax, part of his job as an experimental confederate. In addition to whatever psychological harm this may have caused the subjects, it has been reported that the handsome confederate himself felt badly about having been a party to such deception and questioned whether the value of the research justified the deception involved (Z. Rubin, 1970). Thus, the costs to an experimenter's ethical self-image are also at stake.

Summarizing the Debate

Because our discussion of the role-playing–deception controversy was organized around the issues, it may be useful at this point to summarize the debate from the perspective of proponents of each side.

Arguments Favoring Deception and Against Role Playing

The primary argument in favor of deception and against role playing is that deception experiments better capture spontaneous behavior that is not subject to social desirability biases inherent in reports of what subjects say they would do. It has also been argued that because role-playing studies fail to replicate all but the most obvious forms of social behavior observed in deception studies, the former should not be considered a suitable substitute for the latter.

Arguments Favoring Role Playing and Against Deception

Advocates of role-playing research criticize deception studies on the grounds that they are unethical, create a negative public image of psychologists, and are subject to biases resulting from participants' suspicions and lack of naivete about the deception. On the epistemological side, it is argued that role-playing data provide a broader account of social behavior—one that potentially appreciates the social roles and rules that guide behavior.

Current Status of the Controversy

The controversy over role playing and deception was sparked, in part, by role playing being presented as an alternative to deception (e.g., Bok, 1974; Darroch & Steiner, 1970; M.S. Greenberg, 1967; Kelman, 1967). Today, however, social scientists appear to have reduced their interest in debating whether or not role-playing studies should or could substitute for deception studies in favor of recognizing the virtues of *both* approaches for various purposes. In this regard both Ginsburg (1979) and Krupat (1977) have referred to role playing and deception as "complementary" strategies.

As we have already noted, proponents of the deception approach criticized role playing primarily on epistemological and empirical grounds. However, even early critics who argued that role playing should not be substituted for deception recognized that role playing had some limited value. J.L. Freedman (1969), for example, recognized that role playing could be used to help generate (but not confirm) experimental hypotheses and to provide data in cases where traditional deception methods are impossible. The value of role playing in eliminating or testing for the effects of demand characteristics has also been noted (Orne, 1962, 1969), although this has not gone unquestioned (Kruglanski, 1975).

These same purposes of role playing have been reiterated by more recent observers. For example J. Cooper (1976) and Movahedi (1977) echoed J.L. Freedman's (1969) sentiment that role playing should be reserved for the generation, but not for the testing of hypotheses. J. Cooper (1976) also agreed that role-playing would be an appropriate substitute for a manipulated situation when the behavior in question is too dangerous to actually measure. Like Orne (1962, 1969), so too have Alexander and Scriven (1977) recognized the value of using role-playing as a quasi-control technique to identify demand characteristics in experimental research involving deception.

Recent observers have also argued in favor of several additional purposes for role-playing research that extend beyond those originally recognized. Hamilton (1976), for example, has agreed with J.L. Freedman's (1969) contention that role-playing cannot substitute for deception studies, but may provide useful *explanations* of their results. In this regard Ginsburg (1979) has argued that role-playing data provide a useful way of "disclosing the situational features, including the role/rule framework, which constitute the conditions under which actions occur and by which the actions are guided" (p. 143). In addition to this *discovery* function, Ginsburg argues that role playing can also be used for *verification* purposes—for elaborating and extending other types of data. Other uses, Ginsburg suggests, include synthesizing and analyzing social situations. The analysis of social situations is one of the more common uses of role playing, such as for identifying the situations under which various rules of self-presentation operate (see also Alexander & Scriven, 1977).

Ginsburg (1979) notes, however, that role-playing techniques are unlikely to help achieve insight into the cognitive processes underlying social behavior. In contrast R.M. Baron (1977) argues that role playing can indeed provide insight into social reasoning. This point is argued on the basis of the assumption that the data collected from role-playing subjects are less biased since they are the result of an open, collaborative relationship with the experimenter. Moreover, in many social situations, subjects may be expected to report more honest feelings if they are not apprehensive as a result of suspecting that they are being surreptitiously observed (see also Alexander & Scriven, 1977). On this basis, R.M. Baron (1977) asserts that role playing may be useful as a means of recognizing social system rules, and as a way of studying purposive behavior. His argument is essentially that making these processes focal allows experimenters to better understand how subjects are responding to them without the a priori imposition of interventions. As such, R.M. Baron (1977) asserts—counter to J. Cooper (1976)—that role playing may be superior to deception not only in generating, but in *testing* hypotheses.

In conclusion, there appears to be a place in our methodological repertoire for both role-playing and deception techniques. Current researchers appear to agree with J. Cooper (1976) that the debate over which *one* approach is superior has been misdirected, and that there are good reasons to consider using both. This middle ground appears to have been reached as a result of the many arguments in support of role playing that have generated so much attention in the literature. The result appears to be more widespread acceptance of a greater range of research techniques in contrast to any single standard method.

Chapter 4

The Laboratory Experiment Versus Field Research

At the turn of the century, Norman Triplett (1897–1898) conducted a simple laboratory experiment in which people were asked to wind fishing reels in the presence or absence of others. Triplett's intent was to explain a phenomenon he observed while racing a bicycle—namely, that racers performed better when competing against others than when racing against the clock. By using a laboratory experiment to isolate the variables of interest and testing hypotheses about them, Triplett was among the first psychologists to study a social psychological phenomenon using a method that in this century has gained widespread prominence in the social and behavioral sciences.

Indeed, there can be little doubt about the popularity of the laboratory experiment in the methodological tool kit of today's social scientist. Although the laboratory experiment is not uncommonly used in such fields as sociology (e.g., Scott & Shore, 1979), consumer behavior (e.g., Sirgy, 1983), and organizational behavior (e.g., Fromkin & Streufert, 1976), it is within the field of social psychology that the laboratory experiment has gained particular prominence (e.g., Aronson et al., 1985). As Gergen (1978a) put it, "the practice of social psychology has become unmistakably identified with the experimental method" (p. 507). In support of this claim, one archival study found that 83% of the articles published in the 1972 issues of the *Journal of Personality and Social Psychology* used experimentation (Higbee, Lott, & Graves, 1976).[1] With social science methodology texts referring to the laboratory experiment as "probably the most powerful technique available for demonstrating causal relationships between variables" (R.A. Jones, 1985, p. 282) and "a preferred mode for the observation of nature" (Rosenthal,

---

[1]Similar findings demonstrating the prevalence of laboratory research in an older sample of the social psychology literature (1961–1970) have been compiled by Fried, Gumpper, and Allen (1973). Likewise, the dominance of research reports relying on experimental manipulations has been consistently demonstrated from the late 1950s through the early 1980s (Adair et al., 1985; Higbee, Millard, & Folkman, 1982).

1967a, p. 356), it is not surprising to witness the widespread acceptance of the laboratory experiment.

Such claims about the virtues of the laboratory experiment and the merits of its popularity have not gone unchallenged (for a review, see Locke, 1986a). In fact it was in part a rash of criticisms against the laboratory experiment that fueled the so-called "crisis" in social psychology that occurred in the late 1960s (see Chapter 1). The resulting pleas for a return to the Lewinian (Lewin, 1951) values of studying natural groups (Bickman & Henchy, 1972) marked the so-called "new look" in experimental social psychology (M.B. Smith, 1972). For example, critics have referred to laboratory experiments as being "frivolous" (Ring, 1967, p. 113), as having "reached the point of diminishing returns" (McGuire, 1967, p. 132), and as being "poor indicators of the range and significance of the processes in contemporary social life" (Gergen, 1973, p. 316).

This chapter takes a closer look at the controversies surrounding the use of laboratory experiments and considers the merits of field research as an alternative approach. Questions about the relative merits of both methodologies have been raised in such diverse subfields of psychology as comparative psychology (D.B. Miller, 1977), developmental psychology (Bronfenbrenner, 1976) environmental psychology (Proshansky, 1976), industrial–organizational psychology (Dipboye & Flanagan, 1979; Locke, 1986a), social psychology (Ring, 1967), and perception (Gibson, 1966). Debates also have arisen in other social science fields, such as sociology (Webster & Kervin, 1971), management (Fisher, 1984) personnel administration (Olian, 1986), and marketing (Sawyer, 1975). Given the prevalence of the laboratory experiment in social psychology, it is, not surprisingly, within this field that most of the controversies over the use of laboratory and field research have arisen. Accordingly, although we draw on the literatures from several fields, it is from a primarily social psychological perspective that the controversies are examined in this chapter.

In presenting the various arguments, we focus on two major lines of criticism—the artificiality of laboratory experiments, and the limited generalizability of laboratory findings to nonlaboratory settings. The chapter concludes by assessing the current state of the arguments with respect to the relative viability of laboratory and field approaches to research. Before understanding these analyses, however, we begin by providing some basic descriptions of the laboratory experiment and of field approaches.

Characterizing Laboratory and Field Research

To set the stage for our analysis of the controversies concerning the use of laboratory and field research methods, we review the distinguishing characteristics of each approach.

The Laboratory Experiment

Given that not all experiments occur inside laboratories, it is not merely circular to state that a laboratory experiment is an experiment that takes place in a laboratory setting. Although social psychology experiments typically are conducted inside laboratories, they also have been conducted in field locations as diverse as formal organizations (e.g., Coch & French, 1948), retail stores (e.g., Brock, 1965), cafeterias (e.g., Latané & Bidwell, 1977), park benches (e.g., Sommer, 1969), and dormitories (Siegel & Siegel, 1957), to name just a few. As Fromkin and Streufert (1976) have made clear, an experiment is a research strategy and a laboratory is a research setting.

The most basic question, then, is: What are the characteristics of an experiment? There seems to be general agreement that experiments require the ability to manipulate conditions and to control sources of variation (Fromkin & Streufert, 1976; R.A. Jones, 1985). As summarized by Weick (1965), *manipulation* refers to the experimenter's capacity to cause experimental events to occur at his or her discretion. The manipulation of experimental treatments may be accomplished either by instruction (i.e., by something that is said to the subjects orally or in writing), or by event (i.e., by something that happens to the subjects) (Aronson & Carlsmith, 1968). For experimenters to be able to interpret unambiguously the effects of their manipulations, they also must be able to exercise *control* over extraneous sources of variance— that is, any aspects of the experimental setting or population that could influence the dependent variables.

One potentially problematic source of uncontrolled variance that must be considered is the assignment of subjects to conditions. It is the ability to rule out differences attributable to the subjects themselves (as opposed to the effects of the treatment variables) that is one of the major advantages of conducting experiments in the laboratory as opposed to the field (Aronson et al., 1985). Typically, preexisting group differences may be controlled by either of two procedures: matching (i.e., equating subjects in different conditions on the basis of known characteristics) or randomization (i.e., assigning subjects to conditions such that all subjects have an equal chance of being assigned to all conditions) (R.A. Jones, 1985). These characteristics, although applicable to any experiment, may be more easily accomplished in laboratory settings.

Three different types of laboratory experiments may be identified. First, Aronson et al. (1985) distinguish between impact experiments and judgment experiments. In an *impact experiment* the experimenter creates conditions that affect the subject and those effects are measured. The experiment by Aronson and Mills (1959) is cited as an example. The female college students who served as subjects in this laboratory experiment had to read either obscene words (a severe initiation procedure) or nonobscene words (a mild initiation procedure), allegedly as an initiation into a discussion group. Subjects' attraction to the group as a function of the severity of the initiation procedure constituted the dependent variable. (As expected, the severe initiation procedure induced greater liking for the group.) This is an impact experiment because the experimenters were interested in what happened to the subjects, how their embarrassment influenced them. It is the impact experiment that is considered the prototypical social psychological laboratory experiment. As Fromkin and Streufert (1976) describe such experiments, they are characterized by the use of (1) college students who volunteer for 1 to 2 hours of research experience, (2) two or three independent variables, and (3) two or three dependent variables measured once or twice during the course of the experiment.

A second type of laboratory experiment is the *judgment experiment*. In such experiments "the subject is asked to recognize, recall, classify, or evaluate stimulus materials presented by the experimenter" (Aronson et al., 1985, p. 443). The subject in a judgment experiment is asked to play the role of an observer, someone whose judgments are being assessed. Several examples of judgment experiments in social psychology may be identified. For example many of the experiments on juror decision making (see review by Davis, Bray, & Holt, 1977) may be considered judgment experiments. In many such experiments subjects read a case study or watch a filmed presentation of an event and are asked to judge the guilt or innocence of a defendant or the appropriate severity of punishment for a guilty defendant. Another popular topic on which judgment experiments are common is the area of social cognition, including those on the formation of stereotypes (see review by D.L. Hamilton, 1981) in which subjects are asked to form opinions of stimulus persons described as possessing various traits.

Fromkin and Streufert (1976) identify the *simulation* as another type of laboratory experiment. A simulation is a laboratory experiment that attempts to replicate, to varying degrees, features of real-world environments' or events. For example, in an attempt to study workers' reactions to inequitable payments, Pritchard, Dunnette, and Jorgenson (1972) stimulated a work environment by hiring participants to work as part-time employees over a 2-week period. Realism was enhanced by incorporating many details of the work environment into the experiment (including paying subjects with checks printed with the company's name). (For a more detailed review of simulation methods, the reader is referred to Abelson, 1968.)

Although individual experiments differ with respect to the specific procedures they use, four general stages of laboratory experimentation may be identified (Aronson et al., 1985, pp. 449–466). These include (1) setting the stage for the experiment (i.e., preparing a cover story, a convincing rationale for the study), (2) constructing the independent variables, (3) measuring the dependent variables, and (4) implementing the postexperimental follow-up procedures (such as debriefing; see Chapter 8). Despite the need to make various adaptations to these general procedures—such as for conducting simulation experiments (Fromkin & Streufert, 1976, pp. 442–451)—these four general stages appear to characterize all laboratory experiments.

Field Research

By observing our use of the term "field research" as the focus of our contrast with the laboratory experiment, the reader would be correct in noting that we are comparing several different research techniques in a wide variety of settings with a specific technique in a specific setting. Indeed, as we shall detail, most of the criticisms of laboratory experiments have been directed at the fact that they take place in a laboratory rather than the fact that they use the experimental method (for an exception, however, see Gergen's 1978a critique of the experimental method). The result has been pleas for changes in research settings to the field, whether the method of choice is the field experiment (Bickman & Henchy, 1972), or other data-gathering techniques such as the interview, questionnaire, or systematic observation (Willems & Raush, 1969). (Indeed, analyses of the content of the *Journal of Personality and Social Psychology* have revealed an increase in the prevalence of studies conducted in field settings in the 1970s; Adair et al., 1985.)

Our primary emphasis will be on characteristics of research conducted in field settings. We also will consider the choice of a research method within the field.

Characteristics of Field Settings

Bouchard (1976) has delineated seven special characteristics of field settings. First, independent variables in field settings may have greater *intensity* than they do in the laboratory. Various ethical and practical constraints may make it impossible to mimic, for example, the high levels of stress that workers may experience in response to layoffs or demotions. Extending this idea, the *range* of treatment variation is likely to be greater in the field. For example the size of work groups and the complexity of organizations are variables that must, of necessity, be studied with a more limited range in the laboratory than in the field. Similarly, because laboratory experiments typically are conducted over a short period of time, the *frequency and duration* of the variables studied is likely to be limited. This may be a problem in the case of phenomena that influence behavior when they occur at threshold levels below that which might be manipulated in the laboratory. These three characteristics of field settings influence the point at which behavioral changes occur.

The next two factors typically are sacrificed in laboratory experiments for the sake of experimental control. One comprises *natural time constraints*. This refers to the temporal structure and life span of events, factors that can be studied only in field research. Likewise, field research is necessary to study *natural units* of behavior. Regular behavioral patterns that occur in particular environments (what Barker, 1968, refers to as *ecobehavioral entities*) require investigation in those naturalistic environments. As Mawhinney (1986) notes, subjects in field studies do what they would do even if no study were taking place.

The final two characteristics of field settings identified by Bouchard (1976), although not unique to field settings, enable the field researcher to consider broader questions than that posed by the laboratory experimenter. The first of these, *setting effects*, refers to the possibility that characteristics of the setting may interact with some of the variables studied, producing different effects. Also included in the possible impact of setting effects is the idea that settings are dynamic and may experience changes over time—effects that cannot be observed in a laboratory experiment. Finally, field research is cited for its greater degree of *representativeness* of treatment variables. The complexity of social psychological phenomena may be seen as making it difficult for laboratory experimenters to operationalize conceptual variables in ways that adequately reflect their impact in naturalistic settings.

Although, as we shall see, some of these assertions are debatable, they appear to be a reasonable list of distinguishing features of field research. Indeed, this general framework may be used to help organize various claims that have been made by researchers about differences between the findings of investigations conducted in laboratory and field settings. Consider in this regard Hovland's (1959) analysis of the discrepancies between laboratory experiments showing the effectiveness of attitude change appeals and field data from election campaigns demonstrating their more limited impact. Hovland accounts for this difference by pointing to (1) greater discrepancies between initially held attitudes and advocated attitudes among laboratory subjects, (2) less salient, and therefore more changeable, attitudes addressed in the laboratory, and (3) the delayed timing of attitude measurement in the field setting. These considerations all appear to be accounted for in abstract terms by the characteristics identified by Bouchard (1976) (especially the intensity factor and the setting effects).

With respect to the research techniques used in field settings, a distinction commonly is made between those in which manipulations are made—field experiments—and those in which manipulations are not made—field studies (Kerlinger, 1964).[2] Because most critics of laboratory experiments focus on the setting (i.e., the laboratory) rather than the research technique used (i.e., the experiment), this chapter will pay greater attention to the field experiment than to other field methods. In so doing, we hope to highlight potential differences attributable to the research site.

---

[2]This distinction is further underscored in the literature by the inclusion of separate chapters on field experiments (Cook & Campbell, 1976) and other field research methods (Bouchard, 1976) in Dunnette's (1976) *Handbook of Industrial and Organizational Psychology*.

Distinguishing Field Experiments and Laboratory Experiments

Although the field experiment sometimes is viewed as an alternative to the laboratory experiment, it should be noted that in actual practice the distinction between the laboratory experiment and the field experiment is not a sharp one (Aronson et al., 1985; Jung, 1981; Kerlinger, 1964). Instead, the distinction is a matter of the degree of difference between certain key factors. To illustrate this point, Aronson et al. (1985) describe a series of hypothetical experimental procedures that is worth paraphrasing here. These represent various points along a field-laboratory continuum within the setting of a typical "bystander intervention" experiment (e.g., see Latané & Darley, 1970). Imagine that:

1. You are a young man walking down a New York City street. As an attractive young woman comes within 10 feet of you, she stumbles slightly and drops a stack of books and papers she is carrying. A social psychologist hidden from view observes whether or not, and if so how much, you help the woman.
2. The same events occur, but in front of a university campus.
3. The same events occur, but after you have entered a university building prepared to participate in an experiment.
4. The same events occur, but as you are waiting for an experiment to begin.
5. The same events occur, but after you have participated in a psychology experiment in which an unrelated issue was investigated.
6. Seated inside a university room, you are given a sheet of paper describing a scene in which the same events occurred and you are asked to indicate how you would behave.

Although the first two settings would be considered a field experiment, and the last setting, a laboratory experiment (using role playing, see Chapter 3), the varying degrees of association with a laboratory of settings 3 through 5 leave their status as laboratory experiments or field experiments unclear. For this reason Aronson et al. (1985, p. 444) refer to the distinction between laboratory and field as being "wholly inadequate," one for which there exists "no clear dichotomy," but rather one for which there are "several possible continuua...that cut across one another in complex ways."

Three such continuua are identified. The first deals with a subject's awareness that an experiment is going on. Subjects are more likely to be aware that an experiment is going on in a laboratory than in the field. The second continuum deals with the possibility of random assignment. In the laboratory random assignment of subjects to conditions is more readily accomplished than it is in the field. Finally, laboratory and field sites may be distinguished with respect to the manipulation of the independent variables. In the laboratory such manipulations may be expected to be more precise than they are in the field, where the experimenter typically has less control over extraneous variables.

It probably is not surprising that the very factors that give field experiments a unique advantage over laboratory experiments may be obstacles to conducting field experiments. T.D. Cook and Campbell (1976) identify several such obstacles. Included among these are (1) the difficulty of withholding treatments from no-treatment control groups, (2) the difficulty of being able to randomly assign groups to conditions, (3) a high degree of variability in sampling, (4) subjects' refusal to participate in treatment conditions, (5) high attrition rates caused by the treatment, (6) heterogeneity in treatment implementation, (7) feelings of resentment among no-treatment control subjects, (8) treatment contamination resulting from social comparisons between subjects, and (9) the dubious ethics of unobtrusive measurement. (Further discussion of some of the problems of implementing field research is included in our discussion of quasi-experiments in Chapter 5.)

Given these problems, we may ask: What types of situations are most conducive to conducting field experiments? T.D. Cook and Campbell (1976, pp. 309–318) identify many specific situations, only some of which are identified here. For example, field experiments may be conducted readily in situations in which people expect scarce resources to be allocated through the use of lotteries. Staw's (1974) experiment on the effects of draft lottery number on Reserve Officers' Training Corps (ROTC) students' military attitudes is a good example. In addition, field experiments are facilitated when members of an intact group do not expect changes to be made all at once (such as when innovations are introduced to various organizational or educational units at different times). Field experiments also are facilitated whenever the possibility of communication between experimental units is low (such as when work groups are physically separated). These and other situations noted by T.D. Cook and Campbell (1976) represent those in which the various problems of field experimentation are minimized.

Field Studies

As noted earlier, the experiment is not the only type of research that can be conducted in the field. Also included in the category of field research methods are *field studies*. Kerlinger (1964) defines these as "ex post facto scientific inquiries aimed at discovering the relations and interactions among sociological, psychological, and educational variables in real social structures" (p. 387). Although experiments, both laboratory and field, typically are designed to test the cause-and-effect relationships between theoretically relevant variables (Aronson et al., 1985), field studies can be oriented either toward hypothesis testing or exploration (D. Katz, 1953).[3]

Indeed, it is the heuristic value of methods such as the interview, the questionnaire, participant observation, and systematic observation (see descrip-

---

[3]Although less common, the use of experimentation for discovery purposes also has been advocated (Henshel, 1980).

tion and review by Bouchard, 1976) that have been cited as one of their major advantages. Kerlinger (1964) identified three purposes of field studies: (1) the discovery of significant variables in the field, (2) the discovery of relations between variables, and (3) laying the foundation for later, more rigorous, tests of hypotheses. Given the theoretically less rigorous purposes of field studies, several observers have commented on their lower status among the scientific community. Kerlinger (1964) put it most strongly when he referred to the field study as "a scientific weak cousin of laboratory and field experiments" (p. 390). It is not surprising, therefore, that Bouchard (1976) has noted that "field researchers have not developed adequate intellectual justification for their role" (p. 364).

Controversial Issues

The principal controversy surrounding the use of laboratory experiments revolves around the often cited claim that they suffer from a lack of *external validity* (e.g., Kerlinger, 1964, p. 380). As D.T. Campbell and Stanley (1967, p. 5) originally used the term, external validity refers to the potential for generalizability. Specifically, the question of external validity refers to the degree to which the effects demonstrated in any study may be generalized to other populations, settings, treatment variables, and measurement variables.

Controversies have arisen with respect to two different aspects of external validity: the artificiality of the laboratory setting and the representativeness of the populations used (cf. Calder, Phillips, & Tybout, 1981; Kruglanski, 1975). The controversies surrounding each of these issues are reviewed in the following sections.

Artificiality

The criticism that laboratory experiments are artificial refers to the inability of the experimenter to create conditions within the laboratory that mimic those found outside the experimental setting. In the words of one critic. "The greatest weakness of the laboratory experiment lies in their artificiality. Social processes observed to occur within a laboratory setting might not necessarily occur within more natural settings" (Babbie, 1975, p. 254). Similarly, Harré and Secord (1972) have argued that differences between the social situations studied inside the laboratory and those outside the laboratory make laboratory study "unlikely to discover anything that can be transferred to life situations" (p. 60).

Focusing specifically on the artificially extreme levels of independent variables (treatment conditions) that may be used in laboratory experiments, Borgatta and Bohrnstedt (1974) also criticize laboratory experiments for their artificiality. Other critics' claims of artificiality have been based on the view that the laboratory does not match the world outside with respect to complexity (Fromkin & Streufert, 1976; Zelditch, 1968). Still others have argued that because the laboratory is an unnatural place for human behavior to occur, laboratory experiments involving human subjects are illegitimate and "worthless" (Harré, 1974, p. 146) and yield "misleading findings" (Wachtel, 1980, p. 407). These and other criticisms of the laboratory experiment (e.g., Allport, 1968; Bannister, 1966) have led some to conclude, as Berkowitz and Donnerstein (1982) have observed, that laboratory research "is of little benefit unless its conditions and subjects faithfully mirror 'real people in the real world'" (p. 246).

These various criticisms of the laboratory experiment on the grounds of artificiality have met with spirited rebuttals. In the words of one team of defenders of the laboratory experiment, "the disparaging criticisms of the laboratory as artificial and ensuing proselytizations for greater attention to alternative research methods are unwarranted" (Fromkin & Streufert, 1976, pp. 434–435). On what grounds has the laboratory experiment been defended against claims of artificiality? Three major lines of defense may be identified.

Artificiality Is Irrelevant to Theoretical Research

The major rebuttal to the artificiality criticism is that the issue of artificiality is irrelevant when it comes to the major purpose of laboratory experimentation—theory testing. In fact, with reference to theoretical research, several authors explicitly have referred to artificiality as being a virtue of laboratory experimentation (Berkowitz & Donnerstein, 1982; Calder et al., 1981). Webster and Kervin (1971) captured the essence of this argument when they said:

> The more artificial the setting, in the sense that it contains *all* and *only* the theoretically-specified factors, the more precisely the one theory in question may be expected to predict. Simply to observe that laboratory settings are 'un-natural' is to overlook this point." (p. 268)

Similarly, Kruglanski (1975) has argued that the experimentalist's job is not to create and measure the effects of the outside world inside the laboratory but to create a situation that "captures the intended essence of the theoretical variables" (p. 106). Kruglanski's (1975) argument is aided by a distinction made by Carlsmith and his associates (Carlsmith, Ellsworth, & Aronson, 1976), between *experimental realism*—the effects of the experiment on the subjects—and *mundane realism*—the extent to which the experimental procedure resembles elements in the real world. What really matters in order to test theory, it has been claimed, is that an experiment faithfully operationalize the variables of theoretical interest (i.e., has experimental realism) regardless of whether or not it duplicates the characteristics of certain non-laboratory settings (i.e., has mundane realism) (Aronson et al., 1985; Berkowitz & Donnerstein, 1982; Jung, 1981).

Calder et al. (1981) and Mook (1983) have argued strongly that in the case of theoretical research it is the theoretical explanation and not necessarily the experimental effects themselves that are generalized. As a result, the experimental context is only of interest insofar as it permits a test of the theory. Following Popper (1959), Calder et al. (1981) claim that theoretical research is designed to create testable hypotheses that may lead to the falsification of theories. Mook (1983) makes a similar point:

> In very many cases, we are not using what happens in the laboratory to "predict" the real world. Prediction goes the other way: Our theory specifies what subjects should do *in the laboratory*. Then, we go to the laboratory to ask, do they do it? And we modify our theory or hang onto it for the time being, as results dictate. Thus we improve our theories, and—to say it again—it is these that generalize to the real world if anything does. (p. 383)

According to Calder et al. (1981), after theories survive rigorous attempts at falsification, they can be used as a framework for designing interventions which themselves are subject to testing for falsification. As such, Calder et al. (1981) assert that theoretical research is one approach (the preferred one) to creating real-world applications. Another approach to creating applications, dubbed "effects research," directly attempts to obtain findings that are generalizable to real-world settings, and does so by creating laboratory conditions that correspond to those in the external environment of interest to the investigator (this approach is advocated by Fromkin & Streufert, 1976; see especially p. 432). Calder et al. (1981) argue that criticisms regarding the unrealistic nature of the laboratory experience apply only to effects research, but *not* to theoretical research. The artificiality of theoretical research, they argue, enables strong theories to be developed: "The controlled environment of the laboratory typically allows the researcher to employ true experimental designs, to tailor variables to abstract theoretical constructs, and to minimize extraneous sources of variation" (p. 204). Similarly, Berkowitz and Donnerstein (1982) have argued that "artificiality is the strength and not the weakness of experiments" (p. 256). When conducting theoretical research, field experiments or laboratory experiments diluted with real-world features may actually be "detrimental to achieving a rigorous theory test" (Calder et al., 1981, p. 204).

Artificiality Facilitates Experimental Discovery

Extending the argument that artificiality is a needed feature of theoretical research is the argument that artificiality is a virtue of laboratory experiments designed for the purpose of discovery. In arguing this point Henshel (1980) views artificiality as a more intentional feature of laboratory experiments than we have described thus far. Specifically, he defines artificiality as "the deliberate and calculated introduction into a laboratory experiment of conditions. . .that do not exist even in approximate similarity in the external world" (p. 470). Henshel's (1980) claim is *not* just that artificiality is an acceptable feature of laboratory experiments designed to test theory, but that "artificiality of conditions is a positive virtue, a *sine qua non* that is actively sought" (p. 470) in laboratory experiments designed to discover new phenomena. By creating unique conditions in the laboratory that do not exist within natural settings, scientists can answer "what if" questions (see Schlenker, 1974) that enable them to seek regularities that are capable of existing in the real world under the appropriate conditions (Henshel, 1980; Mook, 1983).

Henshel (1980) gives two examples of important phenomena discovered in the laboratory through the use of highly artificial experimental procedures— biofeedback and language acquisition among apes. In both cases, the phenomena would not have been detected through experimentation that reproduced external world conditions; blatantly unnatural conditions had to be created for these discoveries to be made. Given the usefulness of these discoveries (on biofeedback, see Black & Cott, 1976; on language acquisition in primates, see Patterson, 1978), it is reasonable to assume that some positive effects discovered in the laboratory may be created outside the laboratory by altering the environment. Such an approach to experimentation, popular in the natural sciences, is being advocated by Henshel (1980) for use by social scientists. When such a shift in emphasis occurs, he suggests, questions about the artificiality of laboratory experimentation will cease to be asked.

Dimensions of Similarity Between Laboratory and Nonlaboratory Settings

In contrast to the two previous arguments claiming that issues of artificiality do not adversely affect certain types of research, it also has been argued that even for the types of research in which realism is desirable, a certain degree of artificiality is not problematic. The core of the argument is not that it is unimportant for laboratory experiments to copy real-world conditions, but that it may be impractical or unnecessary to do so with respect to all dimensions (Fromkin & Streufert, 1976; Weick, 1965).

Fromkin and Streufert (1976) couch their arguments in terms of the work organization as the external environment of interest. In this regard they claim, "The argument that realism requires multiple similarities between laboratory and organizational settings seems greatly exaggerated" (p. 441). Similarly, Locke (1986b) has argued that for many social processes operating in organizations, the differences between samples of students and working employees are less than the similarities between them.

Such arguments raise questions about the number and type of attributes that a laboratory setting and an organization must have in common in order for the findings of a laboratory experiment to depict organizational phenomena. Weick (1965, pp. 210–226) has identified five key attributes, which he claims are required to capture the essence of organizational phenomena: (1) work group size, (2) the duration of interpersonal contacts, (3) the ambiguity of performance feedback, (4) the personal value of performance outcomes, and (5) the degree of task interdependence. Although additional criterion variables may be identified, the point is that only a few key variables may need to be manipulated to increase the correspondence between organizational settings and the laboratories within which they are studied.

Commenting on Weick's (1965) list, Fromkin and Streufert (1976) note that "there is little reason to stipulate any normative list of attributes as important to *every* organizational setting" (p. 442). They recognize that experimenters must use judgment in identifying those attributes that are most important to the focal behavior from either a theoretical or practical perspective. A similar plea for the importance of general dimensions of naturalness has been made by Tunnell (1977). To enhance external validity, Tunnell (1977) has claimed, researchers should attempt to capture naturally occurring conditions with respect to three global dimensions—the behavior observed, the setting used as a background, and the treatments used. Decisions about how to operationalize these general attributes must reflect the practical necessity of restricting the number of variables that can be considered in any single experiment.

Fromkin and Streufert (1976) encourage experimenters making these judgments to identify a set of variables, referred to as "boundary variables," that may limit the occurrence of the phenomena under study. They claim that laboratory experiments of organizational phenomena may serve a particularly useful function in identifying such boundary variables.

> Instead of reinforcing the myth that laboratory settings seldom yield data which are relevant to real-world problems, it is proposed that laboratory settings merely impose identifiable limitations upon the range of criterion situations to which a particular set of laboratory findings may be practically applied." (Fromkin & Streufert, 1976, p. 442, emphasis omitted)

Representativeness

The criticism is frequently heard that laboratory investigations rely on subject populations that are not representative of the population to which the results intend to be generalized (e.g., Borgatta & Bohrnstedt, 1974).[4] As the following quotations attest, laboratory experiments have been criticized in particular for their reliance on the use of college sophomores as subjects.

> The existing science of human behavior is largely the science of the behavior of sophomores. (McNemar, 1946, p. 333)

> Often ours seems to be a science of just those sophomores who volunteer to participate in our research. (Rosenthal & Rosnow, 1969, p. 110)

---

[4]Although the question of the representativeness of samples has arisen in social research in which it is assumed that characteristics of the people and their setting may influence their behavior (Gergen, 1978a), it does not arise in research concerned with "socially indifferent" behavior, that which occurs at a more reflexive level (Littman, 1961).

Two issues with respect to representativeness are considered in the following discussion: the generalizability of field studies relative to laboratory experiments and the use of representative samples as a means of ensuring generalizability.

Generalizability of Field Studies

Many pleas for field research are based on the underlying belief that they have greater external validity than laboratory experiments due to their use of subjects drawn from populations to which the demonstrated effects are to be generalized (Harré & Secord, 1972). For example, Gordon, Slade, and Schmitt (1986) found that there was at least one significant difference between student and nonstudent samples in 73% of the 32 studies of organizational psychology they reviewed. Arguments such as this have formed the basis of claims that greater external validity requires the use of field research as an alternative to laboratory experimentation (e.g., Willems & Raush, 1969).

Such claims about the superiority of field studies in providing access to representative samples have been challenged by several theorists. For example, Fromkin and Streufert (1976) have noted that problems of sampling generality also occur in the case of field interviews, field surveys, and field observations, although they are often overlooked when these methodologies are used. Similarly, Tunnell (1977) has observed that many theorists' attraction to field research is due to its presumed external validity, although the mere fact that research is conducted in a field setting does *not* ensure the generalizability of the results.

Extending these observations, Dipboye and Flanagan (1979) launched the most aggressive attack on claims of the allegedly superior generalizability of field research over laboratory experiments. These authors analyzed the contents of the 490 empirical articles appearing in the 1966, 1970 and 1974 volumes of the most frequently cited journals in the field of industrial–organizational psychology: the *Journal of Applied Psychology*, *Organizational Behavior and Human Performance*, and *Personnel Psychology*. They found that the actors, settings, and behaviors sampled in these studies, although different from those typically found in laboratory studies, represented an equally narrow range of choices. Indeed, just as laboratory experiments typically use college students as subjects, the field research surveyed commonly involved self-report data by male, professional, technical, and managerial employees in productive-economic organizations. On this basis Dipboye and Flanagan (1979) conclude that "there is no empirical basis for a belief in the inherent external validity of field research" and that "in some respects laboratory research provides as firm a basis for generalization to the general population of working people and organizations as does field research" (p. 147).

Sampling Limitations and Generalizability

Dipboye and Flanagan's (1979) claim that the narrowness of actors, settings, and behaviors limits the generalizability of research findings—in either the field or laboratory—is related to a more general controversy over the extent to which limitations in the representative of sampling restricts generalizability (see Jerald Greenberg, 1987). Does a representative sample of research participants ensure the generalizability of research findings?

Writing in response to Dipboye and Flanagan (1979), Bass and Firestone (1980) have argued that limitations in the sample used in a study do *not* restrict the generalizability of the findings. Knowing that certain research findings are based on a specific sample, they claim, implies nothing about the generalizability of the findings unless there is some theoretical or empirical basis for expecting certain relationships to be found. Merely considering the subject population used does not address the question of generalizability. "Ultimately, generalizability is an issue for future investigators to demonstrate, either by showing that patterns of relationships remain invariant across types of research settings or respondent characteristics or by providing a sound theoretical rationale for inferring similarity of relationships" (Bass & Firestone, 1980, p. 464).[5] Likewise, Tunnell (1977) has argued that external validity cannot be achieved in any single study.

Earlier, Oakes (1972) made a similar point when he asserted that *any* research population is atypical. Although the generalizability of findings based on laboratory experiments using college students as subjects may be limited, this limitation applies as well to any sample, and the findings of such studies should be considered just as valid as those using more representative sampling procedures. Oakes' (1972) argument was inspired by his attempt to account for the results of a verbal reinforcement experiment in which samples of "true" volunteers responded differently from a sample of "coerced" students (Cox & Sipprelle, 1971). Experiments on many other topics also have reported different results when student and nonstudent samples were used (in particular, see comparisons of students and housewives in consumer marketing studies by Enis, Cox, & Stafford, 1972, and Shuptrine, 1975; for a review, see Sawyer, 1975). Oakes (1972) has argued that just because there

---

[5]In a rebuttal Flanagan and Dipboye (1980) claim that the representativeness of sampling may tell us about the generalizability of the findings because research conducted using a single type of subject, setting, or dependent measure does not permit empirical tests of generalizability. As such, they appear to agree with Bass and Firestone's (1980) argument that generalizability is an *empirical* question and not something that can be assessed on the basis of the characteristics of any single sample used. (See also the response to Dipboye and Flanagan, 1979, by Willems and Howard, 1980, and Dipboye and Flanagan's, 1980, rebuttal. On this same point, see the exchange between Gordon et al., 1986, 1987, and Jerald Greenberg 1987.)

may be differences between subject groups with respect to a certain phenomenon, it does not mean that the demonstrated effect is not valid. Instead, it may be an indication of an interaction between the phenomenon in question and the population used. Such effects, he claims, should be viewed as important to theory development and *not* as problematic.

Lynch (1982, 1983) has made a similar point. He argues that experimenters should attempt to identify a priori any potential interactive factors and include such "blocking variables" in their research designs to ensure the external validity of their findings. Arguing this point, Gordon, Slade, and Schmitt (1987) contend that such an approach is impractical to implement. Likewise, Calder, Phillips, and Tybout (1982, 1983) counter that it is impossible to try to identify all potentially interacting variables. Instead, they advocate including in an uncontrolled fashion the full range of background factors that can be expected to be present in the setting to which the findings are to be applied. Whether the inclusion of background variables is the result of manipulation (blocking on background variables, as advocated by Lynch, 1982, 1983), or selection (including these at a constant background level, as advocated by Calder et al., 1982, 1983), this approach runs counter to the claim that convenience samples are inappropriate and that their use precludes generalizability (Borgatta & Bohrnstedt, 1974; Ferber, 1977). In fact, Lynch (1982) has claimed that random sampling—the alternative advocated for the practice of using convenience samples (Ferber, 1977)—sometimes may be unimportant or *undesirable* inasmuch as using homogeneous groups of subjects may be helpful for testing and qualifying a theory.

By contrast, Calder et al. (1983) assert that whereas background factors should be considered in testing practical interventions (by including them within the context of interest), they have no place in theory testing (where only variables dictated by theoretical interest should be included in the study). Berkowitz and Donnerstein (1982) make a similar point in claiming that theoretically oriented studies need not be as concerned about the representativeness of the sample used as they should be about the internal validity of their operationalizations. Following from Cook and Campbell (1979), Calder et al. (1982) argue that "external validity is not viewed as necessary for achieving a rigorous theory test and, indeed, may be sacrificed in favor of addressing threats to internal and construct validity" (p. 240).

Mook (1983) also agrees that external validity only need be a concern if the experimenter's intent is to predict behavior outside the laboratory. Generalizability is not always the experimenter's intent. Because many laboratory studies are designed to determine whether something *can* happen (such as Milgram's, 1974, demonstrations of subjects' obedience to authority) as opposed to whether it actually *does* happen outside the laboratory, concern over the representativeness of the sample may be misplaced. Kruglanski and Kroy (1976) have criticized the internal–external validity distinction in a similar fashion, arguing that the fundamental validity problem is always the same—representation. They claim that confusion can be avoided if experimenters specify the "domain of quantification," the universe to which they intend their hypotheses to apply.

Current Status of the Controversy

By way of assessing the current status of the controversies surrounding the use of laboratory experimentation and field research, it appears safe to conclude that today's researchers recognize the value of *both* laboratory experiments and field methods as viable research tools. Despite several attacks on laboratory experimentation outlined in this chapter, even the must cursory examination of current psychological journals reveals that the laboratory experiment remains alive and well. As such, there proved to be little accuracy to Bickman and Henchy's (1972) prognostication that, "The time is short when the laboratory may still have hegemony over all social-psychological research efforts" (p. 1). It does not appear to be the case that field research has become an *alternative* to the laboratory experiment. Researchers appear to agree with Fromkin and Streufert's (1976) conclusion that "the artificiality of laboratories is being unjustly elevated to the status of a fatal flaw" (p. 433).

Instead, it appears that researchers have come to recognize the relative merits and drawbacks of both methodologies. As Ilgen (1986) put it, doing research in the laboratory is better recognized as "a question of when, not if" (p. 257). With this has come an increasing awareness of the purposes of various research methods—using the laboratory to test theories and the field to describe the world as it is (Berkowitz & Donnerstein, 1982). Indeed, several observers explicitly have advocated the use of both research methods. Fromkin and Streufert (1976), for example, have stated that "confirming and or disconfirming a hypothesis with different methodologies provides the firmest structure for generalization" (p. 457). Similarly, in concluding their chapter on experimentation in the current *Handbook of Social Psychology* (third edition), Aronson et al. (1985) claim that what is needed is an "interplay between laboratory and field research" (p. 484). The difference between them, to quote, J.P. Campbell (1986), is a "straw issue" (p. 269).

Although some of the exhortations to "go to the field" (e.g., J. Ross & Smith, 1968; Tunnell, 1977) have been viewed as misplaced and based on misunderstandings of the purposes of laboratory experimentation (Berkowitz & Donnerstein, 1982; Calder et al., 1981), it is clear that there has been a shift away from the use of the classic laboratory experiment as the only accepted research methodology among social psychologists. In commenting on changes in experimental social psychology since the 1960s, Aronson et al. (1985) have noted that among other trends, there is a growing interest in field experimentation. Accordingly, it appears that today's social psychological researchers have a broader range of acceptable alternatives available to them than once before—a beneficial state of affairs that appears to have been inspired by much of the debate reviewed in this chapter, a debate that continues to linger in the literature (e.g., see the exchanges summarized in Locke, 1986a, and that between Jerald Greenberg, 1987, and Gordon et al., 1986, 1987).

Chapter 5

Experiments Versus Quasi-experiments

Donald Campbell privately distributed a paper in 1953 entitled "Designs for Social Science Experiments." It became the basis for a subsequent article (D.T. Campbell, 1957) in which the distinction between internal and external validity was first introduced to the psychological literature. That article was especially noteworthy for presenting in detail the formal logic whereby random assignment to conditions (e.g., treatment vs. control) made implausible some specific classes of threats to internal validity. Later this aspect of assignment arrangements, randomization, was used to distinguish "true experiments" from "quasi-experiments" (D.T. Campbell & Stanley, 1963). Indeed, the special relationship of randomization to internal validity was given such prominence that the term *experiment* was taken to mean a randomized experiment unless otherwise noted—a convention we follow in this chapter.

Randomized experiments and quasi-experiments each have their advocates and detractors. Furthermore, opposing viewpoints regarding the merits and demerits of each approach have typically arisen not in abstract, academic discussions about the suitability of methods for advancing science but in considerations of what advice should be given about means for determining the appropriate actions to take in important social settings. The issues involved are of more than theoretical or technical interest; they have practical implications for policy makers and for administrators of educational, industrial, and public programs. In other words the significance of any disagreements about the role of experiments versus quasi-experiments is that these methods are major alternatives for evaluating social programs and innovative treatments.

Anyone faced with a decision about how to evaluate a social program has a right to be somewhat confused about the status of available methodological options, given the competing advice offered from various sources. On the one hand major texts on evaluation research often open by asserting the clear superiority of randomization. The text by Rossi, Freeman, and Wright

(1979), for example, begins a chapter on "rigorous methods of impact assessment" with the following statement: "The randomized controlled experiment is presented in this chapter as the best research design for the purpose of obtaining estimates of the net effect of an intervention" (p. 179). Similar advice has been given by several well-known statisticians (Gilbert, Light, & Mosteller, 1975), whose review of a large number of experimental and quasi-experimental program evaluations led them to the conclusion that "randomized field trials are currently the technique of choice for evaluating the results of complex social innovations" (p. 40). In commenting on papers delivered at a conference on program evaluation, Lumsdaine and Bennett (1975) were likewise struck with the impression that "there seemed to be general agreement on the desirability of randomized experiments" (p. 256).

On the other hand, experimental design methodology is not universally accepted within the area of policy evaluation. Nor can universal endorsement of randomization be found among researchers in general. Lee J. Cronbach, for example, a preeminent psychologist of considerable statistical and methodological sophistication (with a long-time interest in program evaluation), has sharply criticized the view that randomization is essential to successful evaluation (Cronbach, 1982). In this case, as in so many others, statistical authorities seem not to agree among themselves. The value of randomization is touted chiefly among members of the camp whose lineage traces to R.A. Fisher. Fisherian doctrine, in turn, is generally less well received by those more sympathetic to Bayesian statistics. D.T. Campbell and Boruch (1975) claim to have detected a "widespread tendency of Bayesian statisticians to disparage randomization," which they say "is hard to document in writing but seems an important part of an oral tradition" (p. 196).

After giving a preliminary endorsement of randomization, Rossi et al. (1979) remark that the same chapter concludes with an argument for "using both randomization and statistical controls [such as those associated with quasi-experiments], a mixed strategy that has the combined advantages of both approaches" (p. 179). This is but one example of the ambivalence fostered by such controversies. Rather than either randomization or quasi-experimentation having had the final word, a debate has arisen with respect to the applicability of experimental design principles to the naturalistic research milieu encountered in social policy research. We examine that debate in this chapter.

Another feature of the distinction between experiments and quasi-experiments is that the straightforward way in which randomization promoted internal validity stood in contrast to the more problematic reasoning entailed by the absence of randomization. That feature became more prominent when nonexperimental investigations were used to evaluate some of the social reform programs sponsored during the 1960s. Cronbach, Ambron, Dornbusch, Hess, Hornik, Phillips, Walker, and Weiner (1981, p. 34) have argued that "criticisms of the first large evaluations led to attempts to promote an experimental methodology whose results were supposedly less open to challenge." The upshot was a volume entitled *Social Experimentation* (Riecken & Boruch, 1974), commissioned by the Social Science Research Council, in which the virtues of experimental design were extolled and recommended as worthy of importing from the laboratory to the field. Because random assignment can be difficult to implement in field settings generally and in program evaluations especially, this strong call for its use became controversial. Cronbach's comments are representative of those who felt that randomization had been oversold: "As a participant in the Social Science Research Council, I was on the fringe of the effort that produced *Social Experimentation*. . . . I became convinced, however, that this and other pronouncements. . .created an unacceptable imbalance" (Cronbach, 1982, pp. xii–xiii).

This chapter addresses controversies surrounding the relative balance of internal and external validity, as exemplified by the difference that randomization makes in inferences drawn from experiments versus quasi-experiments. Before exploring the issues themselves, however, we first consider the context within which they have emerged.

The Role of Random Assignment in Experimentation

The context of debate about validity priorities in research derives from assumptions about *what* randomization accomplishes, *how* that result is achieved, and *whether* other means of accomplishing the same goal can be comparably efficacious.

The Logic of Random Assignment

Because randomization as an element of experimental design is a way of assigning treatment to some people and not others, the simplest possible case in which these assumptions can be examined occurs when available participants are randomly divided into two groups and only one receives some experimental form of treatment. Randomization is designed to provide confidence that, within statistically specified levels of probability, the two groups were equivalent before the delivery of treatment. Given that they were indeed otherwise equivalent initially, the posttreatment "statistically significant" differences—on some measured dependent variable representing an effect of interest—can logically be attributed to the only other presumed difference between the groups, namely the presence versus absence of the treatment.

This familiar logic shows that the "what" of randomization's accomplishment is a particular type of confidence about cause-and-effect relationships and the "how" is a particular form of equivalence (one associated with a specified probability estimate) between groups. D.T. Campbell's (1957) list of threats to internal validity, along with the Campbell and Stanley (1963) examination of how those threats are handled by experiments versus quasi-experiments, set the stage for debate about the "whether" issue mentioned previously. That is, the between-group equivalence from randomization was said to guard against such threats on the basis of a single (statistical) assumption whose degree of possible error was known. Although quasi-experiments can have other trappings that make them similar to experiments in appearance (e.g., manipulation, treatment, and control groups), their lack of randomization means that they cannot rely on the statistical equivalence assumption as a way of dealing with threats to internal validity.

The threats to internal validity identified by Campbell (1957; Campbell & Stanley, 1963) represent possible alternative explanations for the cause-and-effect relationship under investigation. That is, each such threat is a category of causes, other than the treatment, that are also capable of producing differences on the dependent measure. Statistical equivalence between the groups of an experiment does not eliminate these threats but serves rather to distribute their influence equivalently so that they are presumably neutralized as disturbances. Thus neutralized, they are not even formally considered as plausible alternative explanations.

The Quasi-experimental Alternative

Campbell developed his list of internal validity threats so that these types of alternative explanations, formally ignored in the case of experiments, would be explicitly considered in investigations that did not take advantage of randomization. Interpreting quasi-experiments was thus said to require that alternative explanations be specified and their plausibility examined; potentially extraneous variables would need to be identified and their causal impact assessed. In short, the investigator would have to know a great deal about the phenomenon under study and about the processes by which it might be affected. The investigator who used randomization, on the other hand, could afford to be ignorant about the nature of the multitudinous extraneous causal variables. This ignorance is not presumed detrimental because experiments, as Boruch and Rindskopf (1977, p. 149) comment, "put our ignorance in an explicit form—random error—and more importantly, structure our ignorance so that it does not systematically distort our estimate of a program effect." Randomization is thus seen as a "procedural guarantee" about the impact of those factors that we are ignorant about, a guarantee that "requires the evaluator to know little but distributes his ignorance equitably across treatment and control groups" (Boruch & Rindskopf, 1977, p. 149). Because of the absence of such a procedural guarantee in the case of quasi-experiments, the investigator who uses those designs "can never be sure if this ignorance is working systematically against him, for him, or in a neutral fashion" (p. 149).

This reasoning makes it relevant to investigate the claim that nonrandom assignment might easily lead to erroneous conclusions that are avoided by randomization. In a commentary on experiments and quasi-experiments, Boruch (1975) presents evidence for that claim by reviewing studies in which comparisons can be made between experimentally and quasi-experimentally assigned subjects within the same population. The quasi-experimental design components of these studies involved the identification of a presumably equivalent nontreatment group against which an experimenter-selected or self-selected treatment group was compared, whereas the experimental design components involved the random assignment of other subjects from the same population to treatment and control groups. The review indicates that pre-existing but unknown differences in the quasi-experimental groups, and/or other extraneous factors of which the investigators were ignorant, sometimes operated to make it appear that the treatment was more effective than was in fact the case, sometimes to make it appear that the treatment had no effect, and other times to make it appear that the treatment was actually harmful! These apparent discrepancies were revealed when the experimental design components of the studies were examined; in other words, presumably erroneous conclusions (of different varieties) would have been drawn if the studies had used a quasi-experimental design alone. To cite just two examples, the quasi-experimental component of the Salk vaccine trials *underestimated* the vaccine's effectiveness by 14%, and a quasi-experimental component of a study of a retardation rehabilitation program *overestimated* the program's effectiveness by 9 points on an IQ scale (cf. Boruch, 1975).

Such comparisons obviously assume that random assignment provides the standard of truth against which other types of investigations *ought* to be measured. Questioning that assumption, of course, is part of the controversy. Now that we have set the stage, we examine issues in that controversy explicitly. These issues come in the form of challenges to the goal of using randomization whenever possible. Because the arguments and evidence relevant to these challenges exceed what can be considered comprehensively in this chapter, the interested reader should also consult more detailed sources such as Cronbach (1982) and T.D. Cook et al. (1985).

Controversial Issues

Essentially two types of arguments are advanced against randomization. One form of attack is to charge that although randomized experiments represent a worthwhile ideal, that ideal is virtually impossible to achieve. Given that experiments are infeasible, so this argument goes, we have no choice but to fall back on the available alternatives such as quasi-experiments, which might otherwise be considered less desirable. The second line of argumentation issues a more direct attack on experiments, charging that the ideal they represent is itself misguided. Both types of arguments are discussed in the following section.

The Alleged Infeasibility of Randomization

Arguments against randomized experiments on grounds of infeasibility take several forms. One form asserts that randomization is less feasible than non-randomization, and because nonrandomized quasi-experiments can be equally as valid as randomized experiments, this difference in relative feasibility dictates a preference for quasi-experiments. It is clear that this argument is convincing only to the extent that quasi-experiments *are* as valid as experiments, not merely that they "can be" so. T.D. Cook and Campbell's (1979) analysis suggests that it will be extraordinarily difficult to ensure the validity of quasi-experiments in advance, however, given that much depends on obtaining "ideal" outcomes and adjunct results that render alternative explanations implausible.

A stronger form of argument asserts the infeasibility of experiments in absolute rather than relative terms. Manuals for program evaluators sometimes claim that experiments are impractical (Agency for International Development, 1972) or "rarely feasible" (NIE Task Force on Research Planning, 1974), a judgment with which many researchers seem to agree (Guba, 1985; Stufflebaum, 1969). This opinion is expressed concisely, if somewhat metaphorically, by Edwards and Guttentag (1975): "We strongly agree with the argument that randomization is best when possible. But we must add, 'It's nice work if you can get it'" (p. 458).

According to this view about experiments, there are numerous things that make it virtually impossible to implement randomization. It has been suggested, for example, that only certain types of treatments and social programs are amenable to randomization, hence that true experiments can be conducted only within a considerably restricted range of settings. Excessive, "unnecessary" expense and time are cited as other possible grounds for considering experiments to be infeasible (Boruch, 1975).

Variations on the absolute infeasibility argument have been countered in many ways. Perhaps the most convincing rebuttal to the general notion that experiments are infeasible lies in documenting the variety of experiments that have been conducted. Obviously, no one charges that laboratory experiments involving manipulations of narrowly operationalized theoretical constructs are impossible. At issue, instead, are treatments of social significance administered to people in the natural settings of their daily lives. The recent history of evaluations of social programs does, in fact, provide ample evidence of instances in which experimentation has been possible, and the variety of these programs is impressive. Boruch (1975) has catalogued over 200 social program evaluations that involved randomization, including experiments on plans for negative income tax, housing allowance, and health insurance; programs in police training, juvenile and adult offenders, and mental rehabilitation; as well as numerous treatments in medical and educational contexts.

Boruch (1975) also has addressed the charge that experiments are needlessly expensive and/or time consuming. He points out that cost-accounting analyses for *any* type of program evaluation are hard to find in the first place, which makes the relative expense of quasi-experimental and experimental evaluations an open empirical question. In the only case Boruch was able to uncover in which experimental and nonexperimental costs could be compared directly, randomization required only a 1% budgetary increase. How much time an evaluation will take depends, as Boruch notes, on the nature of the treatment to be implemented and on the importance of assessing long-term effects. Boruch adds, however, that many experimental evaluations of social programs that were short in duration have successfully demonstrated effects.

The larger issue, of course, is whether whatever time and expense an experiment entails is an unnecessary frill or an essential ingredient—or to put it another way, whether the savings produced by not implementing an experiment is a false economy. The answer to these questions depends on one's assessment of how much faith can be put in alternatives such as quasi-experiments. If the money spent on a quasi-experiment is considered a waste because the results cannot be interpreted with sufficient confidence, then the possible benefits of an experiment (the alleged gain in inferential confidence) might well outweigh the costs.

Certain other arguments about the infeasibility of randomization are based on misconceptions about experiments. One claim, for example, is that experiments demand a no-treatment control, and it may not be feasible or ethical to withhold treatment from one group. The logical requirements of an experiment can still be met by randomly assigning different groups to variations of a treatment, however, and such an experiment would reveal which variations are more effective. Another claim is that it will be impossible to randomly assign treatment if a program must rely on volunteers. There is no reason that volunteers cannot be randomly divided into groups, though, either so that some do not receive the treatment or so that different randomized groups receive variations on the treatment. These and other objections to experiments are discussed in more detail by Boruch (1975; see also Boruch, Rindskopf, Anderson, Amidjaya, & Jansson, 1979).

Randomization as a Misguided Ideal

Cronbach (1982; Cronbach et al., 1981) has developed a different line of argument challenging the value of randomized experiments (see also Hultsch & Hickey, 1978; Kruglanski & Kroy, 1976; R.E. Snow, 1974). His position is that experiments have been more highly rated than they deserve to be. Obviously, this judgment also stands in a complementary relationship to the theme that experiments are not very feasible. That is, arguments that experiments are difficult to carry off emphasize the costs of methodological rigor and purity, and Cronbach's position suggests that there is not nearly so much to be gained by incurring these costs as researchers have been led to believe.

Although Cronbach does not explicitly state the issues in quite these terms, a convenient way of examining his position is to describe it as the following two-pronged attack against randomization: (1) the denial that randomization is necessary for important inferences to be made with a reasonable amount of confidence and (2) the charge that randomization is not sufficient for drawing conclusions with genuine usefulness. The first aspect of the attack thus suggests that alternatives to randomized experiments can be equally as helpful, and the second suggests that some alternatives are in fact more helpful. We examine each of these in turn.

Is Randomization Necessary?

Cronbach's position on the necessity of randomization—namely, that it is not necessary—is best understood by contrasting it with a theme found in the writings of Donald Campbell and his colleagues. Campbell has repeatedly recommended the randomized experiment as the most direct and efficacious means for enhancing internal validity (e.g., D.T. Campbell, 1957). Hence, arguments stressing the importance of internal validity imply the special value of randomization. The classic D.T. Campbell and Stanley (1963) monograph, for example, stated emphatically that "Internal validity is the basic minimum without which any experiment is uninterpretable...the sine qua non" (p. 5).

Cronbach (1982) objects to the implications of such strong language. He comments, "Some followers have given the doctrine a weight that was never intended, even using it as a warrant for rejecting out of hand research designs that do not include a randomly assigned control group" (p. 107). The reason why the absence of randomization does not entail uninterpretability, and hence why nonrandomized designs need not be automatically discarded as worthless, is that randomization merely provides a special way of guarding against threats to internal validity—not the *only* way. Furthermore, some threats to internal validity may be so implausible that the application of good judgment and reasoning alone is fully adequate for making an acceptable interpretation. Such cases would obviously indicate that randomization is not essential for drawing safe conclusions.

Cronbach et al. (1981) provide a ready illustration in their discussion of a health program in Nicaragua. The object of the program was to increase a specific health practice: The use of Superlimonada by parents as a remedy for dehydration in children suffering from diarrhea. The program intervention consisted of broadcasts that told parents how to prepare Superlimonada at home and encouraged them to use it. Such broadcasts were made several times daily during a 12-month period.

Studies such as the Superlimonada investigation examine phenomena attributable to the intervention so much more readily than they are attributable to any other conceivable cause that controlling for alternative causal mechanisms seems foolish. In this case the alternative causes that would represent a threat to internal validity amount to "speculation that some freak of cultural change would within one year make Superlimonada popular in the absence of the broadcasts...[but] not even a policy maker hoping to divert the broadcasters' funds to another use could advance that counterhypothesis with a straight face" (Cronbach et al., 1981, p. 290). It is in this sense that a research design involving random assignment to treatment (broadcast) and control (no broadcast) conditions would not be necessary for drawing firm conclusions about cause and effect: No other cause is a plausible candidate for such an unusual and specific event. Logically, although the presence of alternative causes would be possible, Cronbach et al. (1981) note that this possibility is remote and easily ascertainable:

> Moreover the remarkable extraneous events—if any—that influenced the mothers would have been recorded by an alert evaluator. They would not have appeared in all villages all across Nicaragua, so the internal comparison would be enough to assess the spurious influence. (p. 290)

The point is that because there are acceptable alternatives to randomization in the form of good reasoning and careful observation, randomization should not be considered absolutely essential.

Nevertheless, randomization provides a standard way of eliminating major categories of threats to internal validity in all situations, whereas the absence of randomization creates the need for specialized reasoning on the basis of context-specific knowledge (D.T. Campbell & Stanley, 1963). Although the combination of reasoning and knowledge can, *on some occasions*, provide for inferences as confident as would be obtained from randomization, there is no guarantee that such occasions will occur very often; that is, the Super-limonada example may be the exceptional case rather than the general rule. Moreover, the types of inferential threats against which randomization provides a safeguard might be so commonplace as to make experimental control seem the only prudent path to follow. The suggestion that alternative explanations are prevalent without randomization has long been a corner-stone of Campbell's position:

> The sources of invalidity which experimental designs control can be seen as a list of *frequently plausible* hypotheses which are rival to the hypothesis that the experimental variable has had an effect. . . .The "plausible rival hypotheses" that have necessitated the routine use of special control groups [and hence random assignment to treatment versus control conditions] have the status of well-established empirical laws. (Campbell & Stanley, 1963, p. 36, emphasis added)

Thus, the degree of preference for randomization over nonrandom assignment really depends on assumptions about how common and how compelling certain threats are. Neither side can claim the certainty of deductive logic on this point, however, because the prevalence and plausibility of internal validity threats will usually be a matter open for conjecture. As Mark (1986) has pointed out, "The problem is that experience—particularly the systematic synthesis of research—has not yet accumulated to the point where we can confidently estimate the likelihood and magnitude of various validity threats" (p. 62).

Only part of Campbell's position (Campbell & Stanley, 1963), however, rests on assumptions about internal validity threats' being "frequently plausible" in the absence of randomization. As both D.T. Campbell (1969) and Boruch (1975) have noted, the reason why researchers should be concerned about whether such threats are frequent or not has just as much to do with the possible severity of harm done by not controlling them as with their alleged frequency. In the case of inferential errors, where effects are created not by an implemented treatment but by an uncontrolled and unsuspected cause, the danger is that treatment programs of no real value—or worse, those whose harmful effects have been masked—will be needlessly propagated. Similarly, errors involving false null-effect conclusions could do harm by preventing the subsequent implementation of worthwhile programs (cf. D.T. Campbell & Boruch, 1975; T.D. Cook et al., 1985).

The impact of such errors can be more fully appreciated by considering a specific illustration. Imagine, for example, that you are a physician who frequently treats stroke victims. Recently, a new form of therapy for stroke victims, anticoagulant drug treatment, has begun receiving widespread endorsement from other physicians. When asked about the basis for their enthusiasm, however, these colleagues report nonexperimental evidence collected on human beings (let us say, from informal observations). Meanwhile, you have learned that an experimental design has tested the effects of anticoagulant drug treatment on monkeys and has found not only that the drug has no health-promoting impact, but that it actually had some harmful side effects. Faced with these contradictory results, will you listen to the experimentalists or to the nonexperimentalists?

Although the example as described is fictional, it has a basis in fact. In the 1960s, informal observational data collected on humans convinced many physicians of the value of anticoagulant drug treatment (unlike our fictional example, there was no research on animals). When later randomized experiments on humans were conducted, however, it was found that the drug could actually be detrimental to health in some cases, whereas there was no reliable indication of any positive effect (Boruch & Rindskopf, 1977). The point is that if randomized experiments had not been conducted, some patients' health would have been jeopardized by the continued use of a treatment whose initial effects had been spuriously estimated to be beneficial. This example about the dangers of incorrect causal inference illustrates why authors such as T.D. Cook and Campbell (1979) have recommended that researchers ought to take the time and trouble of implementing randomized designs—or at least, to consider seriously "whether the costs of being wrong in one's causal inference are not greater than the costs of being late with the results" (p. 90).

In citing this same passage from T.D. Cook and Campbell's (1979) book, however, Cronbach (1982) has replied to those authors as follows: "Alas, they miss my point: The causal inference even from a true experiment is problematic when the statement extends beyond a trivial summary in operational, past-tense wording" (p. 144). Whether the point was missed or not, it is one that requires some explanation.

Is Randomization Sufficient?

Essentially Cronbach (1982) has argued that internal validity, Campbell's "since qua non," concerns only a single event—the outcome of a treatment being investigated—and as such has no direct bearing on any future events of interest, which makes it trivial. What would make a statement about cause and effect nontrivial is the conclusion that because the treatment was indeed responsible for the observed effect in the investigated instance, a similar impact would be likely to occur in future instances. Such a conclusion, however, would represent a generalization or extrapolation that has nothing whatsoever to do with the logic of having controlled for certain validity threats in the original instance by means of randomization. Randomization may provide certain reasonably good safeguards about what was not allowed to operate in a given study (i.e., the threats that were controlled), but such statements about what *did* happen have no necessary bearing on what *would* happen under other circumstances, at other times, with other people, and involving possible differences in implementation (treatment as operationalized).

Cronbach (1982) believes that the extremely limited type of conclusion to which internal validity refers has been overlooked or not given adequate emphasis: "Deeply buried in Campbell and Stanley (1963, pp. 193–194) and in a rarely cited paper by Winch and Campbell (1969), we glimpse what Campbell has apparently always meant the term *internal validity* to refer to: an inference devoid of generalization" (p. 128). What has apparently gone unrecognized, according to Cronbach, is that the stress on establishing cause-and-effect relationships may represent a search for something that when found turns out to be of little or no value. The following passage makes the point explicitly:

> I consider it pointless to speak of causes when all that can be validly meant by reference to a cause in a particular instance is that, on one trial of a partially specified manipulation *t* under conditions *A*, *B*, and *C*, along with other conditions not named, phenomenon *P* was observed. To introduce the word *cause* seems pointless. Campbell's writings make internal validity a property of trivial, past-tense, and local statements. (Cronbach, 1982, p. 136)

There can be no more stark contrast of the two viewpoints than the juxtaposition of Campbell's sine qua non expression with Cronbach's repeated use of the word *pointless* in this passage.

What appears in sharp relief from isolated passages, of course, often shades into matters of degree when the full context of authors' complete writings is taken into account, and Cronbach (1982) and Campbell (e.g., Campbell & Stanley, 1963) are certainly no exception. A theme emerging clearly from the published works of these authors is that both see their differences as involving relative emphasis rather than either/or statements. Specifically, the issue has become one of the relative emphasis placed on the importance of taking special steps to increase the generalizability of conclusions. Here, the greater emphasis has come from Cronbach. His emphasis is based on judging that internal validity is not sufficient for purposes of generalization. On this point, however, recent trends have seen something of a convergence in viewpoints, and so in the following section we explore the degree of that convergence more extensively by addressing the current status of the controversy.

Current Status of the Controversy

Campbell's frequent collaborator, Thomas Cook, has recently co-authored a chapter that serves as a useful reference on the need to consider more than randomization when generalizability is at issue (T.D. Cook et al. 1985). Specifically, T.D. Cook et al. recommend that social program evaluations use a sequence of steps beginning with those emphasizing external validity at the early stages of research—thereby establishing parameters of generalizability in advance—before moving to those that emphasize internal validity. In this fashion...

> evaluation becomes a funnel, using inexact methods of low cost per site to define classes and to locate the most promising projects, and restricting the use of more precise and more expensive cause-probing methods to a small number of projects that belong to well-validated classes for which there is reason to believe they may be successful by some of the criteria widely believed to be important. (T.D. Cook et al., 1985, p. 740)

This proposal is consistent with a related comment Cook has made elsewhere recently, namely that "we might say that evaluations' major sin of the past has been the *premature* use of experimentation" (Mark & Cook, 1984, p. 80, emphasis added).

Because the last step in the funneling process is the one where "detection of valid causal relationships" is involved, however, T.D. Cook et al. still insist that "causal analysis ought to be as rigorous as possible, which is why random assignment is preferred" (1985, pp. 743, 744) at that point. They likewise continue to proclaim that "the consequences of being wrong about causal connections are greater than the consequences of being wrong about other features of research design" (p. 761). Thus, one aspect of this controversy has remained relatively unchanged—namely, the repeated assertion that when it comes to determining *causal* relationships, experimentation is still the method of choice. Perhaps the only modification is that even its advocates now offer this advice with slightly more of a degree of qualification than before. T.D. Cook et al. (1985), for example, say that "The randomized experiment... although not perfect...is probably still better than the alternatives" (p. 759).

It is tempting to believe that there may nevertheless be something of a resolution to the controversy in such statements regarding a preference for randomization when it comes to causal issues. As Mark (1986) has noted, the history of divergence between Campbell's and Cronbach's perspectives can be traced to the relatively greater emphasis placed by the former on *scientific inquiry* (hence causal issues), versus the latter's relative emphasis on *policy issues* involving a more immediate concern for direct application. Mark (1986) has also commented as follows:

> Campbell's approach seems preferable when a treatment effect is robust across variations in persons and settings, but causal inference is difficult because spurious relationships are likely. In contrast, Cronbach's approach seems preferable when spurious relationships are unlikely or can easily be ruled out, but a treatment effect is not robust. (p. 55)

It should be point out, however, that this is a rather fragile "resolution" of the controversy, for reasons of which Mark is well aware. As he has put it, "Unfortunately, the researcher is not likely to know in advance which conditions hold...[and] thus the dilemma remains" (p. 55).

Although Campbell and Cronbach both continue to insist on their differences being only a matter of degree, and although there exist some partial resolutions of the sort indicated here, some fundamental differences of opinion do still exist. These differences may not be as apparent when the issues are addressed in general terms, but they could well loom large in the context of a particular research effort. As T.D. Cook et al. have so aptly summarized, "The issue is delicate and situation-specific" (1985, p. 761).

Consider as a possible resolution, for example, the classic formulation that there is a place for both internal and external validity. This truism sounds fine in the abstract, but how will such a principle be applied in a concrete instance? When a choice must be made whether to use randomization in a given program evaluation, an advocate of Cronbach's position would still be inclined to avoid experimentation in light of Cronbach's statements about the "pointless" value of causal inference. The decision would also be slanted against experimentation by similar concerns about generalization. On the other hand, advocates of Campbell's position would still be inclined to opt for an experimental design—and would be likely to marshall arguments suggesting that concerns about generalizability are overstated. Indeed, T.D. Cook et al. (1985) have suggested the lines that such a defense might be likely to take:

> But it should be noted that a randomized experiment will rarely be restricted to a single site, a single population of respondents, and a single operationalization of outcome measures. Also, the substantive literature may contain past studies or well-tested theories that facilitate inferences about generalizability. And most experimenters will be able to collect some information that helps causal explanation merely by extending the measurement framework. Thus evaluators who share Campbell's priorities will not be totally powerless to generalize and explain. (p. 761)

Given such beliefs that generalizability can be garnered in a variety of ways, those siding with Campbell most likely will continue to press for randomization.

As we imagine this hypothetical debate over the conduct of an actual evaluation, we see it thus reaching an inevitable impasse—despite the tantalizingly close convergence of current positions—for essentially the following reasons. Cronbach's point about the limited generalizability of a "local" causal inference is compelling enough that some researchers will always view experiments as inadequate to the task of producing useful knowledge. Others, however, will remain convinced regarding the value of enhanced confidence about causal inference obtainable more readily from experiments. Hence, they will insist on randomization as a priority; but they will also seek various generalizability supplements, in the manner suggested by T.D. Cook et al. (1985) from whatever sources might be available. Having become convinced that such sources are plentiful, they will not feel an urgent necessity to abandon randomization.

Does the nature of this impasse—should such a stalemate be inevitable —mean that no progress has been made? We think not. Although the controversy is by no means resolved, those who face the thorny question of whether or not to insist on randomization are now in a position to make a much more considered judgment than earlier "either/or," simplistic prescriptions would have entailed. There are several reasons to take heart about specific signs of progress.

For one thing, Cronbach's (1982) challenge to experimentalists has prompted a renewed search for sources of generalizability in precisely the fashion that T.D. Cook et al. (1985) suggested. Moreover, only naive experimentalists are now complacent about any "guarantees" derivable from randomization. A modern trend linked to Cronbach's criticisms, for example, has been the emergence of increasingly sophisticated treatments of randomization's limitations. Thanks to Cronbach's warnings and the experience of actual program evaluations, it is now clear that field experiments can easily be plagued by numerous problems of implementation (such as subject attrition from groups that were initially assigned to treatments at random). These problems ensure that even the ideal of internal validity is less obtainable than was once presumed (cf. Cronbach, 1982).

Why do we take heart from these developments and see them as signs of progress? The answer is that progress is ultimately more likely from acknowledging the problematic nature of inference, even if proposed solutions fall short of perfection, than from presuming randomization as a panacea. In fact, those who currently view randomized experiments as superior to quasi-experiments, even though continuing to press these claims, have modified their position in ways that will help make researchers appropriately more cautious.

A prime example of this current view is expressed in Mark and Cook's (1984) rhetorical question: "If there are so many problems with implementing random assignment in evaluations, why not aim for a quasi-experimental design in the first place?" (p. 99). Their answers to this question have revealed a tempering of insistence on experiments with some useful caveats.

Specifically, although Mark and Cook (1984) continue to endorse the superiority of experiments over quasi-experiments, their preferences are often stated as matters of degree. This can be seen, for example, in their claim that the bais resulting from a breakdown in random assignment is likely to be *less problematic* than that arising from systematic self-selection (although problematic nevertheless). It is also noteworthy that Mark and Cook indicate that the problems of random assignment are "often manageable, provided... ways of overcoming them have been considered" (1984, p. 99), instead of blindly accepting the logic of randomization. As such, they note that experiments and quasi-experiments pose similar problems for researchers.

To conclude, there appears to be growing acceptance of both experimental and quasi-experimental techniques, replete with the strengths and weaknesses of each. Although advocates of each approach may be easily identified, it seems safe to say that their positions are no longer as sharply identifiable as Campbell and Stanley (1963) and Crobach (1982) initially defined them. As a result, it is difficult to envision that any conclusive resolution of this controversy will be forthcoming. Nevertheless, the course of argument and counterargument clearly has made researchers much more aware of problems to be faced squarely *regardless* of which method is chosen. In the end, this state of affairs might prove to be more useful than premature closure on the issues.

Chapter 6
Subject Roles

There exist today differing viewpoints about the typical perceptions of subjects in an experiment and differing viewpoints about the artifacts that subjects' perceptions might create. Nevertheless, it is clear that the degree of conflict between these differing viewpoints has abated, particularly in contrast to the level of intensity the conflict reached during the mid-1960s. It was then that the prospect of such artifacts contaminating nearly every experiment was seen as "cause for serious and constructive alarm within psychology" (Schultz, 1969, p. 224).

Martin Orne (1962) helped stimulate this alarm by focusing attention on *demand characteristics*, which he defines as "the totality of cues which convey an experimental hypothesis to the subject" (p. 779). The article in which Orne introduced that definition became, in the years 1965 through 1967, the single most frequent citation appearing in the *Journal of Personality and Social Psychology* (Shulman & Silverman, 1972). Yet, only a decade later, Kruglanski's (1975) comprehensive study of this issue led him to the following conclusion:

> The absence of acceptable evidence for subject-artifacts renders unnecessary the various techniques aimed at their elimination. In addition, a detailed examination of these techniques suggests that they may contain several serious difficulties, which render them undesirable as substitutes for current modes of experimentation. (p. 141)

The absence of large numbers of articles on this topic since the time of Kruglanski's (1975) comment makes it appear as if the majority of psychologists have concurred with his opinion, although perhaps Kruglanski said what they wanted to hear! On the other hand the paucity of current literature on the subject may reflect merely a "dip" in a cycle of waxing and waning interest of the kind to which many topics are subject. The appearance of a few recent articles that we will review in the present chapter, moreover, suggest that the issue is far from "dead."

Orne's (1962) paper, as we have noted, serves to identify the point at which research in this area began to crest. That same paper also provided the term most often associated with the methodological issues addressed in this chapter—*demand characteristics*. Unfortunately, this term also has become very strongly associated with some specific characterizations of subjects (e.g., that they are typically motivated to try to confirm the experimenter's hypothesis) that may or may not be accurate. It is possible to agree that subjects are not a neutral (bias free) aspect of experiments while disagreeing with these specific characterizations, and so we refer to *subject artifacts* (Kruglanski, 1975) as a more general descriptive term for the issues to be addressed.

There are, in fact, any number of terms that could be used in reference to these issues, and hence it is necessary at the outset to clarify our focus. As we show in the next section by reviewing the historical context, ideas germane to the topic at hand can be found at various points in psychology's past.

The underlying theme, expressed in various ways and giving rise to various terms, can be described in the most general way as follows: (1) An experimenter's hypothesis describes the experimental setting at the level of abstract concepts. (2) When results confirm the hypothesis, these same abstract concepts are used to make empirical generalizations about the world. (3) The subjects, however, have responded not to abstract concepts but to operational definitions of these concepts (e.g., procedures used to manipulate an independent variable), as well as to various background characteristics of the setting itself. (4) The subjects' interpretations of the situation may not coincide with the experimenter's abstract concepts and characterization of what was going on. They may not have taken the situation seriously, for example, failing to concentrate adequately on the task at hand. They may not have noticed key elements that the experimenter assumed were critical for determining their responses and may instead have responded to aspects of the situation that the experimenter did not even realize were present.

In fact, certain aspects of the situation may be "present" only in the sense that they were perceived as being present by the subjects. The subjects' viewpoints about what is happening in an experiment, for instance, may be colored by various assumptions they bring to the situation or acquire during the course of an experiment. These can include assumptions about the purpose of the particular research project in which they are taking part, as well as assumptions about the proper role of research participants in general.

Collectively, these perceptions and assumptions serve as guides to behavior, and they comprise the subjects' phenomenological definition of the situation. To the extent that the subjects' definition of the situation does not match the experimenter's, the abstract concepts used to describe what happened will be inaccurate, and the empirical generalization false. It is in this sense that we can speak of *subject bias*, or of "contamination" of the results due to the subjects' perceptions. The presence of such bias reflects what Kruglanski (1975) had in mind when referring to *subject artifacts*.

Historically, a diverse literature has contributed to the general notion of subject artifacts. In the modern embodiment of these ideas, however, attention has been focused chiefly on the concept of *subject roles* as a source of bias—probably because the earlier literature addressed the research process in general, whereas more recent writings have tended to concentrate upon the laboratory experiment in particular (as the occasion for a unique human "drama"). Subject roles, in turn, have come to be defined primarily with respect to the experimenter's hypothesis. It is taken for granted that subjects perceive an experimenter as having some hypothesis under investigation. The descriptions of various possible subject roles differ according to the manner in which this perception is thought to influence subjects. Subjects might reach conclusions about what the hypothesis is, for example, and various roles are then distinguished on the basis of whether the subject decides to confirm the presumed hypothesis (the "good subject" role), to disconfirm it (the "negativistic" subject role), or to ignore it completely (the "faithful" subject role). We orient our discussion around these subject roles in order to avoid the confusion that arises when a given term refers both to cues that suggest a hypothesis and to action taken with respect to that hypothesis (e.g., sometimes "demand characteristics" is used as a term to describe hypothesis-related cues and sometimes to describe hypothesis-oriented behavior).

On the other hand an additional subject role (that of the "anxious" subject) can be defined as being adopted independently of perceptions about the experimenter's hypothesis; that is, subjects who adopt this role are said to be more concerned about the social acceptability of their behavior than about the correspondence between that behavior and any scientific hypothesis. The cues that become relevant in this case, therefore, are aspects of the situation that have implications about the social acceptability of subjects' responses. Discussion of this role will reveal that some modern investigations of subject artifacts are really based on postulated *subject motives* (e.g., evaluation apprehension, self-presentation); hence they reflect emerging theories about all social behavior, not just alternative explanations about "artifactual" responses in experiments.

The Context of Concern About Subject Perceptions

Historical reviews (e.g., Adair, 1973; Silverman, 1977) indicate that early investigators of psychological phenomena noted the possible contaminating effect of the subject's own orientation toward the experimental setting. This problem was particularly vexing given that one of the first psychological techniques of investigation was to have a subject act as an "observer" of his or her own thoughts (introspection). The impact that these observers' attitudes might have upon their responses was a source of such concern that reports of introspective reactions were restricted to those obtained from subjects who had received extensive training (Boring, 1953). Even then, many were eliminated because "there are individuals who are entirely incapable of any steady concentration of the attention, and who will therefore never make trustworthy subjects" (Wundt quoted by Titchener, 1895; as reported in Adair, 1973, p. 5).

As we shall see, the question of whether human subjects could be "trustworthy" sources of data continued to haunt psychologists long after they turned away from introspective methods. It is true, though, that attention to subject perceptions and attitudes as sources of bias was restricted virtually exclusively to specific topics. Researchers investigating hypnosis, for example, were notable for their recognition of this type of problem (e.g., Moll, 1898; Sidis, 1906). Other topics whose literatures also contain such warnings even at an initial stage of their development include psychophysical judgments (Fernberger, 1914), personality testing (Vernon, 1934), and conditioning (Cason, 1934). At about the same time as these last two papers, a report by Rosenzweig (1933) appeared that is regarded by many (e.g., Adair, 1973; Lyons, 1964; Silverman, 1977) as being the first extensive critique of laboratory experiments based on the social roles of subject and experimenter (Rosenzweig, 1933).

The gap between these early caveats and the rash of subject-role articles in the 1960s (e.g., Fillenbaum, 1966; Masling, 1966; Orne, 1962; Rosenberg, 1969) should not be taken to mean that psychologists simply forgot about this issue. Rather, concern about the motives, attitudes, and roles adopted by the participants in research investigations simply tended to be focused on contexts other than the psychology laboratory. In particular, two other contexts—the social desirability response set and the "Hawthorne effect"—were quite well known during the period between the 1930s and the 1960s, as we discuss in the following section. It might indeed be argued that the pervasiveness of knowledge about these effects helped provide a background of receptiveness conducive to the general notion of subject artifacts in the laboratory.

Social Desirability and Hawthorne Effects

McGuire (1969) has provided an historical account of psychologists' attention to the problem of social desirability bias, or "faking good," in addition to outlining the history of other response-set biases. According to McGuire, it was Steinmetz (1932) and Kelly, Miles, and Terman (1936) who first highlighted the difficulty of accurately assessing personality from responses to questions whose content implied a normatively approved answer. Later, psychologists working on the MMPI (Ellis, 1946; Gough, 1947; Meehl & Hathaway, 1946) paid considerable attention to the problem and devised various procedures for coping with it (see McGuire, 1969, pp. 18–20). This concern with techniques for identifying the effects of social desirability in the personality-test situation subsequently led to the development of special social desirability assessment measures by Edwards (1957) and Crowne and Marlowe (1964). As has been noted by D.T. Campbell (1957) and by Rosnow and Aiken (1973), survey researchers and interviewers have also long been aware of this type of problem (e.g., Crespi, 1948; Rice, 1929; Stanton & Baker, 1942).

A second precursor to concern over laboratory subject artifacts was widespread publicity regarding what had come to be known as the "Hawthorne effect" (E.E. Mayo, 1933, 1945; Roethlisberger, 1941; Roethlisberger & Dickson, 1939; Whitehead, 1938). Named for the General Electric plant in which a series of investigations spawned the human relations movement, this effect referred to "the observation that the output of the workers seemed to be responding to the transformed interpersonal relationship with the 'boss' (or experimenter)...rather than to the explicitly introduced variations in physical conditions of work" (Bramel & Friend, 1981, p. 870; cf. Roethlisberger & Dickson, 1966). More generally, the term came to refer to the "tendency of human beings to be influenced by special attention from others" (Stagner, 1982). It is noteworthy that the variety of explanations and interpretations of this effect (e.g., Bramel & Friend, 1981; Franke & Kaul, 1978; Landsberger, 1958; Parsons, 1974, 1978) have themselves spawned a running controversy (e.g., first Carey, 1967, vs. Shepard, 1971; then Schlaifer, 1980, vs. Franke, 1980; next Bramel & Friend, 1982, vs. Feldman, 1982; Locke, 1982; Parsons, 1982, Stagner, 1982; Toch, 1982; and Vogel, 1982; and finally Friend & Bramel, 1982, vs. Sonnefeld, 1982).

Reactive Measurement

The social desirability effect and Hawthorne effect were forerunners of the subject artifacts controversy that focused attention away from the laboratory experiment per se and onto field locations (Hawthorne effect) or personality testing (social desirability). It can be argued, however, that laboratory experimenters before the 1960s were also well aware of closely related forms of bias in their own baliwick. As early as 1953, Donald Campbell began privately circulating a paper that, in its published form (D.T. Campbell, 1957) contained the following passages describing the problem of *reactive measurement*:

> A reactive measure is one which modifies the phenomenon under study, which changes the very thing that one is trying to measure. In general, any measurement procedure which makes the subject self-conscious or aware of the fact of the experiment can be suspected of being a reactive measurement. Whenever the measurement process is *not* a part of the normal environment it is probably reactive.... In any of the experimental designs [i.e., those discussed in Campbell's article], the respondents can become aware that they are participating in an experiment, and this awareness can have an interactive effect, in creating reactions to X [experimental treatment] which would not occur had X been encountered without this "I'm a guinea pig" attitude. Lazarsfeld [1948], Kerr [1945], and Rosenthal and Frank [1956], all have provided valuable discussions of this problem.... The direction of the effect may be one of negativism, such as an unwillingness to admit to any persuasion or change.... The result is probably more often a cooperative responsiveness, in which the respondent accepts the experimenter's ex-

pectations and provides pseudoconfirmation....The Hawthorne studies [Roethlisberger and Dickson, 1939], illustrate such sympathetic changes due to awareness of the experimentation rather than to the specific nature of X. (pp. 298–299, 308)

These passages are significant for several reasons. First, the references cited show that Campbell's focus on the unique character of the laboratory subject role was an elaboration of a theme already evident in the literature regarding artifacts in experiments. Thus, the Campbell (1957) article, which was extremely influential, provides evidence that experimenters were probably not completely ignorant of these problems before they gained such notoriety in the 1960s, despite what some accounts imply (e.g., Adair, 1973; Silverman, 1977). Second, this paper, much like the Rosenzweig (1933) article, demonstrates an early awareness of the multiplicity of possible subject roles. Subsequent revisions of the paper amplified this message, as is illustrated by the following comments (D.T. Campbell & Stanley, 1963):

In the usual psychological experiment, if not in educational research, a most prominent source of unrepresentativeness is the patent artificiality of the experimental setting and the student's knowledge that he is participating in an experiment. For human experimental subjects, a higher-order problem-solving task is generated, in which the procedures and experimental treatment are reacted to not only for their simple stimulus values, but also for their role as clues in divining the experimenter's intent. The play-acting, out-guessing, up-for-inspection, I'm-a-guinea-pig, or whatever attitudes so generated...seem to be qualifiers of the effect of X, seriously hampering generalization....Any aspect of the experimental procedure may produce this reactive arrangements effect. (p. 20)

Third, D.T. Campbell (1957) coupled his diagnosis of the problem with a description of tactics for its remediation, and in the following passage he indicates that here, too, he was following the lead of those who had gone before:

In some settings it is possible to disguise the experimental purpose by providing plausible facades in which X appears as an incidental part of the background (e.g., Postman & Bruner, 1948; Rankin & Campbell, 1955; Schank & Goodman, 1939)....The problem of reactive arrangements is distributed over all features of the experiment which can draw the attention of the respondent to the fact of experimentation and its purposes....For communications of obviously persuasive aim, the experimenter's topical intent is signaled by the X itself, if communication does not seem a part of the natural environment....The respondent may say to himself, "Aha, now I see why we got that movie." This consideration justifies the practice of disguising the connection between O [the measurement observation] and X... as through having different experimental personnel involved, using different facades, separating the settings and times, and embedding the X-relevant content of O among a variety of other types. (pp. 308–309)

Finally, the further significance of Campbell's insights is that they became the basis for one of the most widely used treatises on research (D.T.

Campbell & Stanley, 1963); this text became the "bible" of methodology for generations of social psychologists, who thereby had direct exposure to these early warings.

Why, then, does it appear as if there was a sudden uproar about subject-role artifacts in the 1960s? One possible explanation, of course, is that the furor over bias in the laboratory reflected a more general time-bound phenomenon such as "the critical and sometimes anti-intellectual Zeitgeist of the 1960s" (Adair, 1973). Another way of putting it is that these concerns might have been part of the larger demand for "relevance" then so dominant in society (Silverman, 1971). Alternatively, it might simply be that psychology had finally come of age as a discipline and could thus afford the luxury of being more vigorously self-critical, a theme expressed by Silverman (1977) as follows: "Psychology has less need to be defensive [because its] identity crisis is about over.... The integrity of the discipline is inviolate, and the heretic who asks fundamental questions about the validity of our experimental methods can be tolerated" (p. 19).

To fully comprehend the context of the intense debate about subject artifacts, however, it is necessary to recognize ways in which the articles appearing in the 1960s differed dramatically from those preceding them. In particular, although some of the earlier accounts occasionally discussed bias in relatively general terms, these discussions almost inevitably became focused in terms of more narrowly circumscribed topic areas. This tendency is apparent, for instance, in the kinds of examples used by Campbell to illustrate reactivity (D.T. Campbell, 1957; D.T. Campbell & Stanley, 1963). Because of his own interest in attitude change, the examples often concerned persuasive communications and the possibility that respondents might become attuned both to the existence of persuasive intent on the part of the communicator, and to the specific direction of attitude change desired by the communicator and/or experimenter. Thus, the issue of reactivity received greatest emphasis within the context of pretest sensitization. Likewise indicative of a circumscribed focus is the very term so often used to discuss the problem, namely *reactive measures*. When contrasted with *non*reactive measures, there is an implicit narrowing of the magnitude of danger; that is, the implication of a problem with a faulty *measure* is that the solution is as simple as its replacement with a more adequate measure.

An additional reason for the subject-role artifacts controversy's (and the related problem of experimenter bias—see Chapter 7) occupying so much journal space during the 1960s, therefore, is that the context in which it was presented constituted a much broader threat than previous discussions. Specifically, such concepts as demand characteristics raised the possibility that the entire experimental procedure itself, not just particular measures or reasearch in certain types of areas, was suspect. Hence, the issues examined in this chapter are those that pose a general threat to the interpretation of experiments.

Controversial Issues

To the extent that a psychology experiment represents a unique type of social occasion, its participants—both experimenter and subject—might have their behavior influenced by the unique quality of that type of occasion in general rather than by the aspects of it deemed relevant to the particular hypothesis being tested.

Consider, for example, an experimental test of conformity effects. Assume that the hypothesis under consideration concerns the effects of group pressure and that the experimenter uses the Asch (1951) manipulation of "group pressure" by varying the number of confederates whose erroneous responses precede the subject's response. If the "group pressure" aspect of the situation is the basis for interpreting the results, then failures to conform will be considered instances to resistance to pressure. Suppose, however, that the experimental occasion is characterized as being the type of situation in which one person (the subject) has very good reasons to be distrustful of another (the experimenter). Viewed from this alternative perspective, the subject-artifacts perspective, instances of nonconformity are likely to be considered indicative of suspiciousness. Rather than responding to a factor that has been manipulated by the experimenter, the subject (according to this latter perspective) has responded on the basis of an attitude possessed before entering the experiment—an attitude that, in turn, is responsible for the subject's decision to adopt a specific role during the experiment.

The issues surrounding subject artifacts thus concern questions about which roles subjects adopt, how they can be assessed, and whether it is possible to prevent the artifactual impact of subject roles. Each of these issues will be discussed in the following sections.

Varieties of Subject Roles

Subject roles are like the concept of response sets as it is used in the survey research literature. That is, adopting a subject role, like having a response set, influences a person to respond in whatever manner most facilitates a predetermined objective (e.g., the goal of making a particular type of impression on the experimenter or interviewer). In the following presentation we have found it useful to consider these roles in terms of contrasting types of objectives.

The "Negative" Versus "Faithful" Accounts

In the context of the conformity example given above, it was suggested that the experimental laboratory might have become a place in which subjects learned to distrust experimenters. One of the controversies about subject artifacts that has arisen concerns the extent to which this sort of adversary relationship between subject and experimenter has permanently marred psychological research. Do subjects enter the laboratory with a hostile attitude toward experimenters? Jourard (1968), for example, expressed alarm about the antihumanistic consequences of manipulative experimentation, and he alleged that the typical undergraduate comes to view a psychologist as "a trickster, a manipulator" (p. 9). In a similar vein, Argyris (1968) has argued that experiments foster an alienation of subjects vis-à-vis experimenters that is reminiscent of the negative feelings that "organizations create for their lower-level employees" (p. 193).

These concerns have been crystallized in the form of a proposal, subsequently disputed, that a *negativistic subject role* characteristically exists among undergraduate participants in psychology experiments. Best known for this proposal is Masling (1966), who claims this role can lead to a "screw you effect," in which subjects do anything they can to ruin the experimenter's results. It should be noted, however, that Masling provides only anecdotal evidence for such an effect—citing, for example, what is "commonly observed" (p. 95) in operant conditioning studies with human subjects (viz., that there is a reversal of the conditioning effect, apparently at the point when a subject realizes what the experimenter is doing and/or becomes tired of "playing along"). Masling also referred to a report by Goldberg (1965) in which one subject mentioned resenting psychologists' attempts to control their subjects' minds. This subject deliberately produced a response opposite to what she presumed the experimenter had intended her to make. The claim being disputed is that such a response is typical.

Part of the reason that allegations about the existence of a negativistic subject role are controversial is that some investigators portray subjects as characteristically being anything *but* negativistic. Fillenbaum (1966), for example, has described the role adopted by a typical participant in an experiment as being one of a "faithful subject." *Faithful subjects* are those who, if they become aware of the experimenter's hypothesis, avoid responding on the basis of their suspicions. Obviously, subjects cannot be both negativistic and faithful simultaneously. Hence, any evidence in support of one of these roles can be interpreted as raising questions about the existence of the other. It does not follow, however, that evidence against one of these roles necessarily implies the existence of the other. In fact, as the subsequent discussion will show, the evidence regarding each of these roles is suspect. (For reviews of all or part of this evidence see, e.g., Christensen, 1977; Jung, 1982, Kruglanski, 1975; Spinner, Adair, & Barnes, 1977; Weber & Cook, 1972.)

Questions regarding "faithfulness" evidence. Several of the studies that are sometimes cited as containing evidence for "faithfulness" demonstrate instances in which the prior experience of deception seemed to have little effect on behavior in a subsequent experiment, but each of these studies can be questioned. A dramatic example of such a finding, because it involved the greatest amount of previous deception experienced by subjects, can be seen in a study by T.D. Cook et al. (1970, Metaexperiment I). These investigators found that subjects who had been deceived and debriefed in one experiment each week over the course of 4 weeks, showed no evidence of biased responses in a deception experiment conducted during the 5th week. The senior author of this study, however, later admitted that "the rather dull experiments of Cook et al. may have made subjects blasé and submissive, and so they may not have actively searched for any hypothesis or performance-directing cues" (Weber & Cook, 1972, p. 282). Since no attempt was made to access subject suspicion (hypothesis awareness), this interpretation cannot be ruled out. Also, the temporal separation of the experiments from one another made it unlikely that a subject could detect any connection among them (Jung, 1982), and T.D. Cook et al. (1970) went to great lengths to ensure that this was the case. Thus, rather than being faithful to the extent of actively suppressing their own suspicions or behaving in an unbiased fashion despite awareness of the hypothesis, it is possible that subjects may have merely failed to ever become suspicious or to develop a specific hypothesis.

A similar interpretive problem (due to lack of an hypothesis awareness assessment) also surrounds the results of two studies in which the prior deception experience immediately preceded the subsequent experiment used as a test of faithfulness (Brock & Becker, 1966; T.D. Cook et al., 1970, Meta-experiment II). A feature of the Brock and Becker study, however, is that although they did not measure hypothesis awareness, they did manipulate factors presumed to affect the likelihood that subjects would discover the hypotheses (i.e., extent of debriefing and presence of phrases common to each experiment as cues that they might be related; see also Chapter 8). They found that only the combination of (1) a comprehensive debriefing after the first experiment that revealed its deception, plus (2) the presence of a cue to the relatedness of the experiments, yielded any evidence of bias. Because the remainder of the conditions showed no bias, it is tempting to conclude that subjects were predominantly faithful (i.e., actively avoided producing bias). Since bias did arise when subjects were most likely to have actually discovered the hypothesis, however, it is possible that the absence of bias in the other conditions was due to the absence of hypothesis awareness rather than to the presence of a motive to ignore a recognized hypothesis faithfully. This article thus has the unusual distinction of being cited by some authors as evidence for faithfulness (e.g., T.D. Cook & Perrin, 1971; Weber & Cook, 1972) and by others as evidence for negativism (e.g., Jung, 1982). Moreover, Weber and Cook (1972) reanalyzed the data and claimed that the "biased" (negativistic) condition did not differ significantly from the others.

The second "metaexperiment" by T.D. Cook et al. (1970) also failed to assess suspicion, yet one of its conditions is nonetheless claimed to contain evidence of "aware" subjects' faithfulness. The condition in question (labeled "experience of deception–cues" by Cook et al.) involved a prior deception that was of the mildest type imaginable, and the type of cue used to signal the relatedness of the experiments was subtle. As the senior investigator of that study later implied (T.D. Cook & Perrin, 1971), this degree of subtlety may mean that the connection between the experiments was only "hinted at" (p. 208). Furthermore, the cues did not reveal the second experimenter's specific hypothesis (although it conceivably could have motivated subjects to search for one), and so again the absence of an awareness-assessment proves troublesome. If a check on hypothesis awareness is missing, it is impossible to demonstrate conclusively that subjects were aware of the hypothesis, yet "faithfully" chose to be uninfluenced by it.

On the other hand, studies that *have* assessed hypothesis awareness (e.g., T.D. Cook & Perrin, 1971; Fillenbaum & Frey, 1970) are not any less ambiguous in their support of the faithfulness construct. These studies all used an incidental learning paradigm. During a learning–test portion of these experiments, subjects either read or worked on material ostensibly for nonrecall purposes, but then were tested for recall of that same material. After the surprise test, awareness of the hypothesis was measured. As Spinner et al. (1977) have pointed out, this procedure biases the awareness measure in the direction of overestimating the number of people who actually knew the incidental learning hypothesis at the time the relevant behavior was being tested. This bias can thereby result in pseudofaithful subjects, as follows: (1) Subjects do not really guess at the outset that recall will be tested, so they do not try to study the material and do not perform well on it when recall is suddenly tested. (2) The "sneakiness" of the experimenter's having unexpectedly sprung a recall test on them, plus the prompting of the questions designed to assess suspicion, combine to encourage subjects to say that they were aware of an incidental learning hypothesis all along. (3) This correlation of the presence of (apparent) performance awareness with the absence of performance bias is hailed as matching the defining characteristics of faithful subjects. Spinner et al. have demonstrated that the proportion of faithful subjects was in fact overestimated by Fillenbaum (1966). Thus, studies that have assessed hypothesis awareness are inconclusive regarding faithfulness because the measure of awareness may have been seriously biased.

Questions regarding "negativism" evidence. A few of the preceding experiments also contained hints of negativism, a less investigated phenomenon. As noted previously, the evidence for negativism in the Brock and Becker (1966) study has been challenged on statistical grounds. The T.D. Cook et al. (1970) Metaexperiment II found bias in a negativistic direction "only... weakly in interactive contexts" (Weber & Cook, 1972, p. 286). The T.D. Cook and Perrin (1971) study failed to find the same interaction when they used the same attitudinal measure that Cook et al. had used, and the incidental learning measure (which did produce a similar interaction) had been chosen precisely because it differentiated between negativism and an alternative ("vigilance") interpretation. Cook and Perrin concluded that negativism was not a parsimonious explanation for the combined results of these two sets of experiments.

Another investigator has tried to induce negativism deliberately to see when, if ever, it could be provoked (Christensen, 1977). Christansen directed his attention to verbal conditioning, in light of scattered reports of some negativism in this literature (e.g., Alegre & Murray, 1974; M.M. Page & Lumia, 1968). Masling (1960), it will be recalled, had said that this was the area of research in which negativistic results are "commonly observed" (p. 95), although Weber and Cook's (1972) review made reference to "the *minority* of subjects in conditioning experiments who reported awareness of a reinforcement contingency but did not perform the reinforced behavior" (p. 285, emphasis added).

In each of Christensen's (1977) two experiments, subjects were found who were *not* conditioned by the experimenter's reinforcements (i.e., they did not differ from control subjects who received no reinforcements). The only experimental treatment that reliably produced this effect, however, was one that involved the following circumstances: (1) the subject was exposed to a prior experiment with blatantly manipulative instructions, and (2) the manipulative intent was explicitly described in this experiment's debriefing. That is, any antagonism toward the experimenter occurred only in the presence of very heavy-handed experimenter treatment. Furthermore, questions conducted after one of these verbal conditioning studies led Christensen to state that nonconditioned subjects were more interested in avoiding an inappropriate effort aimed at placing them under someone else's control (i.e., confirming that they were not manipulable) than they were interested in "screwing up" someone's experiment out of sheer negativism and hostility toward experimenters in general.

Christensen (1977) summed up the results of his investigations and his review of the literature with the following conclusions as to the highly delimited conditions under which responses even appearing negativistic might be revealed:

> A prior experimental experience generates a resistant response when it consists of a negative experience and/or manipulative cues that are salient and then only on future tasks that are manipulative in nature...and that allow the subject to identify the hypothesis. (p. 399)

Summary of evidence for "faithful" and "negativistic" roles. There is no strong evidence for the existence of either of these roles on a widespread basis. Direct evidence for "faithfulness" requires an accurate assessment of the extent to which subjects were aware of the hypothesis, and this assessment has been either missing or apparently biased in the studies conducted to date. Evidence for "negativism" has been weak, inconsistent, or statistically suspect. Furthermore, given the extremity of the circumstances required before substantial numbers of subjects act contrary to the hypothesis (Christensen, 1977), this behavior (when it does occur) seems more likely to be the product of resistance to unusual and obvious experimenter "pressure" (i.e., perceived manipulative intent that is beyond reasonable bounds) than the product of widespread hostility toward experimenters in general.

"Good" Versus "Anxious" Accounts

Although both negativism and faithfulness have been assumed to be either virtually nonexistent or relatively infrequent (e.g., Jung, 1982; Weber & Cook, 1972), two other subject roles—that of the "good" subject and the "apprehensive" subject—have garnered acceptance as prototypic descriptors of participants in psychology experiments.

Evidence regarding "good" subjects. The concept of the good subject role originated in Orne's (1962) discussion of demand characteristics, the cues that suggest the experimental hypothesis. Orne assumed subjects would be motivated to discover and attend to these cues because of an attitude toward science elicited by voluntary participation in an experiment. That attitude, which Orne claimed is shared by both subjects and experimenters, stems from their mutual desire to advance scientific understanding and thereby contribute to human welfare. The experimental occasion thus takes on the character of a cooperative venture,[1] and the subject's cooperation takes the form of intending to confirm the experimenter's hypothesis (as opposed to the faithful subject's intention not to be influenced by that hypothesis one way or the other).

Much of the evidence that Orne took to be supportive of the good subject role involved illustrations of the generally compliant nature of those who participate in experiments. For example, much was made of the extent to which subjects could be induced to commit acts harmful to themselves or others (Orne & Evans, 1965) or to persist at meaningless, boring, and trivial tasks (Orne, 1962). Of course, being generally compliant is not the same as being "good" by validating the experimenter's hypothesis after it has been discovered. In fact, Weber and Cook's (1972) review of conformity studies, in which subjects knew the hypotheses, showed that the typical response was noncompliance. It cannot be determined whether such a response represents a negativistic motive or merely the desire to maintain a self-image of independence. Clearly, however, the response is not one a "good subject" would make.

---

[1]In a subsequent publication Orne alluded to the possibility (Orne, 1973) that his observations about this cooperative attitude might have been a function of the circumstances of his own research program, which relied almost exclusively on totally voluntary participation. It is possible that these "true volunteers" differ in motivation from the "coerced volunteers" used in the typical psychology experiment. (In fact an additional controversy has arisen regarding so-called "volunteer artifacts" and related sampling-bias problems due to the means whereby subjects are recruited; see Kruglanski, 1975; R. Rosenthal & Rosnow, 1969.) Also, the experimenter relying on volunteer subjects may treat them differently (less like an "object") than the experimenter who has access to a "captive audience," hence engendering a more benign and cooperative attitude from subjects who are thereby inclined to reciprocate good treatment.

Other evidence sometimes offered as support for the existence of the good subject role comes from conditioning and reinforcement studies. Here, the typical finding is that subjects who are aware of the conditioning or reinforcement contingency (e.g., Holmes & Appelbaum, 1970), or who have been in a greater number of psychology experiments (Holmes, 1967), give the hypothesized response sooner and more frequently than those who are unaware or who have had less prior experience. As Weber and Cook (1972) point out, however, there is an alternative explanation that is uniformly applicable to all such findings. Specifically, rather than desiring to *be* good by confiming the experimenter's hypothesis, subjects may have been motivated to *look* good by demonstrating their ability to gain an insight into the "problem" of discovering what was being conditioned or reinforced.

An experiment designed to contrast the "being good" versus "looking good" motives (Sigall, Aronson, & Van Hoose, 1970) has itself been the subject of some controversy (Adair & Schachter, 1972). Sigall et al. used a design that included one condition in which responses due to cooperativeness, versus those due to a desire for positive self-presentation, would presumably be pitted against one another. In this condition the instructions implied that the experimenter was anticipating a depressed level of productivity from subjects. Low levels of output by subjects would thus have reflected a cooperative attitude. The actual results showed high levels of output, however, which presumably resulted because such productivity would reflect positively on the subjects' competence.

Adair and Schachter's (1972) alternative interpretation was that the instructions had not been explicit enough regarding the experimenter's decreased output hypothesis. A redesigned experiment was conducted, in which the original instructions were given to half the subjects and the other half received a more explicit "you should decrease" message along with a rationale for anticipating a performance decrement. Subjects given the original instructions replicated the original finding (high output). Subsidiary analyses by Adair and Schachter also showed that these subjects tended not to recall anything in the instructions that implied low output. By contrast, subjects given the more explicit instructions were more aware of the decreased output hypothesis and actually showed lower levels of productivity.

Obviously a resolution is problematic when the only direct test of two competing motives is susceptible to an alternative interpretation consistent with a subsequent set of findings. The issue is clouded even more by certain ambiguities in the Adair and Schachter (1972) study itself. First, consider the evidence that increased output was associated with lack of an awareness concerning the experimenter's decreased output hypothesis. This evidence is correlational in nature and therefore inherently ambiguous with respect to cause and effect. For example, it is possible that subjects who increased their output could not recall a decreased output hypothesis simply because it is difficult to remember information inconsistent with one's chosen actions. Second, there is a confound in the Adair and Schachter manipulation of explicitness. The more explicit instructions contained a more detailed rationale supporting the experimenter's hypothesis, and it is possible that the content of this rationale was responsible for decreased output. (For example, references to the fatigue-inducing nature of the task may have implied that low productivity was normal and healthy or produced a self-fulfilling prophecy set of lowered expectations on the part of subjects.)

The upshot of these findings has been that the motive to present oneself in a positive vein remains generally applicable to the entire set of investigations reviewed thus far. This motive has been said to be the product of what Rosenberg (1965, 1969) has termed *evaluation apprehension*. Nevertheless, despite the overall post hoc ability of this construct to provide an interpretation for virtually all existing findings, it has been criticized for its inability to provide consistent confirmation of a priori predictions. These criticisms will be illustrated in the following section by Kruglanski's (1975) challenge to Rosenberg's evidence regarding the existence of evaluation apprehension, and Christensen's (1981) evidence disconfirming other aspects of Rosenberg's position.

Evidence regarding "anxious" subjects. Kruglanski (1975) points to two ways in which Rosenberg (1965, 1969) has explored the implications of evaluation apprehension. In the first of these, Rosenberg (1965) sought to reinterpret a dissonance finding as having been due to a confound between the dissonance manipulation and levels of evaluation apprehension. The dissonance finding in question was the inverse relationship between amount of incentive and attitude change obtained in the induced compliance paradigm (e.g., Festinger & Carlsmith, 1959). Rosenberg altered the procedures used by Cohen (reported in Brehm & Cohen, 1962) to produce such results. This alteration, which was designed to eliminate evaluation apprehension, involved separating the dependent variable measurement from the context of the independent variable manipulation. The result was a positive relationship (i.e., a reversal of the original Cohen findings). As Kruglanski notes, however, the earlier Festinger and Carlsmith study had obtained an inverse relationship between attitude change and incentive when the context of the independent and dependent variables was also markedly separated.

Kruglanski (1975) also pointed out that the results of at least one subsequent study (Linder, Cooper, & Jones, 1967) suggest a way in which these seemingly contradictory findings might be reconciled. Specifically, whereas Rosenberg's (1965) procedure apparently did *not* create conditions under which subjects would maximize their perceived volition (i.e., would not see their counterattitudinal arguments as a form of freely chosen behavior), Linder et al. (1967) demonstrated that a high degree of choice *is* a necessary condition for obtaining dissonance effects. That is, Rosenberg's (1965) reversal of a dissonance finding seems to have resulted from his failure to include a theoretically necessary ingredient of dissonance (choice), not from his "removal" of a theoretically extraneous ingredient (evaluation apprehension).

A second tactic of investigation has consisted of Rosenberg's (1969) manipulation of factors said to produce evaluation apprehension. In reviewing these investigations, Kruglanski has drawn attention to a distinction between two key factors: (1) the presence or absence of a cue describing certain behavior in emotion-laden terms, and (2) the interaction of cuing with levels of apprehensiveness. The evaluatively toned cues used by Rosenberg were typically references within the instructions as to what patterns of responding the experimenter considered indicative of someone well adjusted (normal). Virtually all of Rosenberg's studies demonstrated a strong effect of this cue, such that subjects consistently behaved in the "desirable" manner. Kruglanski argues, however, that this cuing effect can be alternatively interpreted as the product of a self-fulfilling prophecy involving mere subject *expectations*, not anxieties (apprehensiveness about being evaluated). That is, subjects might combine information from the cues about what was normal with their own belief that they were normal people to produce an expectation that they would perform in the normal manner. It is possible that subjects were merely guided and influenced by these reasonable expectations, rather than anxiously being driven to do whatever would make themselves look good in the eyes of the experimenter.

The possibility of such a self-fulfilling prophecy led Kruglanski (1975) to insist that a stricter criterion of evidence be used to judge the evaluation-apprehension hypothesis (cf. Blake & Heslin, 1971; Burkart, 1975). Specifically, if anxiety (rather than mere expectation) about appearing normal and well adjusted was the source of cuing effects, then these effects should be stronger under conditions of high anxiety than under conditions of low anxiety. Kruglanski thus reviewed Rosenberg's (1969) studies for evidence of this apprehensiveness-by-cuing interaction. The evidence was inconsistent. Some of Rosenberg's studies actually contain instances in which low-anxiety subjects produced larger cuing effects than high-anxiety subjects. Clearly these inconsistencies suggest that the construct of evaluation apprehension has not yet been specified in a theoretically coherent way, and Kruglanski concluded by citing Rosenberg's own remark about the investigations' being "decidedly preliminary" (Rosenberg, 1969, p. 321).

An effort to go beyond these preliminary stages has been made by Christensen. As he points out (Christensen, 1981), the cuing effect is actually only one of three components in the evaluation-apprehension construct entailed by Rosenberg's theoretical position. A second necessary element (cf. Rosenberg, 1969, p. 281) is subjects' assumption that the experimenter is actually interested in evaluating their emotional stability. Christensen sought to determine the prevalence of this orientation by asking introductory psychology students what they thought psychology experiments were all about. The descriptions of ascribed purposes were coded by blind raters. Regardless of the time of the semester during which independent groups of students were asked the question, the frequency with which responses were coded as falling into the category of an emotional-stability assessment never exceeded 12%.

The third component of evaluation apprehension is the arousal of anxiety.

Christensen's (1982) review of evidence pertaining to this component cited only two studies in which self-reported anxiety was properly influenced by an evaluation apprehension manipulation (Henchy & Glass, 1968; Rosenberg, 1969). In contrast, four studies were cited in which self-report measures yielded no such effect (Burkart, 1975; Innes & Young, 1975; Minor, 1970; C.W. Turner & Simons, 1974), and one additional study (Henchy & Glass, 1968) failed to find evidence for differentially induced anxiety on a physiological measure. Nevertheless, Christensen suggested that this lack of evidence was inconclusive, because anxiety generally had been assessed postexperimentally, whereas an assessment of anxiety conducted at the beginning of an experiment or during the course of an experiment might be more likely to produce confirmatory evidence. Using the Speilberger, Gorsuch, and Lushene (1970) State-Trait Anxiety Scale, Christensen (1981) set out to assess momentary anxiety before, during, and after conditions that Rosenberg (1969) had previously reported as producing evaluation apprehension. The experiment successfully obtained the cuing effect obtained by Rosenberg. Its results call into question the conclusion that cuing is mediated by differences in anxiety arousal, however, in that no such differences were obtained on the assessment-of-anxiety measure.

Such results, along with the general inconclusiveness surrounding the evidence with respect to Rosenberg's (1969) formulation, has led Christensen (1981) to propose a subject role that is similar to evaluation apprehension but is devoid of its negatively toned, anxiety-related components. Christensen identifies this new subject role with the motive of *positive self-presentation*. Such a motive has its roots in the concept of ingratiation (E.E. Jones, 1964; E.E. Jones & Wortman, 1973) and in impression-management accounts offered as alternative explanations of dissonance phenomena (e.g., Schlenker, Forsyth, Leary, & Miller, 1980; Tedeschi, Schlenker, & Bonoma, 1971). Christensen's review indicates that self-presentation has already been used to provide an alternative interpretation of a wide range of social psychological phenomena (e.g., Bradley, 1978; Pendleton & Batson, 1979; Reis & Gruzen, 1976; Snyder & Swann, 1976) and that it can be used in a similar fashion to reinterpret existing evidence regarding each of the other subject roles proposed to date. Rather than focusing exclusively on post hoc reinterpretation, however, Christensen reviews the literature to provide an outline of those factors having self-presentation effects that can be predicted a priori. Programmatic subject-role research based on this outline has yet to be conducted.

Summary of evidence regarding "good" and "anxious" accounts. Because almost any evidence for cooperativeness (the "good subject" role) also can be interpreted as a instance of evaluation apprehension (the "anxious subject" role), two experiments have attempted to pit these roles against each other. Unfortunately, these experiments are inconclusive. One supports the anxious subject role (Sigall et al., 1970), but both are susceptible to alternative interpretations. Efforts to test a theory about the determinants of evaluation apprehension (Rosenberg 1965, 1969) have produced results likewise subject to an alternative explanation (Kruglanski, 1975), namely that allegedly "evaluative" cues produce behavior-guiding expectations rather than anxieties. Further tests of Rosenberg's theory have suggested that a motive for positive self-presentation might more parsimoniously explain the entire range of subject-artifact results to date (Christensen, 1981).

Techniques for Assessing Subject Roles

The evidence reviewed here has shown that disagreements exist regarding which subject role, if any, typifies the participants in laboratory psychology experiments. Over and above the conflict of *which* role is most often operative, there has been additional controversy concerning *how* the evidence of subject roles and their effects should be gathered. In the following section we examine the issues raised with respect to the adequacy of each of three techniques generally proposed for assessment purposes.

Postexperimental Inquiry

Orne (1959) advised that discussions between subject and experimenter immediately after an experimental session had been completed would often be helpful in discovering both the extent of subject suspiciousness and the aspect of the situation responsible for suspicion. Page has actively explored this technique and has developed perhaps the most extensive set of questions designed to probe for suspicion (see, e.g., M.M. Page, 1973). A more detailed examination of controversies surrounding this particular technique is given in a separate chapter (Chapter 9), but the following points noted briefly are worth underscoring in the context of the present chapter.

First, certain areas of research have been steadily subjected to the claim that their effects are mediated by hypothesis awareness, without any apparent consensus emerging despite the extensiveness of attention directed toward the issue. Kruglanski's (1975) review illustrates this point. He notes that whereas there has been a continuing effort to demonstrate the awareness-mediated nature of verbal conditioning (e.g., Holmes, 1967; M.M. Page, 1968, 1972), a previous review (Greenspoon & Brownstein, 1967) had already "cited numerous well-conducted experiments in which conditioning without awareness had been found" (Kruglanski, 1975, p. 126).

Similarly, in the area of the classical conditioning of attitudes, evidence adduced in support of awareness-mediation (M.M. Page, 1969) has been seemingly controverted by opposing evidence of conditioning without awareness (A.W. Staats, 1969), but differences of methodology and interpretation have allowed the controversy to continue unabated (e.g., M.M. Page, 1973; Weber & Ridell, 1975; see Jung, 1982, for a review). The same is true regarding the continuing debate between proponents of the thesis that the classical conditioning of aggression is mediated by hypothesis awareness (e.g., Adair, 1982; M.M. Page & Scheidt, 1971) and their antagonists (e.g., Berkowitz, 1971; Berkowitz & Donnerstein, 1982).

Kruglanski's (1975) comments on this technique suggest one reason inconclusiveness may be endemic to it: When awareness is correlated with behavior, there is inevitably a problem of establishing cause and effect (e.g., the relationship might be spuriously caused by a third variable). A second problem is that the procedures designed to assess awareness are themselves inherently susceptible to the same charge of reactivity as the experimental manipulations they may cast doubt on. (Both these points are considered at greater length in Chapter 9.) It should also be noted that in Orne's writings on this subject (e.g., Orne, 1959, 1962, 1969, 1973), he has consistently expressed an awareness of the problematic nature of the evidence obtained by means of the postexperimental inquiry. The following quotation (Orne, 1969, pp. 154–155) is illustrative:

> A subject might "catch on" to a verbal conditioning experiment only at the very end or even in retrospect during the inquiry itself, and he may then verbalize during the inquiry an awareness that will have had little or no effect on his performance during the experiment.

The Nonexperiment

This technique, proposed independently by Orne (1959) and Riecken (1962), is a variation of role-playing procedures, and as such it has the same air of controversy about it that surrounds these procedures in general (see Chapter 3). Participants are asked to imagine that they are really subjects. Having been exposed to all the accoutrements of the experimental setting, they are given a detailed description of the procedures "in such a way as to provide them with information equivalent to that which would be available to an experimental subject" (Orne, 1969, p. 155). They are then tested in ways comparable to experimental subjects (i.e., the same dependent measures are taken).

Kruglanski (1975) has criticized this procedure on the same grounds as the second point made previously regarding the nonexperimental inquiry—namely, by stating that both techniques tend to introduce a special mental set. Allegedly, this perspective is unique to role-playing subjects, and hence their responses cannot be considered as isomorphic with those of the experimental subjects even if the results appear identical.

The difficulties of trying to settle arguments based on role-playing data can be illustrated by looking at the history of a controversy involving one of the investigations Orne (1969) chose to emphasize as "an elegant application of [these] techniques" (p. 157). The original investigation was conducted by Bem (1967) as part of his attempt to supplant dissonance theory with self-perception theory. Bem replicated dissonance-theory findings with Orne's nonexperimental (role-playing) procedure. Because the nonexperimental replication subjects never directly experienced the negatively toned affective state said to characterize cognitive dissonance, Bem and others assumed that the construct of dissonance was superfluous and that the construct of self-perception was more parsimonious. Interpretive difficulties in the self-perception account were soon unearthed by those in the dissonance camp, however, and the ensuing debate (e.g., Bem, 1968; R.A. Jones et al., 1968) continued to produce sporadic outbursts of heat (e.g., Fazio, Zanna & Cooper, 1979; Ronis & Greenwald, 1979) without accompanying increases in the amount of light shed on the subject. One observer of the debate has argued that both theories are too ambiguous to allow a conclusive confrontation (Greenwald, 1975b), but it may be the case that the ambiguity of the nonexperimental procedure is also at least partly to blame. Again, Orne was prescient in forewarning others of this ambiguity, as the following passage indicates:

> Direct comparison of non-experimental and actual experimental data is therefore possible. But caution is needed. If these two kinds of data are identical, it shows only that the subject population in the actual experiment *could* have guessed what was expected of them. It does not tell us whether such guesses *were* the actual determinants of their behavior. (1969, p. 156, emphasis added)

Simulators

The final technique proposed by Orne involves "simulators" who "are asked to pretend that they have been affected by an experimental treatment which they did not actually receive or to which they are immune" (Orne, 1969, p. 158). For example, nonhypnotized subjects (often chosen from among people who cannot be hypnotized) are asked to feign hypnosis for experimenters who are blind as to which of their subjects are simulating and which are not. The objective similarity of the responses of simulators and nonsimulators, as well as any inability of the blind experimenter to detect differences subjectively, raises the possibility that a demand characteristics explanation might offer the most parsimonious account of the behavior of both groups. Once more, however, Orne's cautions regarding the tentativeness of this inference should be noted. The following passage describes the caveat in his own words:

> To the extent that an unhypnotizable, simulating subject is able to do this [i.e., behave the same as a nonsimulator] without special training, we must conclude that an alternative hypothesis [demand characteristics] *could* explain the behavior. . . .It of course says nothing about the treatment itself. Thus, the simulator may merely know enough to predict accurately how a given treatment would affect the subject. . . .Consequently, we will often find no differences in behavior between hypnotized and simulating subjects even though there are differences in the *mechanism by which the behavior is elicited*. (Orne, 1973, p. 175, emphasis in original)

An investigation by Carlston and Cohen (1980) has added a twist to the simulation procedure in a unique attempt at explicating subject roles, although this procedure also has come under attack (Christensen, 1982). Carlston and Cohen essentially altered the simulation technique by asking subjects to feign a particular subject role rather than any psychological state pertaining to substantive theory. The subjects were told of the investigators' alleged interest in "how different kinds of people might react" to the experimental situation and were instructed "to pretend that they were the sort of subject described" (Carlston & Cohen, 1980, p. 859) in a brief paragraph written specifically for this purpose. Different paragraphs were assigned to different subjects, and the text of each had been prepared to capture the essence of a separate subject role. The roles of good, faithful, negativistic, and apprehensive subjects were portrayed. A further group of subjects, those given no assigned role, served as controls. In addition some subjects (those given the "curious" role) were asked to "try hard to figure out what the experiment is really about...[and] act in accordance with your theory rather than what the experimenter said" (p. 860). All subjects were exposed to the identical experimental procedure, which involved their selecting nonsense syllables to memorize and then being tested subsequently for recall. Demand cues imbedded in the procedure, which were also presented in identical fashion to all subjects, had been carefully prepared so that each cue pertained differently to separate role instructions (e.g., an explicitly presented hypothesis that the investigators expected right-handed people to focus more attention of the right-hand side of the visual display served as a cue to differentiate "good" subjects from "negativistic" ones).

The results of this experiment led Carlston and Cohen (1980) to two major conclusions. First, they calimed that their evidence confirmed a link between descriptions of motives stated in *general* terms and patterns of particular behaviors that had been predicted in the subject-role literature to be the consequences of these antecedent motives. Second, they offered reassurances that "subject role playing may be fairly uncommon" and that "role responding seems likely to be the exception rather than the rule" (p. 870). The basis for this second conclusion was that control subjects displayed behavior that was not precisely duplicated by subjects given any one set of role instructions. Furthermore, the pattern of control subjects' responses was neither especially confirming nor especially informing of the bogus hypothesis about handedness tendencies.

Christensen (1982) took exception to both of these conclusions. In regard to the first point, he argued that Carlston and Cohen (1980) had been *too* explicit in their instructions—that is, so explicit that it would be difficult to imagine how subjects, knowing what they did, could possibly have acted otherwise. For this argument to be compelling, however, it must plausibly refute the counterclaims implicit in Carlston and Cohen's account of their experiment. With respect to the role of good subject, for instance, Carlston and Cohen indicate they do not think that the instructions to provide "valuable scientific data" were specific enough to entail only hypothesis-confirming responses. Thus, while these responses were in fact obtained, Carlston and

Cohen think their subjects might just have easily responded "naturally" instead, thereby "providing valuable data by giving their true responses" (p. 867). The relative plausibility of these two opposing accounts is, of course, a matter of opinion.

In another vein relevant to Carlston and Cohen's (1980) first conclusion, Christensen (1982) comments as follows:

> Carlston and Cohen's (1980) data does [sic] seem to reveal that subjects given role-play instructions will attempt to portray their assigned roles. However, little information seems to be presented regarding the existence or nonexistence of the four subject roles in psychological research. (p. 581)

This point is valid in that any evidence showing how subjects *can* behave when explicitly instructed does not necessarily imply the pervasive presence of that same behavior in ordinary experiments, where the deliberate attempt is made to *avoid* such cuing instructions (cf. Kruglanski, 1975). Christensen is probably guilty of attacking a straw man in making this point, however, since Carlston and Cohen never claim that behavior guided by subject roles is pervasive. In fact their second conclusion was that subject role playing tends to be uncommon, not pervasive.

Nevertheless, Christensen (1982) is also reluctant to accept the validity of Carlston and Cohen's (1980) second conclusion (viz., that their control subjects were uncontaminated by any subject-role orientation and that a corresponding absence of subject role playing is usually the case). The grounds on which Christensen attacks this conclusion are instructive because they indicate the quintessential difficulty of obtaining definitive results in this area. Basically, Christensen argues that control subjects were motivated to perform well on the memory task itself. This focus on performance allowed them to disregard other (seemingly irrelevant) aspects of the instructions. These same aspects were relevant as cues to role-instructed subjects, however, who were thereby distracted in various ways and whose performance was influenced correspondingly. Christensen's conclusion is that "the lack of correspondence between the performance of control subjects and role-play subjects may be due to the different underlying motives generated by the task and the instructions given to subjects and not because psychological paradigms are not influenced by subject roles" (1982, p. 582). In line with this conclusion, Christensen offers the following two alternative interpretations of the data: "(1) all possible subject motivations were not represented or (2) the task was not appropriate for investigating the influence of the stated subject roles" (1982, p. 582).

There are few rejoinders that can be made to such an unassailable position as that represented in this last quotation. The reason this is the case, however, has more to do with logic than it has to do with any empirical truth. *Any* failure to find evidence for a particular subject motivation or set of motivations could *always* be due to the omission of some yet unspecified motivation. This problem corresponds to Hume's demonstration of the inconclusiveness of induction (cf. Popper, 1959): It is always logically possible for a counterexample to any inductive truth to lie "just around the corner." Likewise any failure to find evidence for *anything* can always be chalked up to test conditions that are "not appropriate." This problem is characteristic of any null-hypothesis finding (cf. Greenwald, 1975a; Popper, 1959).

Techniques for Preventing Subject-Role Contamination

Numerous procedures have been suggested as countermeasures designed to guard against possible bias due to role-motivated behavior (e.g., see D.T. Campbell, 1969; Carlsmith et al., 1976). One of these, deception designed to disguise the true hypothesis, has been the source of a controversy that is detailed elsewhere in this book (Chapter 3). The remainder of the bias-prevention techniques have been largely uncontroversial as regards their methodological effectiveness when properly implemented. For example, if the dependent measure is administered by someone other than the original experimenter, and in a completely different context, there is little doubt that a subject's efforts aimed at impressing or cooperating with the first experimenter are minimized—provided, of course, the subject does not realize that the separation is a ruse. Other controversy associated with bias-reducing tactics of this sort centers on ethical issues, particularly in the case of those techniques that seek to achieve nonreactivity by making people unaware that their behavior is being studied (see Folger & Belew, 1985).

There are two procedures whose effectiveness in reducing subject-role bias has been challenged by Orne (1973). One of these, which Orne claims is "widely believed to be effective in controlling demand characteristics" (p. 181), involves minimizing or eliminating verbal instructions. As Orne notes, however, the absence of such instructions does not entail the absence of subject perceptions about the purpose of an experiment, nor does it prevent the subject from having these perceptions influenced by features of the experiment other than the instructions. At best, this technique reduces the cues stemming from one source of demand characteristics, leaving other sources free to operate. And, even if all such sources could be eliminated, there would still be nothing to prevent a subject (motivated by a given set of role considerations) from simply taking a wild guess about the experimenter's hypothesis and behaving in a biased manner as a result of that guess. It is for this reason that Carlsmith et al. (1976) recommend presenting a false hypothesis rather than none at all. Accordingly, they claim that it is better to convince subjects of a bogus hypothesis designed to avoid bias than to leave them on their own to invent hypotheses, some of which might bias their behavior.

A second controversial prevention technique has its origin in investigations of the faithful subject role. On the basis of results from his own investigation of that role, Fillenbaum (1966) proposed that experimenters might be able to obtain subjects' cooperation in remaining unsuspicious by deliberately providing cues that elicited the faithful subject role. Weber and Cook (1972) echoed that suggestion, as have Carlsmith et al. (1976). In both these latter instances, however, the authors recommended that this technique be restricted to experiments in which evaluation apprehension was low.

The T.D. Cook and Perrin (1971) experiment illustrates one way of attempting to elicit the faithful subject role. One of the manipulations in that experiment involved telling subjects that they were in "one of those experiments whose true purpose cannot be revealed to you right now" (p. 211). The results of that instruction appeared to produce unbiased behavior. Cook and Perrin cautiously suggested that such an instruction "might sometimes eliminate the need for deceptions" (p. 220). At the same time, however, they admitted that "it seems reactive to say that the purpose of a study cannot be revealed" (p. 220).

Another approach to capitalizing on the faithfulness of subjects is to abandon deception completely, taking care to inform subjects fully regarding the exact purpose of a study (see Chapter 3). This approach is founded on the principle that honesty begets honesty. Orne (1973) emphatically opposes such a tactic, and his criticism of it seems to apply with equal force to the other variations of this approach. In essence, Orne sees the problem as one of control over subject perceptions, which is impossible to achieve by an instructional set alone. Regardless of what an experimenter says—be it bogus or real—a subject may choose not to believe it. Orne (1973) has aptly summarized his critique as follows:

> Unfortunately, some honest explanations about experiments are less plausible to subjects than some of the better deception instructions. At times, subjects find it hard to believe that the investigator is really interested only in what he honestly describes as his purposes....The consequence is exactly the same as in an unsuccessful deception study: It is what the subject perceives which determines his behavior, and this need not be what the experimenter had intended. (p. 182)

Current Status of the Controversy

The heydey of research on subject roles has passed. Other than a few scattered articles, not many papers are currently beings written on the subject. In terms of the sheer volume of output on the subject, there has been a return to the level of inactivity that existed before the 1960s.

Perhaps part of the reason for this decline has been the absence of conclusive proof that a subject-role orientation has been responsible for an artifactual finding. As can be seen from the preceding review of evidence, the inconclusiveness of results has dogged researchers in this area throughout its history. Especially problematic has been the absence of what Kruglanski (1975) has called "straightforward tests" on artifacts. This approach requires delimiting the allegedly artifactual elements of a procedure so that they can be manipulated orthogonally to the independent variable of interest. Kruglanski was able to find only two such tests in the literature. The first, relevant to demand characteristics (Orne & Evans, 1966), produced results that were not consistent with a phenomenon mediated by demand awareness. The second, relevant to evaluation apprehension (Rosenberg, 1965), was consistent with subject-role mediation but was subsequently called into question on other grounds (Linder et al., 1967) as being artifactual itself.

The decline in research should not be taken as a sign of closure on debate, however. It is notable that quite recently, in fact, advocates of the experiment (Berkowitz & Donnerstein, 1982; Jerald Greenberg, 1987) felt compelled to defend it against demand characteristics and related charges (see Gordon et al., 1986). Among the various responses to this defense, Adair (1982) in particular takes a stance that serves to illustrate the current nature of the controversy. Adair notes that the Berkowitz and Donnerstein article includes a defense against charges that the classical conditioning of aggression (the so-called "weapons effect") was due to demand characteristics. Part of this defense involved calling attention to the correlational, hence causally ambiguous, nature of evidence in support of demand mediation. In response, Adair offers the following comment:

> Berkowitz and Donnerstein argue that this correlational relationship does not *prove* that awareness caused the behavior. Such a statement overlooks the fact that the onus is on the researchers who are alleging that their study *proves* the weapons-effect hypothesis to rule out plausible alternative explanations...not the reverse. (1982, p. 1407)

What Adair's (1982) remarks suggest is that the controversy as it is currently engaged boils down to questions about where the burden of proof lies, since neither side seems to have effectively demonstrated the validity of its own position beyond a shadow of a doubt (or at least, not to the satisfaction of the other side). Unlike a court of law, where the precedent of "innocent until prove guilty" clearly places the burden of proof in one camp, there may continue to be disagreement concerning which side of this issue is duty bound to provide supportive evidence. In the absence of such established criteria, however, practitioners of social psychology seem to have yielded to tradition—that is, the laboratory experiment still appears to be given the benefit of the doubt (see Chapter 4). Even so staunch a proponent of research on demand characteristics as Orne himself, for example, has concluded that although "research with human subjects is far more difficult and complex than has generally been recognized, no adequate viable alternative to the experimental method is available" (Orne, 1973, pp. 182–183).

Orne's own most recent extensive discussion of demand characteristics (Orne, 1973) provides a number of statements that can serve as our conclusions. First, "it is always possible to raise doubts about whether subjects really perceived the situation as they were supposed to" (p. 182). Second, any procedure designed to investigate this problem is itself open to the same doubts, leading to "the infinite regress implicit in criticisms arguing that a given effect is due to demand characteristics" (p. 182). Therefore, given this logical impasse, the use of such techniques as quasicontrols for demand awareness might be most fruitfully applied during pilot investigations as tools for the design of better experimental procedures. It is during pilot testing and the prior review of pertinent literature that one should be on the lookout for "hints...which ought to alert an investigator...to the likelihood that demand characteristics are important variables" (p. 108). Orne goes on to note a number of these signposts of danger (e.g., results that differ from one investigator's laboratory to the next). Our own sense of current trends in social psychology leads us to add one final note: Pilot work aimed at developing procedures to circumvent a subject-role alternative interpretation will become increasingly necessary to the extent that a viable theory of self-presentation is expanded to make predictions about a greater number of laboratory phenomena.

Chapter 7
Experimenter Bias

During the 1960s, a series of reports by R. Rosenthal (e.g., 1963, 1964a, 1966, 1967b, 1967c) focused on the experimenter as a source of bias in scientific research. These reports called attention to problems considered serious enough that the number of investigations studying them has reached, by recent count (R. Rosenthal, 1981; R. Rosenthal & Rubin, 1978), a total of at least 345. It is safe to say that this topic area has been one of the most heavily researched in the modern history of social psychology.

Modern social psychology was not, however, the inspirational source of all this research. Rather, the origins of interest in experimenter bias can be traced to the study of animal learning in general, and to one animal in particular—the infamous "Clever Hans." (Numerous accounts of this horse exist, including several contained in a collection of articles edited by Sebeok & Rosenthal, 1981.) Clever Hans was owned by a former high school teacher in Germany, a Mr. von Osten, who succeeded in training the animal to perform feats that amazed audiences during the early 1900s. Apparently, the horse could solve problems of mathematics, answer a variety of other kinds of questions put to him verbally, and even "read." Experienced trainers of the day were unable to determine what made Hans so clever. It was only after an extensive investigation by Pfungst (1904/1965), an experimental psychologist, that evidence emerged regarding the lack of any true reading or mathematical ability on the part of the horse. Pfungst's most conclusive demonstrations came from creating conditions under which Clever Hans was *not* able to perform correctly, namely when no one in the horse's presence knew the appropriate response.

There are still a number of questions surrounding Clever Hans' remarkable behavior (e.g., Chevalier-Skolnikoff, 1981; Heidiger, 1981). Clearly, the essential secret of his success, however, was his ability to detect aspects of *human* behavior that gave away the answers. That is, certain behavioral manifestations of the trainer (or even of persons in the audience who knew the answer) were sufficient to signal Clever Hans when his hoof pawing, for example, had reached a total matching the sum of an addition problem. The humans involved were themselves unaware of these cues. The horse, on the other hand, was apparently able to use even slight inclinations of his questioners' heads or bodies as indicators that guided his responses. A lesson for behavioral science was in the making: Without proper precautions, the responses of subjects might be biased by unintended, unconscious cues emanating from an experimenter.

Psychological research on animal learning did not have to wait long before encountering difficulties of this sort. According to several sources (e.g., Heidiger, 1981; R. Rosenthal, 1981; Sebeok, 1979), the story is as ancient to psychology as that of Pavlov's (1927) work. In some of his many investigations, the renowned Russian physiologist at first thought he had obtained evidence proving the Lamarckian theory that behaviors learned in one generation could be passed by inheritance to later generations. With each successive generation of Pavlov's mice, the number of trials-to-criterion on an experimental task was reduced. Eventually Pavlov (1927) discovered, however, that the intergenerational improvements of the mice were due to differences in handling procedures by his research assistant, Studentsov.

Social psychologists were not immune from such errors. One of the founding fathers of the discipline, McDougall, was also erroneously convinced of Larmarckianism by virtue of related mistakes in experimental procedure that went uncorrected (see, e.g., accounts by Heidiger, 1981; Katz, 1937; Munn, 1933). Oddly enough, McDougall erred despite his own self-avowed attempts to guard against obtaining the positive results he desired (Hardy, 1965; Heidiger, 1981).

A list of historical figures who have contributed to an awareness of experimenter bias and related problems is not complete without the name of Robert Merton. Merton (1948) introduced to sociology the concept of the "self-fulfilling prophecy." The term refers to the influence of one person's expectations on another person's behavior. The mediation of the effect occurs as person X's behavior toward person Y is altered because of X's expectations about Y. Person Y is affected by this expectation-guided treatment from X. The eventual result is that Y's behavior conforms to X's expectations. Serious problems of mistaken inference arise when person X is an investigator who does not realize that (1) his or her unintended treatment of subjects has been a function of differential expectations and (2) the confound between expectations and the independent variable of interest makes the results uninterpretable.

Some of the most dramatic data attributed to the process accompanying a self-fulfilling prophecy are those of R. Rosenthal and Jacobsen (1968). These investigators studied the extent to which teachers' expectations could influence their pupils' performance—a phenomenon known as the "Pygmalion effect." Some elementary school teachers were led to expect that certain students possessed an unusual potential for dramatic gains in intellectual capability. Other teachers had no such differential expectations manipulated. The expectation that some students were intellectual "bloomers" apparently did not have an effect on their subsequent test scores, although the evidence has not gone unchallenged. (For criticisms, see Elashoff & Snow, 1971; Jensen, 1969; Thorndike, 1968. On the rebuttal side, see R. Rosenthal, 1969, 1976a; R. Rosenthal & Rubin, 1971, 1978.) This type of work has illustrated that the potential impact of self-fulfilling prophecies has important and far-ranging implications for practice in many applied domains (e.g., see also Brophy & Good, 1974; R.A. Jones & Cooper, 1971; Snyder, Tanke, & Berscheid, 1977; Word, Zanna, & Cooper, 1974).

Despite the "age" of the issues involved, the extensiveness of effort devoted to investigating them, and the practical significance of resolving them, they remain controversial. The various issues are examined in this chapter after a brief description of their underlying dimensions.

Dimensions of the Controversy

Chapter 6 focuses on aspects of the subject role that can bias research outcomes; the present chapter focuses on similar biasing possibilities inherent in the role of the experimenter. The two can be related. Suppose, for example, that a given subject is inclined toward the role of maximizing a favorable self-presentation. Further suppose that the subject perceives the experimenter as an important and authoritative source of what constitutes a "favorable" response, given the ambiguities of an experimental situation (i.e., one in which the social desirability of responses is not immediately and/or consensually apparent). The subject may hence be motivated to attend to cues from the experimenter (one form of demand characteristics) that serve to define what is appropriate, just as Clever Hans became attentive to the human cues that revealed correct answers for the problems put before him. Meanwhile, the experimenter is supposed to be following a rigidly standardized protocol—but he or she may in fact be deviating unconsiciously from the "script" because of expectations derived from the hypothesis being investigated. In this fashion the subject's orientation and that of the experimenter might interact to produce biased results (cf. Minor, 1970).

Besides illustrating one possible relationship between the roles of subject and experimenter, this hypothetical example singles out one way that experimenters might bias their findings. It is not, however, the only way. In fact much of the controversy in this area revolves around ambiguities concerning which of several possible sources of bias was primarily responsible for the effects obtained in a given study. The dimensions underlying these sources are outlined in the following sections. (The reader is referred to reviews by T.X. Barber, 1976, and Rosenthal, 1976b, for further examples and references.)

Who Does the Biasing?

As noted previously Chapter 6 is devoted exclusively to the role that the attitudes, perceptions, and motivations of subjects play in biasing research findings. The emphasis of the present chapter is on those persons formally associated with an investigation other than the human objects of study themselves (although we also noted that the behaviors of the two sets of people may interact in ways tending to blur the conceptual distinction). Here, we are concerned with making the further distinction between someone who actually collects the data and someone who "decides that a study is to be conducted, how it is to be designed and carried out, and how it is to be analyzed and interpreted" (T.X. Barber, 1976, pp. 1–2). These two roles may of course reside in the same person, and it is also possible for several people to be responsible for each role in a single investigation. We will follow the lead of Barber (1976; see also T.X. Barber & Silver, 1968a, 1968b) in calling the former the role of *experimenter* and the latter the role of *investigator*.

Ample documentation exists to indict each role as a potential contaminating source (e.g., T.X. Barber, 1976; Rosenthal, 1976b). In the next two sections, we elaborate on the variety of ways contamination can occur. At this point, however, a fundamental caveat is in order. Even when two reviewers agree that a given study provides an example of bias, they may not agree on which role—experimenter or investigator—accounts for more variance in the bias effect. Often, it appears that both the experimenter *and* the investigator may have had a hand in the processes leading to bias (e.g., the experimenter may have provided unintentional cues that biased subjects' behavior in a hypothesis-confirming direction, and the investigator may have incorrectly analyzed the data in a manner biased toward confirmation of the hypothesis). The interpretations drawn from a given study or from a literature review, not to mention the implications for ways to conduct unbiased research, will depend on conclusions about the relative contributions of these two roles. To the extent that it is difficult to disentangle the size of these contributions, "conclusions" will be perpetually controversial.

What Is Biased?

A second distinction concerns instances in which the actual behavior of subjects was affected by some source of bias, versus those instances in which the subjects' behavior was not (cf. Rosenthal, 1969, 1976). The former might include situations in which the experimenter's demeanor differs between treatment and control conditions, and the subjects are influenced by these differences in demeanor rather than by the presence or absence of the experimental treatment. Other cases of actual bias in subjects' responses might stem from decisions made by the investigator, such as his or her choice of an experimental design that failed to control for some confounding factor (e.g., the bias of practice or fatigue in a within-subjects design without counterbalanced treatments).

Whereas the preceding examples illustrate ways that the actual behavior of subjects might be biased, both the experimenter and the investigator are also capable of biasing *results* even without biasing the subjects' *responses* per se.

Unbiased behaviors might be susceptible to biased perceptual distortion (mis-observation) on the part of the experimenter, who might also simply misrecord some observations. Likewise, the investigator might err in computations, or bias the results by the choice of an inappropriate method of data analysis.

Sadly, we must allow for the possibility that at times errors are made deliberately. Even some of the most notable figures in the history of science seem not to have been immune from the temptations of what T.X. Barber (1976) has called the "fudging effect." For example, Westfall (1973) argues that some of Sir Isaac Newton's data exhibited a degree of precision unobtainable from the measuring instruments used—an instance of "'small scale' fudging" (T.X. Barber, 1976, pp. 36–37). Barber also notes the contentions of Brush (1974) that Dalton's data on chemical atomism and Mendel's data on genetics apparently show similar signs of tampering; the original data set in Mendel's case was shown by Sir Ronald Fisher to be so statistically improbable that it was beyond belief (Koestler, 1971). A goal of science, of course, is to use replications by sceptical, independent investigators as a safeguard against intentional fudging.

What Mechanisms Are Involved?

Each of the types of bias described previously—whether stemming from the experimenter or the investigator, and whether leading to biases in actual subject behavior or in the report of that behavior—can occur in a variety of ways. Merely identifying these sources in 2 (experimenter vs. investigator) × 2 (behavior vs. report) fashion does not explicate the processes responsible. A given source of bias might have the magnitude of its effects mediated by any of several means. True understanding of bias requires a specification of the underlying causal mechanisms responsible for different forms of bias.

Rather than expand our taxonomy of bias sources by introducing another general bifurcation, one for different types of causal mechanisms (e.g., presence vs. absence of intent to influence), we want to narrow the focus at this point. Suppose that the subjects' behaviors are actually biased, and that this bias does occur because of something done by the experimenter rather than something done by the investigator. In such cases it is important to identify which aspect of the experimenter's behavior was responsible for the bias, because any remedy for bias will need to focus on those aspects and not others. Two such aspects occupy our attention.

One is under the general rubric of "nonverbal communication" and represents the source of bias that allowed Clever Hans to amaze his audiences. An experimenter's expectations regarding the behavior of subjects in a given treatment condition might operate like the knowledge of someone posing a question to that famous horse: In both cases, information as to what constitutes a "correct" response might be unintentionally transmitted to the respondent. The information comes not from the content of what is said but from *how* it is said. Variations in tone of voice (one example of *paralinguistic cues*) might be responsible, for instance, or subtle changes in such physical aspects of the experimenter's demeanor as his or her facial expression and posture—the range of *kinesic* cues (Hall, 1959) made famous by popular treatises on "body language" (e.g., Fast, 1970).

Other aspects of experimenter behavior are not nearly so subtle, nor so likely to be unwittingly transmitted—namely, ways that the experimenter can depart from the procedure devised by the investigator. An experimenter committed to obtaining the hypothesized results at all costs, for example, might try using verbal reinforcement to operantly condition the desired behavior. Or suppose treatment conditions as designed by the investigator are hypothesized to result in performance differences. If an experimenter were determined to obtain such differences but did not trust the manipulated independent variable to produce them, he or she might implement the manipulation in ways that added extraneous performance-facilitating features to one condition and performance-hindering features to the other condition (e.g., by systematically varying the speed or care with which instructions were transmitted).

Obviously, this latter form of experimenter influence constitutes "unscrupulous" behavior because it violates the scientific canon of objectivity. That is, it is scientifically unethical practice when an experimenter's subjective desires to obtain hypothesized results lead to deliberate, willful attempts to "help" the operationalizations of independent variables by deviating from the prescribed procedure. The scientific community can hope, of course, that proper "moral education" of its practitioners will reduce the occurrence of this form of bias. Careful instruction and training of experimenters, with emphasis on the importance of standardization, clearly is required.

The significance of the Clever Hans phenomenon, on the other hand, is its implication that even well-intentioned, scientifically scrupulous experimenters, who faithfully implement all procedures as prescribed and follow a script word-for-word, might still inadvertently bias behavior. This possibility is especially troublesome to the extent that influence can be conveyed nonverbally and unintentionally. It is Rosenthal's contention that such an effect is indeed possible and might well be pervasive (e.g., R. Rosenthal, 1976b).

Implications

The distinctions made previously are essential to understanding what is controversial about the material reviewed in this chapter, and Table 7-1 has been prepared as an aid to understanding the significance of these distinctions. First, it is essential to realize that the controversy is chiefly focused on questions regarding the extensiveness of one particular category relative to the others—actual biases caused by the experimenter. The reason for this focus is that this category has, if it is extensive enough to warrant attention, implications for research practice that are quite different from the others. For

Table 7-1. The "Investigator" and the "Experimenter" as Sources of Bias: A Summary

Type of bias	The *investigator* as cause	The *experimenter* as cause
Errors in reporting	Fudging Inappropriate analyses	Misobservations Misrecording Fudging
Actual bias in subject behavior	Confounds Faulty designs	Failure to implement procedure Extraneous verbal reinforcement or other differential treatment Unintentional Nonverbal behavior Paralinguistic and kinesic cues

example both categories of errors in reporting might be avoided by the practice of having independent investigators attempt replication, but it is clear that any number of independent investigators could be equally fooled by a situation such as that involving Clever Hans. It is likewise the case that the standard sound design practices followed by a competent investigator could easily fail to prevent the problems of biases caused by the experimenter. Thus, it would be necessary to take special steps if actual biased behavior due to the experimenter is a prevalent phenomenon, and the degree of necessity is controversial to the extent that assessments regarding the degree of prevalence is controversial. Assessments of prevalence become controversial when an effect said to be an instance of bias caused by the experimenter is susceptible to alternative interpretation as an instance of other biasing factors.

Furthermore, even when there is agreement that what has occurred represents an instance of experimenter bias, there may be controversy regarding *how* that occurrence was made possible (i.e., whether it was the result of a failure of implementation, or the result of nonverbal cues). Quite simply, if actual biased behavior occurs because the experimenter failed to implement the procedure as directed (including the failure to refrain from extraneous verbal reinforcement), then the procedure itself is not at fault—it should be sufficiently corrective to find ways that the procedure is in fact implemented as it was supposed to be (e.g., emphasis on word-for-word recitation of a script). On the other hand if the experimenter's tone of voice and "body language" can influence the subject's behavior even without the experimenter's awareness (i.e., unintentionally), then it is difficult to think of instructions about implementing the procedure that could avoid this problem.

Controversial Issues

For the sake of simplicity, we identify an effect as an instance of *experimenter bias* (EB) if it refers to an influence on actual subject responses that the experimenter produces unintentionally through his or her expectancy-guided nonverbal behavior. We organize questions about the pervasiveness of the EB effect in the following manner. We first consider results attributable to the experimenter and examine the extent to which *intentional* influences can be ruled out. Next, we consider the investigator's influence in selecting data analytic techniques. Finally, we also address issues concerning the potential for control of EB and its elimination as a form of bias.

Experimenter Intentional Influence

The literature on EB is voluminous (for representative summaries, see, e.g., T.X. Barber, 1976; R. Rosenthal, 1969, 1976b), and we are selective here of necessity. One way of narrowing attention to a key set of studies is to focus on those singled out on methodological grounds by the two principal protagonists, Robert Rosenthal and Theodore X. Barber. Both authors have suggested criteria by which to distinguish studies that are in some respects "purer" than others (e.g., Barber, 1976; Barber & Silver, 1968a, 1968b; R. Rosenthal, 1969, 1976b).

R. Rosenthal (1969) has identified a small number of studies that address the issue of recording errors and fudging by the experimenter. Because a much larger number of studies have not provided for control of these factors or for estimations of their influence, he has also provided (R. Rosenthal, 1969) the following general comment:

> Analysis of the films of...experiments [on EB] ([R.] Rosenthal, 1966) in which experimenters did not know they were being filmed, gave no evidence to suggest any attempts to cheat on the part of the experimenters. Similarly, other analyses of the incidence of recording errors show their rates to be too low to account for the results of experimenter expectancy or most other studies for that matter. (p. 247)

Our review of these studies with special controls will focus on two groups of studies—those studies reported only by Rosenthal and those reported by Rosenthal that Barber also has examined.

In a section on "Expectancy Effects as Artifacts," R. Rosenthal (1969) cites three studies that do not receive critical attention in any of Barber's writings. One of these, a convention presentation by Hartry (cited in R. Rosenthal, 1969), involved planaria conditioning. Rosenthal's description says that "experimenters were given more intensive training, an instructor was present during the conduct of the experiment, and three observers were present to record the worm's response" (p. 246). Despite these controlled conditions, "experimenters expecting more responses obtained an average of 211 percent more responses than did the experimenters expecting fewer responses" (p.

247). Elsewhere, T.X. Barber (1976) has criticized planaria studies in general as being particularly susceptible to errors in judgment and scoring, because the size of these organisms makes their behavior ambiguous. Rosenthal's description suggests that this ambiguity may have been ameliorated by Hartry's procedure to the extent that it followed T.X. Barber's (1976) admonition to "pay careful attention to clarifying for the student-experimenters what criteria they are to use to score the animal's response" (p. 80). This extent is unknown.

The two remaining studies not examined by Barber (1976), one by Weick, and the other by Persinger, Knutson, and Rosenthal, have not been published. The special precautions taken in the Weick study consisted of its being administered "under the watchful eyes of students in a class in experimental social psychology" (R. Rosenthal, 1969, p. 246). The other study allowed independent observers to check tape recordings of the original experiment, and the transcription errors discovered were of such trivial proportions that they did not influence the results. It should be noted that in this study, "experimenter expectancy interacted with another variable" in a manner that is not described (see R. Rosenthal, 1969, Table XI, pp. 224–225). T.X. Barber and Silver (1968a) stated that "copies of these reports were not available when we reviewed the literature" (p. 382, footnote 7), and no subsequent work by Barber makes reference to them.

The same section of R. Rosenthal's (1969) book chapter examined two additional studies on which Barber has commented. An experiment by Adair and Epstein (1967, Experiment 2) used instructions taped from an earlier study in which experimenters had obtained results biased by expectations. These covertly taped instructions alone were sufficient to bias the responses of a new group of subjects who had no live contact with the experimenters. R. Rosenthal's (1969) interpretation is that "tape recordings cannot err either intentionally or unintentionally" (p. 246). T.X. Barber and Silver (1968b), on the other hand, argue that intentional biasing cannot be ruled out. They are willing to admit that when the experimenters biased the original subjects' behavior during the initial "live" session, subtle paralinguistic cues may have been responsible. There is no way of knowing, however, whether these cues were given intentionally or unintentionally. If they were given intentionally during the live rendition of the instructions (e.g., by the tone of voice used to introduce the task), then the tape of that performance would also be conveying the same intentional alterations in inflection, changes in pitch, and so on.

The significantly biased effects of an experiment by Johnson (1967, 1970) were cited by R. Rosenthal (1969) because its electronically recorded responses were tallied by someone blind to the expectancy conditions under which subjects had been run. T.X. Barber (1976) has included this study in a list of those that give "stronger evidence...that the experimenter's expectancies or desires can be communicated to their subjects by verbal, facial, or gestural cues and that the subjects may then respond in such a way as to fulfill the experimenters' expectancies" (p. 77). Barber's list includes four others in the same category (Marwit, 1969; McFall & Schenkein, 1970; K.A. Miller, 1970; Zobel & Lehman, 1969).

A later publication by R. Rosenthal (1976b) mentioned two other specially controlled studies that Barber has also examined. Both experiments were by Johnson and Adair (1970, 1972). In each case it was possible to determine the extent to which misrecording by experimenters occurred. Such errors were present, but their implications are subject to alternative interpretations. For example, T.X. Barber (1976) reports that Johnson and Adair's (1972) female experimenters obtained biased data "by systematically misrecording the data" (1976, p. 58), implying that such misrecording was the only—or was at least the primary—source of bias. Rosenthal's (1976) alternative account is as follows:

> In both experiments the overall effects of interpersonal expectations were modest...and cheating or recording errors accounted for 30% of these effects....Thus, even where cheating and/or recording errors can and do occurs, they cannot reasonably be invoked as an "explanation" of the effects of interpersonal expectations. (pp. 456–457)

Interestingly, when Johnson and Adair (1972) themselves reviewed explanations for the bias obtained, they concluded that "none...are unequivocal" (p. 93).

To summarize, it is possible to draw differing conclusions from this selective review of "methodologically purified" studies. On the one hand several (Johnson, 1970; Marwit, 1969; McFall & Schenkein, 1970; K.A. Miller, 1970; Zobel & Lehman, 1969) studies seem to have met even Barber's stringent criteria for an EB effect mediated precisely along the line implied by Rosenthal. It appears experimenters *can* influence subject behaviors in ways so subtle (e.g., by paralinguistic and kinesic cues) that the experimenters themselves may be unaware of the bias introduced by their own expectations.

On the other hand, even tightly controlled studies are occasionally prone to forms of bias that are not unintentional. Cheating and misrecording seem to be extremely difficult to eliminate entirely; and even though their effects may be minimal when "the best" of studies are examined, these sources of bias have gone largely unexamined in the bulk of the literature. Furthermore, the same nonverbal cues that are perhaps being conveyed unintentionally in some studies could just as easily be used intentionally by experimenters in other studies.

In this connection T.X. Barber (1976) has reviewed studies directly manipulating experimenters' behavior rather than manipulating experimenters' expectations (the indirect mediation with which Rosenthal has been most concerned). Such studies have shown that bias can be obtained by differential emphasis on one word in the instructions (Duncan, Rosenberg, & Finkelstein, 1969; Duncan & Rosenthal, 1968; Scherer, Rosenthal, & Koivumaku, 1972) or differential eye contact (R.A. Jones & Cooper, 1971). Thus, while evidence exists that EB can occur nonverbally and unintentionally, the studies cited to indicate its pervasiveness may contain other sources of bias as well. Some of these may be intentional, and some may represent biased reports rather than instances of biased subject behavior.

Statistical Analysis of Individual Studies

Apart from the extent to which experimenters can bias their subjects' behavior, or misrecord and misreport it, the analysis of data from an experiment is an additional context in which errors can occur. No one can take exception with such a statement (viz., that errors *can* occur). Labeling one form of analysis as an "error" and another as "correct," however, is a process subject to considerable disagreement. In fact Barber and Rosenthal do not see eye-to-eye on the way data from an individual study should be analyzed.

Too much space is needed to present the fine points of all the statistical issues being debated (details can be found in T.X. Barber & Silver, 1968a, 1968b; R. Rosenthal, 1968), so again we must be selective. First we present brief highlights of some of the major points made in discussions of the research in this area in general. Then, to illustrate these issues, we examine the controversies involving two particular examples (T.X. Barber et al., 1969; Rosenthal, Persinger, Mulry, Vikan-Kline, & Grothe, 1964).

T.X. Barber and Silver's (1968a, 1968b) objections to methods of EB data analysis include a number of major charges. Fundamental to several of these is that a traditional hypothesis-testing use of p values has sometimes been undermined because of ways the p values were calculated. Traditionally, a predetermined cut-off point (i.e., $p < .05$) is used to make an either/or decision whether to "accept" or "reject" the null hypothesis of no difference between treatment conditions. This hypothesis-testing orientation also contributes to a tendency for alpha-level protection against type I errors to assume more importance than safeguards against type II errors. Given these features of the decision-making procedure, a p value that is somehow "suspect" will be cause for alarm.

One way such suspicions can be raised is by claiming that a given p value has "capitalized on chance" in, for instance, not taking into account the number of statistical tests performed on overlapping data sets (e.g., data arbitrarily divided in half 100 different ways for pairwise comparisons could produce five tests "significant" at $p < .05$ by virtue of chance alone). The safeguards customarily recommended include omnibus tests (e.g., an "overall F" at $p < .05$ required before performing subsidiary analyses such as post hoc contrasts), subsequent replication, use of multivariate procedures that make adjustments for possible capitalization on chance (e.g., Duncan, Scheffé, and other "data snooping" tests). Essentially Barber and Silver have charged Rosenthal with ignoring all of these safeguards, but the bulk of the statistical controversy has centered around omnibus tests and replications.

These two issues have become interrelated in some of the discussions. Not using an omnibus test (or ignoring "nonsignificant" results from such a text) can be justified to the extent that the subsidiary test in question represents a "planned" contrast identified on a priori grounds. An attempt to replicate a previously discovered finding would constitute one source of such justification, and it is on these grounds that Rosenthal (1976b) defends some of what Barber and Silver have called his "postmortem" tests. T.X. Barber and Silver (1968b), however, argue that Rosenthal has stretched the term *replication* to include instances of phenomena that have not been reliably demonstrated.

Other controversial matters regarding the use of omnibus tests are separate from the issue of what constitutes a replication. A key problem is that there is usually more than one type of overall test possible. R. Rosenthal (1968, p. 395) argues that it would be unfortunate if key differences in subsets of data were ignored "only because an insufficiently powerful overall test was employed." Elsewhere, when commenting on procedures he used to tabulate statistical summaries of several studies, by a variety of researchers, R. Rosenthal (1969, p. 206) noted that "sometimes. . . it was necessary to decide on the most appropriate overall test," and he also mentioned that "many secondary analyses [were] performed when the original was felt to be inappropriate." Given this opportunity for the analyses reported to be at the discretion of the person doing the reporting, there is always a potential for controversy. We examine two such illustrative cases in the following section. (A third example, not reviewed because of space limitations, prompted journalistic exchange, resulting in what may be the largest number of articles devoted to a single data set in this literature: Harrington, 1967; Harrington & Ingraham, 1967; Ingraham & Harrington, 1966; Rosenthal, 1967a, 1967b.)

Rosenthal et al. (1964): An Illustration

The first example is a study by Rosenthal et al. (1964) that T.X. Barber and Silver (1968a) criticized on the following grounds: (1) An appropriate omnibus test had not been performed. Furthermore, such a test would have revealed something different than originally claimed—nonsignificant results instead of significant ones. (2) Data contradictory to the hypothesis were excluded from the analysis that yielded the significant results, and this exclusion was produced by the use of an after-the-fact criterion rather than a predetermined procedure. R. Rosenthal (1968) responded that although an overall analysis had not been reported, the appropriate overall analysis was a test for bimodality—a bimodality so readily apparent (because the scores contradictory to the hypothesis were such clear outliers) that formal statistical tests had been deemed unnecessary. Formal tests of bimodality did in fact confirm that the three scores opposite to the hypothesis differed significantly from the 17 scores in the direction of the hypothesis.

In responding to these criticisms, T.X. Barber and Silver (1968b) reiterated their qualms about the absence of a predetermined basis for categorizing the subjects into two separate groups for purposes of analysis. Their objection centered on the use of the dependent variable alone to subcategorize; in other words, first examining the results, then determining which subjects' data were used in the analysis designed to test the hypothesized effect. Such a "test," argue Barber and Silver, is inevitably biased in favor of one's hypothesis, since it removes for *separate* consideration and analysis the statistical "outliers" that have the greatest potential for disconfirming the hypothesis. They allege that Rosenthal's procedures "did not allow for the possibility that the null hypothesis may be correct" (T.X. Barber & Silver, 1968b, p. 153; cf. Chapanis & Chapanis, 1964).

Barber et al. (1969): Another Illustration

A second case of disagreements about statistical analyses involves the data from a set of experiments by T.X. Barber et al. (1969). In each of the five independently conducted studies that made up this data set, there was a failure to obtain an EB effect. R. Rosenthal (1969) attributed this outcome to several differences between these studies and the one they were designed to replicate (R. Rosenthal & Fode, 1963, Experiment 1). In addition Rosenthal performed alternative statistical analyses that suggested interpretations differing from the ones drawn by Barber et al. Thus, issues of both replication and data analysis were raised.

R. Rosenthal (1969, p. 7) charged that the research by T.X. Barber et al. (1969) "can by no stretch of the imagination be regarded as a serious effort at replication in the usual sense." In particular he argued that the "replication" procedures differed from the original (R. Rosenthal & Fode, 1963) study's along the following key dimensions: (1) type of subject, (2) number of subjects per experimenter, (3) sex of experimenter, and (4) status of experimenter. T.X. Barber et al. (1969) responded by offering counterarguments with respect to each of these.

The Rosenthal and Fode (1963) studies had used as subjects students in a coeducational state university, whereas only 18% of the students used by Barber et al. were of this same "subject type"; as T.X. Barber et al. (1969) pointed out, however, attributing replication failure to such a factor would severely limit the generality of the EB phenomenon. To Rosenthal's criticism that Barber et al. had used a relatively small number of subjects per experimenter (less than 10, as opposed to the Rosenthal and Fode figure of 20), Barber replied that there was no reason to think an analysis involving 51 experimenters and 501 subjects (Barber et al.) would be any less powerful than one using 10 experimenters and 206 subjects (Rosenthal and Fode). It should be noted that elsewhere R. Rosenthal (1976b) has recommended fewer subjects per experimenter as a bias-reducing technique. This recommendation is made because bias allegedly increases as a given experimenter contacts more subjects. Rosenthal's own review of the evidence pertaining to this assumption, however, reports inconsistent findings (R. Rosenthal, 1969, pp. 255–

256). T.X. Barber et al. (1969) also note inconsistencies in the evidence Rosenthal has reviewed with respect to each of the other two procedural matters raised (experimenter sex and experimenter status). Further evidence cited by Barber additionally challenged Rosenthal's contentions regarding these latter procedural factors (e.g., there was no effect of experimenter sex in the Barber et al. data).

Despite Rosenthal's calling into question the status of the Barber et al. studies as replication attempts, he nonetheless purports to find in them evidence challenging the conclusion that no biasing occurred. This evidence comes from a special partitioning of the data, for which Rosenthal obtained a significant overall chi-square. Barber, however, reexamined Rosenthal's overall chi-square by means of separate chi-squares for each of the partitioning intervals. These analyses revealed that the frequencies did *not* differ significantly in 11 of the 13 instances. The two intervals where response frequencies did differ significantly by expectancy, moreover, were problematic theoretically and of questionable general interest.

T.X. Barber and Silver (1968a, 1968b) purport to find numerous instances in which studies cited as supporting EB have been inappropriately analyzed. Most of the criticism directed against these analyses has suggested that they underestimate the extent to which chance may have been responsible for the findings obtained. Part of Rosenthal's reaction to these critiques has been emphasis on the replicability of the phenomena in question, but Rosenthal and Barber cannot seem to agree on what constitutes a replication.

One of the studies supervised by Rosenthal and one supervised by Barber were chosen to illustrate some of the interpretive issues surrounding data analysis. In the former case differing conclusions could be drawn about the reliability of the phenomenon, depending on how subjects were categorized for analysis, and disagreements exist regarding when this categorization should take place (before vs. after the data have been collected). In the latter case the procedures used to attempt replication were questioned by Rosenthal, who also reanalyzed the data to draw different conclusions than Barber had. Barber's conclusions, on the other hand, were supported by his own subsequent reanalysis. Regardless of the analysis used, the results did not support the EB hypothesis as originally formulated.

Techniques of Control

A great many procedures have been recommended for the detection, minimization, and elimination of EB effects. We do not review all of these techniques, as extensive descriptions have been provided by T.X. Barber (1976, Chapter 10), by Carlsmith, Ellsworth, and Aronson (1976, Chapter 9), and by R. Rosenthal (1976b, Chapters 19–24). Our discussion focuses on three procedural matters regarding which differing forms of advice have been given.

Hypothesis Blindness and Reduced Investigator–Experimenter Contact

Hypothesis blindness and reduced investigator-experimenter contact are closely related techniques whose advisability has been questioned for similar reasons. Hypothesis blindness involves using "student research assistants who could be kept uninformed of the hypothesis and overall design of the experiment" (Rosenthal, 1976b, p. 368). An experiment by R. Rosenthal, Persinger, Vikan-Kline, and Mulry (1963), however, indicated that the expectancies of investigators who instructed these research assistants might be transmitted unintentionally and nonverbally—even though the instructions themselves did not mention what to expect, and the persons giving the instructions had been warned not to convey any such information. Based on these results R. Rosenthal (1976b) has recommended that minimal contact between an investigator and an experimenter be used to reduce the possibility of the experimenter's discovering the research hypothesis.

Carlsmith et al. (1976) question the utility of both techniques because of a faulty underlying assumption the two have in common. This assumption is that if a hypothesis has not been communicated (overtly or covertly) to the experimenter, he or she cannot bias the results. What Carlsmith et al. point out is that the absence of a communicated hypothesis does not prevent experimenters from developing hypotheses themselves. The experimenter-formed hypothesis, of course, might systematically bias results even if it is not the same as the uncommunicated hypothesis formulated by the investigator. In addition to stating their reasons for believing that these procedures will not work, Carlsmith et al. also argue that there are reasons why experimenters *should* know the research hypothesis. Explicitly communicating the hypothesis to the experimenter serves important training and educational functions, they claim. More complete participation (knowing the hypothesis) means that more effective learning occurs, and "the experimenter's ignorance of the hypothesis or a reduction of supervisory contact does the student a disservice" (Carlsmith et al., 1976, p. 296).

Condition Blindness

Another technique can be used to eliminate EB effects. Rather than keeping experimenters unaware of the hypothesis, steps can be taken to prevent them from discovering the conditions to which subjects have been assigned. The logic of this approach is that if an experimenter does not know about differences in assignment, expectations cannot systematically alter the experimenters' behaviors in ways that coincide with these differences. This technique is a long-standing practice in pharmacological research, where it is called the *double-blind* procedure (see, e.g., Beecher, 1959; Levitt, 1959; E.B. Wilson, 1952). Its use can be illustrated by a hypothetical experiment about the effects of a new drug in capsule form. Subjects assigned to the control group receive a placebo (an inert substance with no pharmacological effect). If identical-appearing opaque capsules are used, detection of what is inside (drug vs. placebo) can be made impossible. The experiment is typically called *single-blind* if only the subjects are thereby prevented from determining which substances they have ingested (analogous to the use of deception as a safeguard against bias stemming from demand characteristics). If the experimenter who administers the capsules is similarly prevented from knowing which capsule contains which substance, the double-blind nature of the experiment is complete. Note that in terms of our description, an experiment is still double-blind even if the experimenter knows what the new drug is and has a hypothesis about what its effects will be.

Carlsmith et al. (1976) devote virtually all of their discussion of EB control techniques to this procedure, which we will call *condition blindness*. It is called a theoretically "*complete* solution to the problem of experimenter blindness" (p. 296, emphasis in original) as well as "the ideal solution" (p. 297). These authors go on to note that although condition blindness is ideal in principle, it may sometimes be difficult to achieve in actual practice. They then describe several ingenious methods whereby most of these difficulties could be surmounted, including variations on what might be called "partial" condition blindness (e.g., experimenter condition blind to one independent variable in a factorial design, thereby ruling out EB as an explanation for a main effect of that variable or significant interactions between it and other independent variables). Carlsmith et al. (1976, p. 301) conclude by saying that "it is a rare experiment which, with some ingenuity, cannot be built in such a way as to allow the experimenter to be kept ignorant of at least one critical aspect of the subject's condition."

We do not wish to exaggerate the difference in attitudes toward condition blindness between Carlsmith et al. (1976) and Rosenthal (1976b). Any differences that exist are matters of degree, involving subtle shifts of emphasis. It is true, for example, that Rosenthal (1976b, p. 373) says the technique "gives virtually complete assurance of the maintenance of experimenter blindness," hence prevention of EB. Nevertheless, he expresses some concern about ways that the experimenter's initial blindness to conditions can subsequently break down, and he therefore urges further corrective measures.

R. Rosenthal (1976b) discusses this issue by alerting investigators to the problems of treatment "side effects" (pp. 369–70) and experimenter "code-cracking" (p. 377). He uses the example of an experiment in which anxiety is manipulated. Suppose levels of anxiety are predicted to influences affiliative behavior (e.g., Schachter, 1959). Differing levels of anxiety are initially induced in subjects without the experimenter's knowledge. Highly anxious subjects, however, may behave differently from less anxious subjects in a variety of ways (side effects) that the experimenter can detect before administration of the affiliation measure. That is, even though the experimenter may not have been privy to the manipulated basis for coding subjects into conditions, it might be possible for the code to be cracked on the basis of behaviors that are extraneous to the theory being investigated. When such code cracking occurs, it circumvents condition blindness and the experimenter is no longer prevented from biasing the results. Thus, condition blindness is theoretically a complete cure for EB effects, but these effects might still intrude on actual practice if such blindness is not effectively maintained in ways that prevent code cracking where side effects are present.

A response to this challenge for condition blindness is difficult to formulate without more extensive information regarding side effects and code cracking. How often, for example, are these side effects of manipulations likely to occur? Are they restricted to particular classes of manipulations more than others? If so, on what basis might these manipulations be identified? R. Rosenthal's (1976b) discussion does not provide answers to these questions.

Similarly, the prevalence of code cracking is unknown. It occurs to us, however, that there is a simple procedure for assessing the existence of code cracking in some experiments. The type of experiments to which we refer are those in which the experimenter does not see the subjects' behaviors that constitute the dependent measures (e.g., questionnaires filled out in the experimenter's absence and examined only by the investigator). Because experimenters in such studies do not observe the dependent measure responses, only any manifested side effects would provide clues as to the condition of a particular subject. If experimenters were asked to guess which condition each subject had been assigned to, their guesses would provide a measure of the extent to which any side effects were detectable. Of course, the ability to detect side effects does not necessarily entail an EB effect. For an EB effect to occur, information about side effects must be *used* (effectively!) in a way that actually biases the subjects' subsequent behavior.

Condition blindness is more effective than the technique of keeping the experimenter uninformed as to the hypothesis since experimenters can generate hypotheses on their own. The technique of condition blindness is itself relatively noncontroversial. In theory it is a perfect way to prevent the EB effect. R. Rosenthal has raised questions about its effectiveness in actual practice, but answers to these questions await further information on the prevalence of manipulation side effects and the capacity of experimenters to use such effects as a basis for inferring a subject's assigned condition.

Current Status of the Controversy

The absence of systematic investigations concerning manipulation side effects and experimenter code cracking suggests that social psychologists have felt secure about the effectiveness of condition blindness in preventing EB effects. Condition blindness has become the standard of acceptable practice for experiments in social psychology (Carlsmith et al., 1976). Given the acceptance of this "cure," interest in the "disease" itself has diminished. This currently quiescent status of a once more-animated controversy can be understood in terms of an implicit cost–benefit analysis. That is, the benefits of the status quo (accepting condition blindness without question) are apparently seen as outweighing the costs of change (further modifications in procedures).

What costs of change are being resisted? One particularly salient cost seems to be the risk of what might be called "overmechanization." If the presence of an experimenter might produce bias even when he or she is blind to the condition, then one approach to avoiding all possibility of EB effects is to remove the experimenter entirely and rely exclusively on written instructions, tape recordings, video presentations, and so on. A point that comes across very strongly in the Carlsmith et al. (1976) discussion of experimental methods, however, is that a "live" experimenter may often be essential to maintaining subjects' interest and involvement in the experiment. Indeed, capturing the subjects' attention and having them become caught up in the flow of events (increasing what Carlsmith et al. term the *experimental realism* of the situation) is promoted as being absolutely essential to capturing subject responses that are genuine and spontaneous rather than artifically induced by role expectations (see Chapter 6). It is clear, then, that advocates of condition blindness such as Carlsmith et al. perceive a high cost in alternative techniques that reduce the degree of experimenter–subject interaction.

For what reasons, on the other hand, has Rosenthal (1976b) insisted that it may be important to go beyond mere condition blindness and investigate the effectiveness of additional safeguards against EB effects? The answer lies in his estimates of the magnitude of these effects. For him the costs of ignoring *any* possibility of EB are too high because the risks of a "finding" being a mere artifact are too great.

Here, then, is the crux of the matter: How well established is the EB phenomenon? Are these effects so prevalent as to call for even "extreme" measures such as total mechanization of an experiment? Our review of the evidence suggests that there are still questions as to the strength and prevalence of the effect. In particular the inconclusiveness of the evidence stems from the frequent lack of control for other sources of bias in a study in addition to EB (i.e., experimenter fudging, experimenter inadvertant misrecording or failure to follow the procedure, and inappropriate statistical analyses).

Chapter 8

Debriefing

It was in response to the onslaught of ethical outcries against the use of deception in experiments (see Chapter 3) that the practice of "debriefing" research participants developed. In the 1960s, when deceiving experimental subjects became commonplace (cf. Adair et al., 1985) observers of the research scene began voicing concern over the possible long-term effects of these deceptive practices, and noted the ethical obligation of the researcher to "undo" any such effects in postexperimental sessions known as debriefings (Aronson & Carlsmith, 1968). In addressing the 1965 meeting of the American Psychological Association (APA), Herbert Kelman reflected this sentiment when he advised that "a subject ought not leave the laboratory with greater anxiety or lower self-esteem than he came with" (Kelman, 1968, p. 222).

It was soon thereafter that the APA formed its Committee on Ethical Standards in Psychological Research, headed by Stuart Cook (S. Cook et al., 1971), to draft a formal set of ethical standards. The resulting formal codification of these ethical standards (Ad Hoc Committee, 1973) clearly highlighted the ethical necessity of debriefing research participants. This is especially apparent in Principle 8, which requires experimenters, following data collection, to "provide the participant with a full clarification of the nature of the study and to remove any misconceptions that may have arisen" (Ad Hoc Committee, 1973, p. 77). Adding to this function, Principle 9 states that "Where research procedures may result in undesirable consequences for the participant, the investigator has the responsibility to detect and remove or correct these consequences, including, where relevant, long-term after-effects" (Ad Hoc Committee, 1973, p. 83). These admonitions were subsequently incorporated into a revised version of the APA's *Ethical Principles* ("Committee," 1982), where they reside in Principles H and I. The debriefing procedure is placed in a position of "pivotal importance" (Holmes, 1976a, p. 858) in removing these misconceptions and undesirable consequences.

Interestingly, rather than dissuading experimenters from relying on deception, the formal acceptance of deception procedures with suitable postexperimental debriefings appears to have given experimenters implicit approval to continue deceiving their subjects (Tesch, 1977). The remarkable prevalence of deception techniques in today's experimentation (see Chapter 3) attests to researchers' faith in the effectiveness of their debriefings in correcting any misinformation given subjecs and removing any harm. As Tesch (1977) put it:

> It apparently became an article of professional faith that debriefing suffi-ciently minimized or eliminated any serious vilification of devious experimen-ters, that it functioned remedially to disabuse participants of any negative affect or outcome, and that it justified the experimenter's actions to the participants. (p. 218)

Indeed, a survey of empirical studies published in major social psychology journals reveals a strong trend for debriefings to become more prevalent as more deceptions are carried out—from 17% with no deceptions to 100% with five deceptions (Adair et al., 1985).

To what extent is debriefing effective in meeting its goals? Does it actually disabuse subjects of misinformation and remove harm, or does it just create new bases of misinformation and distress for the subject and methodological problems for the experimenter? These are the issues about debriefing that have been raised in the literature. Before considering them we will first take a closer look at the nature of the debriefing process, focusing on the specific functions of debriefing and the methods by which debriefings are conducted.

The Nature of the Debriefing Process

Today's research methodology texts variously refer to debriefings as attempts to describe to subjects "the true nature of the experiment and the reasons for the deception" (Carlsmith et al., 1976, p. 102) and to minimize among them any "negative impressions of self" and "any feeling that they might have been manipulated, made fools of, shown to be gullible, or revealed character weak-ness" (Kidder, 1981, p. 404).

The Functions of Debriefing

The preceding descriptions highlight the two major functions of debriefing that have been identified in the literature—the educational function and the ethical function (Tesch, 1977).[1] Holmes (1976a, 1976b) distinguishes between these functions by using the term *dehoaxing* to refer to the educational func-

---

[1]There is yet a third function of debriefing identified by Tesch (1977)—the methodo-logical function. This refers to interviewing subjects about the effectiveness of the experimental manipulations (see also Kidd, 1976). However, inasmuch as using post-experimental debriefings as checks on the validity of experimental manipulations is typically not considered a function of debriefing by others writing on this topic (e.g., Holmes, 1976a, 1976b) and is covered in a separate chapter (Chapter 9), the methodo-logical function will not be considered here.

tion and *desensitizing* to refer to the ethical function. Specifically, he notes that *dehoaxing* focuses on the experimenter's deception: "the process of convincing subjects who had just been deceived that the information they had been given was in fact fraudulent"; and that *desensitizing* focuses on the subject's behavior: "the process of helping the subjects deal with new information about themselves acquired as a consequence of the behaviors they exhibited during the experiment" (Holmes, 1976b, p. 868).

Educational Function

Given that the vast majority of laboratory research participants are undergraduate college students drawn from departmental "subject pools" and are procured to fulfill a course requirement (Jung, 1969; Menges, 1973; Schultz, 1969; Smart, 1966), it is incumbent on researchers to meet the APA's ethical standard of giving subjects "a full clarification of the nature of the study" (Ad Hoc Committee, 1973, p. 77). Doing so, Tesch (1977) argues, is necessary to give subjects the educational benefit promised to them to justify their participation (a better understanding of and appreciation for behavioral science by experiencing experimentation first-hand).[2] It should not be surprising, then, that the educational benefits to be derived from research participation are most frequently cited by psychology department personnel as the justification provided for requiring research experience (Jung, 1969).

Kidder (1981) identifies seven goals of debriefing, four of which may be considered as serving an educational function. These include (1) communicating to subjects the potential value of the research, (2) apprising subjects of their contributions to the research, (3) educating subjects about the social science phenomena relevant to the research in which they were involved, and (4) informing subjects about the sometimes necessity of having to use deception in attaining answers to research questions.[3] Knowledge of this type may be assumed to leave research participants with an "identifiable benefit" from the research experience, as stipulated by the APA's (Ad Hoc Committee, 1973, p. 11) code of ethics. As such, the need exists to debrief all experimental subjects, even those who were not deceived (Tesch, 1977).[4]

---

[2]As Perry and Abramson (1980) note, debriefing is too often omitted from experiments using nonstudent populations, but they argue that it should not be, because experimenters need to educate their subjects in return for their participation, regardless of the population from which they are drawn.

[3]Although many experimenters certainly attempt to meet these goals in good faith (e.g., Davis & Fernald, 1975), some have noted that experimenters merely use their didactic role, their authority as experimenters, to manipulate subjects' impressions of the educational value of the experiment (Tesch, 1977).

[4]Despite this, a recently conducted survey at the University of Georgia shows that better debriefings are conducted when subjects are deceived than when they are not deceived (S.S. Smith & Richardson, 1983). Given the fact that great care is needed to disabuse subjects of erroneous information and possible stress created by experimental deception (Mills, 1976), this is not particularly surprising.

Another explicit educational purpose of debriefing is inherent in Holmes's (1976a) notion of dehoaxing. That is, subjects need to be informed about the true nature of the experiment they were in and what was being studied. Any deception has to be revealed. Thus, debriefing may serve an educational function by informing subjects about (1) the truth concerning the experiment, (2) the nature of the phenomenon being studied, and (3) the experimental process itself.

Ethical Function

In addition to these educational functions, debriefing is also used for ethical purposes. According to Kidder (1981), these include (1) immunizing participants against negative self-impressions, (2) convincing them that the investigator regrets having deceived them, and (3) minimizing any negative feelings that may have resulted. If these functions are not adequately served, participants may well feel foolish in addition to misinformed. One subject in a study on hypnotism and problem solving, for example, reported feelings resentment at "being dropped like a cold jellyfish" (Hunt, 1982, p. 142) in response to an inadequate debriefing.

Of course, the functions of debriefing are much easier to identify than to bring to fruition. To demonstrate these difficulties, consider attempting to implement them following Milgram's (1963, 1974) obedience studies. If a subject believes he or she engaged in an inappropriate behavior (allegedly administering high doses of electric shock to another), it cannot be denied that the subjects actually pressed the lever; it cannot be disproved (like fraudulent information about the purpose of the experiment). Moreover, subjects' beliefs in the inappropriateness of the behavior in question (harming another) is probably well ingrained into their value systems (Holmes, 1976b). Such sensitive situations demand an especially effective debriefing by the experimenter (one that some have argued was not carried out in Milgram's research; e.g., Baumrind, 1964). Holmes (1976b) recommends two interrelated tactics. He suggests that experimenters point out to the subjects that their behavior was situationally induced, and as such, that it was *not* abnormal; most people behave that way (i.e., they are obedient to the experimenter's commands to administer shock).

Whether or not such debriefings actually work is a topic we consider later in this chapter. It is, however, possible at this point to note the irony involved in the experimenter's attempts to undo the very effects he or she strived so hard to create in the first place. Commenting on this paradoxical "eraser function" of debriefing, Tesch (1977) has said:

> On one hand we devise marvelous manipulations and hone them for maximum impact upon our participants. On the other hand, we apparently assume that the effects produced conveniently cease when the participants leave our experiments. Have we discovered the best of all possible worlds, in which events happen when we wish and do not when we turn away from them? (p. 219)

Methods of Debriefing

It is surprising that very little is known about the debriefing practices of researchers despite the prevalence debriefing is accorded as an ethical tool ("Committee," 1982) and despite the admonition by Aronson and Carlsmith (1968) that "The art of debriefing should be an important part of research training" (p. 70). We know, however, that reports of debriefing are becoming increasing common in social psychology journals. For example, after examining the 1971 issues of five journals (*Journal of Personality and Social Psychology*, *Journal of Abnormal Psychology*, *Journal of Educational Psychology*, *Journal of Counseling Psychology*, and *Journal of Experimental Psychology*) and the 1961 issues of the *Journal of Abnormal and Social Psychology*, Menges (1973) reported that debriefings were reported in only 10% ($n = 993$) of the studies reported. More recently, Perry and Abramson (1980) noted that debriefing was reported in 35% of the articles appearing in the 1975 issues of the *Journal of Personality and Social Psychology*, and 11% of the articles appearing in the *Journal of Consulting and Clinical Psychology* for the same year. By 1983, Adair et al. (1985) found that debriefings were included in 45% of the empirical studies published in the *Journal of Personality and Social Psychology*; 66% in the case of deception studies.

Moreover, Perry and Abramson (1980) found that among the studies in which debriefing was reported, over half failed to specify any specific debriefings procedures used (51% in the case of the *Journal of Personality and Social Psychology* and 63% in the case of the *Journal of Consulting and Clinical Psychology*); it was usually just stated that "subjects were debriefed." More recent data reveal that not much has changed (Adair et al., 1985). Arguing that knowledge of debriefing procedures is useful, Sieber (1979) recommends that authors specify their debriefing procedures in their articles. Perry and Abramson (1980) echo their sentiment, but take it a step further by recommending that journal editors reject articles that fail to thoroughly report debriefing procedures.[5]

Although little has been written about *how* to debrief subjects (Adair et al., 1985), a few researchers have described the debriefing procedures employed in their laboratories. Judson Mills (1976), for example, has described the approach used in over 20 years of his own and his students' research. This method involves preparing a detailed script, a "debriefing scenario," that serves the purposes of (1) explaining the general reason for using deception, (2) explaining the purpose of the study and the deception used, (3) relieving subjects' anxieties about their experimental performance, and (4) explaining the need for them to maintain secrecy about the study. These points are ex-

---

[5]Leak (1981) has noted his objections to these recommendations on the grounds that complete reports of debriefings are not required by the *Publication Manual of the American Psychological Association* and that the "method" section of an article is not the appropriate place to pass judgment on the ethics of another's research.

plained to subjects very gradually and thoroughly until the debriefer is assured that the subjects understand them. Mills explains that this is necessary in order to get subjects to reorganize their thoughts about the experiment, especially if the deceptive cover story was convincing. This slow process also provides the experimenter with the opportunity to monitor subjects' emotional responses and to gain their sympathetic understanding.

This approach is very much in keeping with Carlsmith et al.'s (1976) recommendation for experimenters to "spend more time with the subject after the experiment is over than during the experimental session itself" (p. 102). Both Mills (1976) and Carlsmith et al. (1976) emphasize the necessity of the experimenter's being sincere and showing honest concern about the subject's welfare and regret for having engaged in deception. Similarly, Sieber (1983) advocates the practice of debriefing by a skilled and sympathetic professional for fear of doing more harm than good. For the experimenter to be smug about the subject's uneasiness, under the assumption that these reactions are justified by the scientific value of the experiment—an assumption subjects might not share (e.g., Baumrind, 1985; Tesch, 1977), is deemed inappropriate and does not preclude the need for a thorough debriefing. Mills emphasizes that it is at least as important, if not more so, to train researchers in the art of debriefing as it is to train them to run complicated deception experiments. Although a movement toward systematic graduate-level training in debriefing methods has been called for (Smith, 1983), there is evidence of only scant teaching of such techniques (Adair, Lindsay, & Carlopio, 1983).

Sometimes it is necessary for experimenters to make an elaborate show of the fact that they actually deceived their subjects. After all, why should subjects now believe someone who just admitted having deceived them (S. Cook et al., 1971; Tesch, 1977)? Providing concrete proof has been useful in proving deception in some experiments. A good example is provided by Milgram's (1963, 1974) showing his subjects that they had not actually harmed the "learner" in his experiment. Sometimes, debriefings about even more innocuous manipulations benefit from direct demonstrations as well. For example, in proving to their subjects that the experimenter actually gave them false feedback about their test performance, Bennett and Holmes (1975) produced the sealed envelope containing the test that supposedly provided the basis for that feedback. Such demonstrations provide further examples of the lengths to which experimenters must go to adequately debrief their subjects.

Although these careful debriefing techniques involve a great expenditure of time and effort, they are generally considered "well worth the price" (Carlsmith et al., 1976, p. 103). The benefits of scrupulously ethical treatment are derived by both the subject (who is made to feel good and is given an educational experience) and the experimenter (whose conscience is cleared of guilt for having been deceptive). The careful debriefing sessions described by Mills (1976) also provide a potential opportunity for subjects to become enthusiastic about the topic under investigation and the experimental process in general. Experimenters may also benefit by using postexperimental interviews to find out what subjects were thinking about during the study (particularly in pilot studies) and to provide valuable information about the validity of their manipulations (see Chapter 9). In sum, then, lengthy postexperimental debriefings, such as those outlined by Mills (1976), appear to be valuable to both subjects and experimenters alike.

In recognition of this importance, formal debriefing sessions have been made part of the experimental participation requirements of most colleges and universities (Jung, 1969) and represent an important part of the considerations of institutional review boards (Smith, 1981; Suls & Rosnow, 1981). The debriefing procedure followed in the psychology department of the University of New Hampshire (UNH), as described by J.R. Davis and Fernald (1975), provides a good example of the care taken by some institutions to formally ensure the educational benefits of debriefing. Researchers at UNH are required to hold formal postexperimental debriefing sessions during which (1) subjects' questions are answered, (2) the independent and dependent variables used are identified, (3) the importance of the study to the field is discussed, and (4) the practical significance of the work, if any, is identified. These small group meetings with experimenters are deemed beneficial inasmuch as they provide students with first-hand knowledge about experimental procedures and exposure to new faculty members. On the basis of these meetings, subjects are required to prepare a report of one to two pages in length that describes the experiment. Students surveyed about these experiences reported that both the laboratory report and the experimental experiences themselves were worthwhile, beneficial, and should be continued. In personal communication with James R. Davis, the authors are assured that the practice of requiring debriefing sessions and laboratory reports have indeed continued at UNH.

Small group debriefing sessions held after the experiment is completed have also been reported by Abramson (1977; Perry & Abramson, 1980) in his research on human sexual behavior. Abramson offered subjects (introductory psychology students) additional experimental credit for attending a 1-hour debriefing session scheduled during an evening 2 weeks after the study was completed. The debriefing consisted of a detailed lecture and discussion about the experimental procedure and results, and was assumed to be responsible for the largely positive reaction to the research. Interestingly, the use of research credit for attending the debriefing session proved to be an effective incentive for subjects, as it was attended by virtually all the participants.

Both Abramson's (1977) debriefings and those conducted at UNH (J.R. Davis & Fernald, 1975) were not held immediately after the experimental session, before participants were dismissed. Such delayed debriefings are not uncommon. In fact, in Jung's (1969) survey of debriefing practices in 45 American psychology departments it was found that among the 62% that required formal debriefings, 32.3% of these usually held delayed debriefings. The majority of the departments, 53.2%, reported that immediate debriefings were usually held (the remaining 14.5% reported both immediate and de-layed debriefings).

Although the educational benefits of delayed small group discussions are apparent, the delays they require dictate limiting their use to extremely in-nocuous experiments—those in which the need to disabuse subjects of poten-tially sensitive or harmful matters is nonexistent. The educational function of debriefing might be very well served in delayed small group meetings, al-though the ethical function requires immediate debriefings. The potentially harmful effects of delayed debriefings in a stressful setting have been demon-strated by Holmes (1973). This study found that subjects who were immediate-ly dehoaxed about receiving painful electric shocks in the future demonstrated significantly lower physiological arousal, as measured by both pulse rate and self-report measures, than those whose debriefings were delayed. Although delayed debriefings are not always less effective than immediate ones (espe-cially in nonstressful settings; L. Ross, Lepper, & Hubbard, 1975), they are generally not recommended. Carlsmith et al. (1976), for example, argue that the ethical risks of delayed debriefing (prolonging possible distress) outweigh the potential economic and procedural benefits of delaying debriefing until the experiment is over (saving time by debriefing *en masse*, and minimizing the chance for subjects to contaminate the responses of future participants by informing them about the study).

Controversial Issues

Two distinct categories of issues regarding the use of debriefing procedures have been noted in the literature. The first concerns the very basic question of whether or not debriefing is actually effective in meeting its educational and ethical goals. The second issue concerns the methodological and ethical prob-lems caused by debriefing. We turn our attention to each of these issues in this section.

Effectiveness of Debriefing

Our discussion of the effectiveness of debriefing is organized around the evi-dence bearing on each of the debriefing functions identified, educational and ethical. As such, two effectiveness criteria are used: the extent to which de-briefing disabuses subjects of erroneous information and the extent to which it minimizes potentially harmful aftereffects of research participation.

Correcting Experimentally Created Misinformation

The inherent difficulty in dehoaxing experimental subjects is that they may be reluctant to suddenly trust an experimenter who admitted having once deceived them (S. Cook et al., 1971). The shift in role from experimenter-deceiver to debriefer may be jarring, and experimenters are cautioned against assuming that the participant has made an analogous shift in orientation (Tesch, 1977). Indeed, unless subjects come to believe that the experimenter is now being truthful, debriefings may unintentionally confirm the apprehension and skepticism of naive subjects (Schulman & Berman, 1975). Subjects may well question whether they are actually being "set up" for another deception (multiple deception is not unusual, as typified by the research of Ring et al., 1970). They may also suspect that the debriefing information is simply presented in an attempt to assuage their feelings in reaction to inadvertent exposure to negative information revealed during the experiment (Holmes, 1976a).

Given these difficulties, several studies have been designed to specifically test the effectiveness of dehoaxing procedures.[6] Among the first studies in this area was a Master's thesis conducted by Abrahams (1967), described in detail by Holmes (1976a) and by Walster, Berscheid, Abrahams, and Aronson (1967). Abrahams (1967) gave subjects false feedback about their creativity and maturity after completing two personality tests and subsequently debriefed them by admitting that this feedback was false. To determine the degree to which the debriefing information was successful in disabusing subjects of the erroneous personality information, comparisons were made of the self-ratings of creativity and maturity of subjects who were initially led to believe they were creative and mature with those of subjects led to believe they were uncreative and immature. The results were inconsistent with respect to the two self-report test measures. After the deception was admitted, subjects who were initially told they were uncreative and immature did not rate themselves significantly differently on creativity than subjects initially told they were creative and mature. This suggests that the debriefing successfully minimized potential carry-over self-impressions (although more meaningful pre-postdebriefing comparisons were not reported). With respect to self-rated maturity, however, Walster et al. (1967), in reanalyzing Abrahams's (1967) data, found a marginally higher level among subjects who were initially led to believe they were higher along this dimension, suggesting that the debriefing was not completely effective.

Abrahams (1967) also tested for secondary side effects of debriefing by comparing subjects' own performance evaluations before and after they had been given false feedback and were debriefed about it. Not only were no significant differences in performance evaluations found, but actual task performance differences also failed to reach significance. These findings suggest that subjects accepted the debriefing information inasmuch as they failed to

---

[6]We do not consider here more indirect evidence based on studies conducted for other purposes (reviewed by Holmes, 1974, 1976a) showing that material repressed in response to an experimentally induced threat is returned when the threat is eliminated, such as through debriefing.

use the false feedback to achieve consistency by reinterpreting their self-impressions.

Following up on Abrahams's (1967) study, Walster et al. (1967) used a similar paradigm. After taking a personality test, subjects were successfully led to believe that they were either high or low on sociability (i.e., they had either well-developed or poorly developed social skills). Soon afterward they were debriefed and asked to complete a questionnaire (containing a self-rating of sociability) to indicate what they were really like. As in the Abrahams (1967) study, the results were inconclusive regarding the effectiveness of debriefing. Specifically, the primary effects showed that debriefing was ineffective; self-ratings of sociability were significantly higher among subjects who were earlier misled into believing that they were highly sociable than among those who were led to believe they were low in sociability. In contrast, subjects who thought they scored high in sociability did not rate their performance on an earlier interview (allegedly designed to measure ability to make a good impression) as being any different from subjects who thought they scored low on sociability. Although this implies that the debriefing was effective in eliminating secondary effects, this conclusion must be considered tentative inasmuch as the design of the study did not peremit a determination of whether or not there were any secondary effects created in the study that possibly could have been eliminated through debriefing (Holmes, 1976a).[7]

A methodological and conceptual extension of the Abrahams (1967) and the Walster et al. (1967) studies was attempted by L. Ross et al. (1975), who were also concerned about the degree to which experimentally created impressions survive debriefings. In the first of two studies, Ross et al. found that subjects' positive self-impressions created by false task performance feedback persevered after debriefings (5 or 25 minutes later) in which the false feedback was admitted. These effects were eliminated, however, in a second experiment under conditions in which debriefings consisted of telling subjects that their performance outcomes were bogus and also that this sometimes leads to the perseverance of erroneous impressions—what they call "process debriefing." Apparently, simply telling subjects that their performance feedback was bogus was ineffective in changing the self-perceptions they may have formed as a result of such information. In contrast, providing explanations about the impression perseverance process (in addition to disclosing the fraudulent information) quite effectively dehoaxed subjects; the self-ratings of those given positive feedback did not differ significantly from those who were given negative feedback. Although the authors admit that the demonstrated effects of process debriefings may have been the result of demand

---

[7]Walster et al. (1967) also considered the possibility that it would be more difficult to debrief (return to a preexperimental state) subjects who received false information about themselves that was relevant to their current concerns than those who received irrelevant information about themselves. No significant evidence in support of this possibility was reported (although Holmes, 1976a, describes a provocative trend).

characteristics, their findings strongly indicate the effectiveness of thorough debriefings.

The effectiveness of debriefing has also been examined by Bowerman (1976), and in a follow-up by Holmes (1976c) in studies using a mailed questionnaire to assess deception-related attitudes. Bowerman dehoaxed subjects after giving them false information regarding either positive or negative performance on a bogus intelligence test. To assess the long-term effectiveness of the debriefing, a questionnaire was mailed to subjects 2 months later. Bowerman found that subjects who initially were misinformed of their low intelligence subsequently rated their intelligence as being lower than those who initially were misinformed of their high intelligence, suggesting that the subjects were not disabused of their experimentally created impressions. However, inasmuch as subjects in Bowerman's two groups showed differences in their initial (predeception) self-perceived intelligence levels, Holmes (1976a) has argued that Bowerman's results are invalid. In a direct replication using groups with equivalent predeception beliefs about their own intelligence, Holmes (1976c) found no differences in perceived intelligence 2 months later. Although Holmes (1976c) concludes that these data indicate the absence of long-term aftereffects, we should note that the failure to immediately assess the effects of the intelligence feedback manipulation makes it impossible to allege that there were any immediate effects that were subsequently reduced.[8]

Before concluding this section one additional aspect of the educational function of debriefing needs to be mentioned. This concerns the extent to which debriefings successfully lead participants to appreciate the need for deception (Tesch, 1977) and to agree to maintain secrecy about the investigation so as to avoid contaminating the responses of future subjects (Mills, 1976). Evidence revealing that subjects are very reluctant to admit to being tipped off by another (Golding & Lichtenstein, 1970; Levy, 1967; Newberry, 1973) suggests that it would be difficult for experimenters to accurately detect their subjects' disloyalty to requests to maintain secrecy about the study. Despite this, Wuebben (1967) found that 64% of subjects who promised during

---

[8]Both Bowerman (1976) and Holmes (1976c) used an additional measure of debriefing effects as well. Reasoning that an ineffective debriefing could be detected by a decrease in self-ratings on failure-relevant dimensions after deception/debriefing compared to before deception/debriefing, Bowerman had subjects rate themselves on a variety of dimensions at the present time and as they stood at the time of their high school graduation. Bowerman found that subjects who were told of their poor performance on an intelligence test did not rate their present intelligence as being any lower than it was at the time of their high school graduation. Although Holmes (1976c) did find some significant reductions in his subjects' self-ratings, he argues that these are questionable measures, inasmuch as they "can be attributed simply to the occurrence of political events, personal maturation, and the fact that for the 'present' ratings, subjects were using as a reference group a selected college population rather than a general high school population" (Holmes, 1976a, p. 864).

the first of two experimental sessions that they would not discuss the experiment with anyone until it was completed admitted at the time of the second session, 1 week later, that they had talked to at least one other person about it. Several other investigators (e.g., Farrow, Lohss, Farrow, & Taub, 1975; Horka & Farrow, 1970; Lichtenstein, 1970) likewise have reported that many debriefed subjects discussed their experiences in an experiment with classmates who subsequently participated in that same study. In one investigation it was found that swearing subjects to secrecy was found to reduce the rate of disclosure (Walsh & Stillman, 1974), although this practice is infrequently used by social psychologists (Adair et al., 1985).

In contrast, following a deception study by Aronson (1966) in which debriefed subjects were given "a long and vivid description of the consequences of testing sophisticated Ss" (p. 238), not one of the nine subjects who were subsequently approached by a confederate who attempted to get them to reveal the true nature of the study did so. Although Aronson's findings are based on a very small number of cases, they suggest that educating subjects about the importance of maintaining secrecy about experiments may be an effective way of getting them to maintain secrecy. If secrecy can be maintained through appropriate debriefings, this would not only minimize the possibility of problems arising from contamination, but it would also be a useful indication of subjects' understanding and acceptance of postexperimental information itself. Research on the effectiveness of this aspect of debriefing is sorely lacking and has been identified as a useful topic for future research (Tesch, 1977).

To summarize, experimental tests designed to determine the extent to which postexperimental debriefings are successful in disabusing subjects of experimentally created impressions (one of the educational functions) have yielded mixed results. Self-ratings consistent with experimentally created misinformation have been found to persist after debriefings in which the misinformation is revealed for some, but not all of the relevant rating dimensions (Abrahams, 1967; Holmes, 1967c; Ross et al., 1975; Walster et al., 1967). In no case, however, were subjects' self-impressions on dimensions related to the misinformed dimension found to be affected by the deceptive information (Abrahams, 1967; Walster et al., 1967). The preservation of self-information obtained from deception was shown to be effectively reduced by debriefings in which these perseverance effects were explained (L. Ross et al., 1975).

In commenting on this literature, it is curious that critics have drawn different conclusions about the effectiveness of dehoaxing. Although Holmes (1976a) concludes that "dehoaxing is a viable postexperimental technique for eliminating misinformation acquired by a subject as a consequence of deception" (p. 866), Tesch (1977) reads the same literature as indicating that "typical [dehoaxing] procedures may not necessarily correct misinformation or correct emotional upset" and are inadequate in providing subjects "with a full appreciation of and disclosure on their experiences in our laboratories" (p. 218). Not only do these divergent conclusions reveal a great deal about the biases of the observers, they also serve to highlight the mixed nature of the results.

Eliminating Potentially Harmful Aftereffects of Research Participation

A second purpose of debriefing is to eliminate any potentially harmful effects created by the research. This is an especially important concern to researchers who employ procedures that may be noxious or stressful to participants, whether or not they are the results of deception. The charge to researchers is clearly stated in "Principle I" of the APA's *Ethical Principles*: "Where research procedures result in undesirable consequences for the individual participant, the investigator has the responsibility to detect and remove or correct these consequences, including long-term effects ("Committee," 1982, pp. 66–67).

Clearly, the most publicized case concerning the elimination of potentially harmful aftereffects is Milgram's (1963, 1974) research on obedience to authority. In order to dehoax his subjects, Miligram (1964) reportedly revealed the deception (by telling them that the "learner" had not actually received any electric shocks) and demonstrated that the alleged "victim" was not actually harmed. Subjects were also sent a written report detailing the experimental procedures and results. The desensitization aspect of the debriefing procedure primarily consisted of assuring obedient subjects that their behavior (going along with the experimenter's commands to administer high levels of electric shock to another) was "entirely normal and that their feelings of conflict or tension were shared by other participants" (Milgram, 1964, p. 849). In some instances this required having lengthy, detailed discussions with participants.

The effectiveness of these procedures in eliminating potential harm to subjects (the result of self-knowledge that one is capable of inflicting harm on another; see Baumrind, 1964) is attested to by the results of a follow-up questionnaire and psychiatric interviews. The relevant questionnaire item, completed several months after the experimental session and mailed in conjunction with the debriefing letter, asked subjects to indicate how glad they were to have been in the experiment now that they have read the debriefing report. On the basis of the finding that 84% reported being glad to have participated and only 1.3% indicated negative feelings (the remaining 15% reported neutral feelings), with negligible differences between obedient and defiant subjects, Milgram concluded that his desensitizing procedure was successful. However, Holmes (1976b) contends that caution is needed in drawing conclusions from the results of a single questionnaire item, especially one that asked subjects to consider their feelings about having been in the experiment instead of the more relevant issue of their views about themselves as a result of having participated. Moreover, Holmes (1976b) contends that strong demand characteristics (see Chapter 6) may have biased subjects' responses inasmuch as (1) the debriefing letter was designed to enhance subjects' reactions to the value of the experimental experience, and (2) subjects were instructed to respond to the question while taking the letter into consideration.

Although the psychiatric interviews also revealed that there were no harmful aftereffects, these too are subject to question. One year after the experimental program was completed, an experienced psychiatrist interviewed 40 participants who were believed to be most likely to have suffered consequences from participating (Errera, 1972). The psychiatrists report revealed that none of the subjects showed any signs of harm or traumatic reactions resulting from the experiment (Errera, 1972; Milgram, 1964). Holmes (1976b), however, has questioned these conclusions, pointing to the low reliability and validity of psychiatric interviews, the demand characteristics of the interviews, and the incomplete nature of the psychiatrist's report as factors indicating the low confidence that should be placed on this information.

A more thorough attempt to systematically assess the aftereffects of a Milgram-type procedure is represented by the work of Ring et al. (1970). These experimenters conducted an investigation similar to Milgram's (1963, 1974) except that subjects were led to believe they were administering painful blasts of sound instead of painful doses of electric shock. As in the Milgram studies, most subjects were obedient (over 88%) and found the experimental experience to be stressful. After subjects either refused to administer any more sound blasts, or had completed the "learning trials," they were assigned at random to either a nondebriefing control condition or to one of two debriefing conditions. Subjects in the debriefing conditions were told that the experiment was actually concerned with obedience to authority and were then provided a justification for either obedient or defiant behavior. In the obedience-justification condition, subjects were told that obedient behavior (going along with the experimenter's commands) was associated with positive personality characteristics (subjects who did so were said to have "higher ego strength," to be "better adjusted," etc.). In the defiance-justification condition, subjects were told that defiant behavior (not going along with the experimenter's commands) was associated with the same positive personality characteristics. Finally, subjects in the no-debriefing, control condition neither were told anything about the purpose of the study nor were misinformed of the implications of either obedient or defiant behavior.

To determine reactions to the debriefings, the experimenters had subjects anonymously complete a questionnaire (tapping their reactions to the experiment and their feelings about themselves) that was allegedly used to evaluate students' reactions to research participation in their department. These ratings revealed that subjects responded most positively when their obedient behavior was justified than when either justification was provided for defiance, or when no information was given at all. (Because only 5 out of the 57 subjects were defiant, only obedient subjects were used in the analysis, and a parallel test of the effects of justifying defiant behavior to defiant subjects was not possible.) Subjects who were told of the (erroneous) positive implications of their obedient behavior tended to feel less emotionally upset, less depressed, and more pleased with themselves than those led to think badly of their actions. Interestingly, though, these subjects redirected their anger away from themselves and toward the experimenter. However, debriefings successfully led all subjects except one to believe that the experiment was ethical and to not resent having been deceived or to regret having partici- pated. In contrast, approximately half of the not-debriefed subjects regretted participating and reported feeling that the experiment should have been stop- ped. The debriefing that justified subjects' behavior was apparently successful at getting them to feel better about themselves and the experiment itself.

Two problems with the Ring et al. (1970) investigation, a methodological one and an ethical one, have been identified by Holmes (1976b). The first problem is that although obedience-justified subjects may have been less upset than controls, prestress levels of arousal were not measured, thereby making it impossible to determine whether subjects were returned to the state they were in before the study began (i.e., whether stress levels were reduced *enough*). A second problem is that possible distress due to deception (sub- jects' believing that they were harming another) was reduced by recourse to another deception (false information about the personality characteristics of obedient or defiant subjects), which is an ethically dubious procedure.

Reaction to these problems stimulated Holmes (1976d) to conceptually rep- licate the work of Ring et al. (1970) using an improved procedure. Holmes' (1976d) follow-up investigation included a no-stress control group condition to provide a base rate level of anxiety and used a more ethical debriefing pro- cedure (some additional variables were also included that are not reported here). This debriefing procedure consisted of telling subjects, in 3- to 4- minute sessions, that their obedient behavior was (1) normal and quite typi- cal, (2) mild compared to behaviors exhibited by participants in other studies, and (3) unlikely to be generalized outside the laboratory. Although the ex- perimental experience was successful in generating stress reactions, subjects who were immediately debriefed demonstrated no difference in physiological reactions following debriefing than control subjects who did not experience any stress at all. Moreover, immediately debriefed subjects displayed more positive attitudes toward the experiment than those who were not subjected to stress (see also Holmes, 1973; Holmes & Bennett, 1974).

Further evidence of the effectiveness of debriefings in eliminating the poten- tially harmful aftereffects of participation in stress-inducing research is pro- vided in a report by S.S. Smith and Richardson (1983). These investigators surveyed 464 University of Georgia students 1 week after they participated in various psychological experiments. Participants who felt they were harmed during the course of the study but believed they were successfully desensi- tized before leaving the lab not only recognized the educational benefit of participating, but also perceived their experimental experience as positively as those who were not harmed at all. Interestingly, these findings corrobo- rate the anticipated positive reactions to debriefing revealed in a noninvolv- ing role-playing study by Berscheid et al. (1973). Although the Smith and

Richardson survey findings do little to guide experimenters in the use of debriefing techniques, they suggest that the everyday debriefing practices employed by psychologists at one institution, whatever they may be, had positive benefits.

We may conclude this section by noting that the evidence regarding the effectiveness of debriefing in eliminating the negative aftereffects of research is more consistently positive than the evidence on the effectiveness of debriefing in disabusing subjects of misinformation. Although the evidence is scant and subject to problems, mostly consistent results over a series of progressively refined investigations suggest that debriefing techniques *can be* effective in eliminating experimentally induced levels of stress.

Problems Caused by Debriefing

Beyond the issue of the effectiveness of debriefing in meeting educational goals and resolving ethical problems is the question of whether or not debriefing procedures can actually cause problems. Some attention has been paid to both ethical and methodological problems potentially caused by debriefings. These problems are anticipated by Menges' (1973) question, "how may the subject's right to maximal learning from his experience, including debriefing, be furthered when debriefing information may contaminate performance of potential subjects or when the subject's reflections on his performance may damage his self-image?" (p. 1030).

Potential Ethical Problems

Given that so much attention has been paid to the ethical benefits of debriefing, the reader may find it curious that there also may be potential ethical problems arising from debriefing. In its most general form, the problem is that subjects may feel that they were "suckers" or "dupes" for having believed the experimenter's cover story. In fact, "The more elaborate the deception and the more successful it is in deceiving them, the more likely the subjects are to feel very disturbed upon learning the true nature of the experiment" (Mills, 1976, p. 3). Most experimenters feel that they are ethically obligated to reveal their deceptions to their subjects, despite the fact that it may be anxiety provoking, but recognize the special obligations they have to do an effective job of disabusing subjects of any such feelings (Mills, 1976). As Aronson and Carlsmith (1968) put it, "if harshly presented, the truth can be more harmful than no explanation at all" (p. 31).

A more difficult ethical dilemma arises in cases in which honest debriefings leave subjects in a worse condition than if no debriefing occurred. Diener and Crandall (1978), for example, suggest that if subjects have been preselected because they possess an undesirable trait (e.g., low self-esteem), the investigator will probably leave the subject in better condition if he or she omits this fact from the debriefing.

In a similar manner Kidder (1981) questions the ethics of debriefing subjects about experimentally induced behaviors that may have raised their self-
esteem. If the deception feels better than the truth, should that deception
stand? A typical reaction to this question is represented by Blanchard and
Cook's (1976) study on helping. Among other results they found that military
servicemen who were induced to help a less-competent group member were
more satisfied with the group experience and liked that group member more
than when he was helped by someone else. Was it ethical to threaten the self-
esteem of these subjects by dehoaxing them? It is certainly easier to ignore
the question, accepting that "ignorance is bliss," than to confront subjects
with a potentially stress-inducing (instead of stress-reducing) debriefing. However, Blanchard and Cook (1976) chose to debrief their subjects. They did so
in small groups (of 4 to 6 participants), holding discussions that averaged 1
hour in duration. This care was apparently necessary in order to explain the
need for deception and guard against threats to subjects' self-esteem. It appears that they were successful: In responding to anonymous questionnaires
at the end of the debriefing session, only one of the 64 participants expressed
concern about the deception. (Of course, in the absence of other criterion
measures, and a design that compared debriefing with no-debriefing, the true
impact of debriefing cannot be determined.) This experiment appears to be
typical in that the investigators opted to debrief their subjects, which is not
surprising in view of the formally codified mandate to debrief ("Committee"
1982) to which experimenters usually must adhere to meet the requirements
of their institutional review boards (Suls & Rosnow, 1981).

A related issue regards the ethics of debriefing subjects in field experiments. Some have argued that so long as the field manipulation is ethical itself, it is appropriate to dispense with a debriefing (D.T. Campbell, 1969).
Consider the case presented by Schaps' (1972) field experiment on helping in
which a female experimenter posing as a potential customer visited a shoe
store and rejected whatever the salesman showed her. D.T. Campbell (1969),
in commenting on an earlier report of Schaps's study, argued that it would be
painful for the salesman to learn in a debriefing that he had "been had," but
that the experimental treatment probably did not result in a higher than usual
level of frustration experienced by the salesman.[9] We should also probably
add that naive passersby in a naturalistic field study may make poor
candidates for debriefings inasmuch as they never agreed to have an "educational experience," and may be annoyed at, and misunderstand the intentions
of, a stranger telling them that they were unwitting participants in an
experiment. As D.T. Campbell (1969) put it, "Some damage to the future

[9]Interestingly, Wilson and Donnerstein (1976) found that 72% of subjects surveyed
about field experimental procedures reported that they would have felt harassed if
they were in the Schaps (1972) experiment, 65% would have minded being a subject in
it, and for 68%, it would have lowered their trust in social scientists.

utility of natural settings would result...and the possibility of journalistic publicity would be greatly enhanced" (p. 377).

On fewer occasions experimenters have elected to debrief participants in a field experiment. An investigation by Darley and Batson (1973) provides an excellent example of some of the considerations involved in doing so. These researchers examined the influence of various situational variables on helping behavior by having seminary students pass a slumped victim (actually an experimental confederate) in an alleyway while on their way to a building to complete an experiment in progress to see if they offered assistance. (They found that subjects who were in a hurry were less likely to help than those who were not in a hurry, but that those who were on their way to deliver a talk on the parable of the Good Samaritan were no more likely to help than those who were on their way to talk about a nonhelping-related topic.) Subjects were subsequently debriefed by (1) informing them of the exact nature of the study, including the deception, (2) explaining the reasons for using deception, (3) discussing their reactions to the alleged victim, and (4) discussing the role of situational variables on helping behavior. The authors report that the debriefing was successful inasmuch as "All subjects seemed readily to understand the necessity for the deception, and none indicated any resentment of it" (Darley & Batson, 1973, p. 104).

The key to the decision to debrief subjects in field studies appears to be subjects' knowledge that they were being studied in *some* way. Darley and Batson's (1973) subjects knew they were taking part in a study, although not at the time the primary dependent measure was taken. Other studies in which observations are made of the reactions of naive passersby in naturalistic settings as they witness an experimentally created situation, such as a person in need of help (e.g., Piliavin, Rodin, & Piliavin, 1969), typically do not involve debriefing participants (who unknowingly happen to "walk into" an experiment). A related consideration is that because seminary students agreed to participate in an experiment and might potentially derive a valuable lesson from understanding their behavior in the experiment, the experimenters were ethically obligated to provide that benefit. Although experiments on nonstudent populations also warrant debriefings (Perry & Abramson, 1980), these are typically not given when the participants have not agreed to be studied.

Finally, a more subtle ethical problem is that the debriefing may lead subjects to believe that their experimental responses were only important as the experimenter interprets them. In addressing this possibility Tesch (1977) has argued that the experimenter unintentionally promotes his or her own explanation as being better than the subject's, leaving the implicit message that they were fooled. "In this way," he notes, "debriefings lead us to an ethical dilemma: In the experiment we invade participants' privacy under the principle of informed consent, and in the debriefings we tacitly minimize their own understandings of what they have experienced" (p. 221).

Potential Methodological Problems

A second potential problem of debriefings lies in the threats to experimental validity caused by subjects using the information obtained in one study to influence their responses to other studies. In Chapter 3 we established that subjects who suspect that they are being deceived sometimes produce biased data. Here we note the contribution of prior experimental debriefings to this effect. What, then, if any, are the effects of previous experimental debriefings on subsequent experimental performance?

Experimental results bearing on this question have yielded mixed results (see Kruglanski, 1975; Weber & Cook, 1972). The initial studies suggested that debriefing had only a negligible effect on subjects' subsequent experimental performance. Fillenbaum (1966), for example, found that recall in an incidental learning task was unaffected by previous dehoaxing about a character sketch. These results are interpreted by Fillenbaum as evidence of subjects' interest in playing the "faithful subject" role—what Orne (1962) has called the "good subject"—by attempting to act as if they were unaffected by the previous information. This explanation is consistent with the finding of Silverman et al. (1970) that deceived and debriefed subjects are more sensitized to the possible ulterior purposes of experimenters and present themselves in a more favorable manner than subjects who have never been deceived. Similar to Fillenbaum (1966), Brock and Becker (1966) also found little effect of previous debriefing on subsequent experimental performance. They varied degree of dehoaxing about compliance effects (none, partial, or complete) in one experiment to determine its effects on a subsequent experimental request to sign a counterattitudinal petition. It was found that dehoaxing was effective in reducing compliance only when it was complete and when there was a great similarily between the subject matter of the dehoaxing and subsequent experimental experiences. Under other conditions, Brock and Becker (1966) note that "Massive debriefing, even immediately prior to the test experiment, did not affect sensitivity to the new treatment" (p. 232). Similar results have also been reported by T.D. Cook et al. (1970), T.D. Cook and Perin (1971), and by Fillenbaum and Fry (1970).

However, not all studies leave us with the impression that the residual transfer effects of debriefing are inconsequential. Several studies reveal that subjects with prior information about an experiment use it to "improve" their performance. For example, Levy (1967) found that subjects with advance knowledge about the reinforcement contingencies used in a verbal conditioning experiment appeared to learn more rapidly than those without such knowledge (see also Page, 1969, 1970, 1972). Similarly, Newberry (1973) reported superior problem-solving performance among subjects having advance knowledge about the problems than those without advance knowledge. More recently, Gruder, Stumpfhauser, and Wyer (1977) found that subjects who were given false feedback about their intelligence test scores and were subsequently debriefed performed better on a parallel version of the same test administered 1 week later. Debriefed subjects also can use the debriefing information to improve their self-presentations. Subjects in a study by Silverman et al. (1970) who were deceived about their performance on a variety of tasks and then debriefed were found 1 week later to present themselves (on a battery of tests) as being more psychologically strong and stable than those who were not deceived and debriefed. These studies, revealing subjects' tendencies to improve their performance in some manner, suggest that experimental debriefings may in fact bias subsequent experimental responses in a way that casts doubt on their validity.[10]

One particularly interesting manifestation of this idea is inherent in Gergen's (1973) notion of *enlightenment effects*; i.e., "sophistication as to psychological principles liberates one from their behavioral implications" (p. 313). Simply put, Gergen's idea is that once the public becomes familiar with a behavioral phenomenon, that phenomenon is likely to change, often because people attempt to compensate for it (see Chapter 1) Stricker et al. (1967) make a similar point with respect to doing conformity research: enlightened subjects often fail to conform.

The literature on prosocial behavior provides a good case study of how such enlightenment (a byproduct of debriefing) may alter social behavior patterns, although in a socially facilitative manner. Experiments on bystander intervention (for a review, see Latané & Darley, 1970) typically lead subjects to believe they have witnessed an emergency while in the presence of a varied number of others while observations are made of the subjects' helping behavior (whether or not they offered help at all, response latency, etc.). In general it is found that as the number of bystanders increases, the probability decreases that any one will offer help, hence the phenomenon of "bystander apathy." The study by Latané and Rodin (1969) is typical of these. After they found their subjects to be apathetic, the experimenters thoroughly debriefed them. The debriefing was successful inasmuch as almost all the subjects indicated that they understood the true purpose of the experiment and appreciated the justification for using deception. What are the effects of such knowledge? Will persons enlightened about bystander apathy remain

---

[10]The transfer effects noted in these studies are not unlike the one exception in Brock and Becker's (1966) experiment: Transfer effects occurred when sufficient information about the first experiment was provided and a second, similar study was experienced soon afterward. The cautious experimenter would certainly want to avoid contaminating subjects by running experiments soon after similar ones in which subjects were debriefed. Although this advice is obvious in the case of extreme temporal closeness or conceptual similarity, little is known about how long a wait or how similar a study can be tolerated without risking bias, making this a topic of needed research. The danger must be recognized that even if the second of two closely run studies is highly dissimilar to the first one, it may be contaminated by subjects' beliefs about it, whether or not they are relevant or accurate.

apathetic, or will they use their knowledge to react against it, to be more helpful, thereby altering the phenomenon?

This question was central to a pair of studies conducted by Beaman, Barnes, Klentz, and McQuirk (1978). After hearing a lecture or seeing a film on Latané and Darley's (1970) bystander intervention research, subjects were sent to another building or another room, making it possible for them to come into contact with a stranger in need of help (the alleged victim of a bicycle accident in one experiment and a person sprawled out on the floor in the other experiment). In comparing the helping rates of these subjects with control subjects (who either heard a lecture on another topic or no lecture at all), it was found that significantly more enlightened subjects (those who were informed about the bystander apathy effect) offered assistance to the person in need of help in both experiments. These data provide a clear example of how subject enlightenment (not unlike the information provided in a typical debriefing session) may markedly alter behavioral patterns, albeit in a potentially socially desirable way.

To summarize, there exists convincing evidence that subjects who are "enlightened" by behavioral science phenomena in debriefing sessions will behave differently from "unenlightened" subjects in later experiments. Although no one has as yet recommended that this consideration be used to justify abolishing debriefings, or even altering debriefing practices in any way, it has provided the foundation for arguments about the need to detect the possibility of subject suspiciousness and to assess its impact (e.g., Newberry, 1973).

Current Status of the Controversy

The body of empirical research and critical observation that comprises the literature on postexperimental debriefing suggests that such debriefings, although not uniformly effective, *can be* made to be effective. As several authors point out (e.g., Holmes, 1976b; Mills, 1976; Tesch, 1977), the crucial question is not whether or not subjects should be debriefed at all, but *how* these debriefings should be conducted. By looking at what approaches have been recommended and the experimental conditions under which debriefings seem to work, a happy state of agreement may be noted. Critics appear to be recommending techniques that work; in general, immediate, detailed debriefings—interviews in which subjects are not only apprised of the deception, but are led to appreciate the importance of the work to which they have made a contribution. The point is that although effective debriefings are possible, it is each experimenter's responsibility to ensure that they are adequately conducted. Some even recommend that the effectiveness of debriefing procedures be regularly monitored (e.g., Holmes, 1976b; S.S. Smith & Richardson, 1983; Tesch, 1977).

In concluding, we should note strong agreement with the argument that evidence of the effectiveness of debriefing should *not* be taken as a license to use deception without good reason (Holmes, 1976b; Mills, 1976; Smith & Richardson, 1983; Tesch, 1977). Those who have noted the effectiveness of debriefing (e.g., Holmes, 1976a, 1976b), even cynically (e.g., Tesch, 1977), caution against using this information to justify deception research without consideration for the hidden costs of such investigation (see Chapter 3). These include not only the practical cost of jeopardizing the usefulness of future generations of subjects (Newberry, 1973) but also the costs of derogating the public image of psychological experimenters in the public eye (Z. Rubin, 1970) and in the eyes of subjects themselves (S.S. Smith & Richardson, 1983).

Chapter 9
Postexperimental Inquiries: Assessing Demand Awareness and Treatment Effectiveness

The preceding chapter discusses debriefing procedures—postexperimental sessions during which experimenters attempt to disabuse their subjects of experimentally created misinformation and eliminate any negative after-effects caused by the research. The focus in debriefing is on the experimenter's *telling* subjects about the study. However, postexperimental sessions are also used to *ask* subjects about the study. Specifically, experimenters attempt

> to judge the degree to which the manipulations and measures were appropriate and effective, to determine the extent and accuracy of participants' suspicions, and to verify that the participants construed the situation as intended (e.g., accepted the "cover story") and were involved with it. . . . (Tesch, 1977, p. 219)

Therefore, in addition to the ethical and educational functions discussed previously, postexperimental sessions also may be used to serve a methodological function.

It is these postexperimental inquiries into subjects' reactions to experimental methodology that concern us in this chapter. Specifically, we begin by describing the various functions served by postexperimental inquiries and then examine some of the controversial issues surrounding them.

Functions of Postexperimental Inquiries

Typically, postexperimental inquiries are made with two functions in mind. One such function is to assess subjects' awareness of any experimental deceptions (see Chapter 3) and to ascertain the extent to which their experimental behavior was the result of demand characteristics (see Chapter 6). A second function of postexperimental inquiries is to determine whether or not the experimental manipulations had the intended effects on subjects. Such inquiries are typically referred to as *manipulation checks*. This section of the chapter takes a closer look at each of these functions.

Assessing Suspiciousness About Manipulations

In view of the prevalence of deceptive practices in social psychological research (see Chapter 3), surprisingly little is known about the extent to which subjects are aware of the deceptions employed. In most cases investigators identifying suspicious subjects merely state that a certain number of subjects were found to express "suspicions about the manipulations," or reported admitting "prior knowledge about the experiment." Readers of journal articles in social psychology are only rarely informed of the accuracy of these suspicions, or of the nature and extent of subjects' advance information (for one such rare example, the reader is referred to the unusually detailed report of subjects' expressed suspicions about false feedback in a study by Jeff Greenberg, Pyszczynski, and Solomon, 1982). Neither are they usually informed about the criterion level of suspiciousness used to identify suspicious subjects as such. Likewise, it is rare that the method used to assess suspiciousness is reported.

A major reason for this, Stricker (1967) has suggested, is that "experimenters may be hesitant to classify subjects as suspicious and exclude them from their studies, being unwilling to discard data they have labored to obtain or to cast doubt on the validity of their studies" (p. 19). Therefore, there may be a general reluctance to assess suspiciousness at all (i.e., to look for trouble), or to label only the *most* suspicious subjects as being suspicious. Even then accurate assessments of suspiciousness are difficult to obtain inasmuch as (1) some suspiciousness is probably the result of overgeneralized suspiciousness of psychologists in general (Stricker, 1967), and (2) implicit demands to provide "useful" data may discourage some subjects from admitting harboring any suspicions (Orne, 1970).

More basic than the fact that the criteria for identifying suspicious subjects are frequently unreported is the fact that the *possibility of suspiciousness* usually goes unreported in studies using deception (see Chapter 3). In fact information about suspiciousness was reported in only 23.9% of the 88 studies using deception published in the 1964 issues of the *Journal of Abnormal and Social Psychology, Journal of Personality, Journal of Social Psychology*, and *Sociometry* (Stricker, 1967). Within these, the median reported percentage of suspicious subjects was only 3.7%. More recently, reviewing, the 284 empirical studies appearing in the 1979 issues of the *Journal of Personality and Social Psychology*, Adair et al. (1985) found that checks for suspiciousness were reported in 11% of the studies, with the mean identification rate of suspicious subjects only 0.08% (these figures were higher in deception studies—19% and 1.85%, respectively).

There would appear to be four reasons for the low suspiciousness rate. One possibility is simply that the experimenters are actually quite adept at skillfully deceiving subjects. Another possibility is that subjects may not want to admit their suspicions, preferring instead to take a "pact of ignorance" (Orne, 1962). It is also possible that the experimenter's threshold for identifying suspicious subjects is set extremely high, so that only the most extremely suspicious subjects are identified. Finally, of course, experiments with extremely high suspiciousness rates may never be published, thereby attenuating the range of suspiciousness rates likely to be encountered in published reports. After all, such works, if submitted for publication, would be likely candidates for rejection by journal editors on the grounds that the procedure was probably not valid. Experiments in which many subjects report suspicions about the manipulations may not even be submitted for publication by researchers who recognize that a high rate of suspiciousness may signal a problem with their experimental procedure.

Assessing the Effectiveness of Manipulations

Postexperimental inquiries providing information about subjects' perceptions of the independent variables used to determine their effectiveness are referred to as *manipulation checks*. More formally, Cherulnik (1983) has defined a manipulation check as, "A method used to assess the degree to which an experimental treatment produced the intended effects on the subjects" (p. 362). These are measures apart from the dependent variable; they are independent assessments of the manipulations themselves (Kidd, 1976; Mills, 1969). In practice, they are often considered "secondary measures" (Hendrick & Jones, 1972, p. 27). Refining these ideas, Wetzel (1977) has noted that manipulation checks cannot prove that a manipulation is successful; it can only demonstrate the possibility of *disproving* it, of falsifying its effects. As such, he notes that manipulation checks can be used to warn researchers that an independent variable is (1) not properly operationalized, (2) confounded, and/or (3) not having the theoretically intended effect on the independent variable.

   As a typical example of manipulation checks in social psychological research, let's consider Robert A. Baron's (1974) investigations of the aggression-inhibiting influence of heightened sexual arousal. The men in Baron's study were exposed to manipulations designed to make them feel either angered (they were verbally and physically provoked by a confederate) or not angered (they were treated neutrally by the confederate). After this they were either made to feel sexually aroused (by being shown photographs of attractive nude women from *Playboy* magazine) or not aroused (by being shown photographs of scenery, furniture, and abstract paintings). To determine whether the impact of these variables on subjects' subsequent aggressive behavior could be reasonably interpreted in line with the hypotheses it was necessary to determine whether or not subjects were aroused and angered as intended. Questionnaire items were used to assess subjects' feelings of arousal in response to the photos and their anger in response to the provoking confederate. Because subjects reported feeling significantly more aroused in response to the erotic than the neutral photos, and significantly more angered by the behavior of the provocative confederate than the nonprovocative confederate, it appeared that both manipulations were effective.

   Of course, all we know from these questionnaire findings is that subjects in one group *reported* feeling relatively more or less angry and more or less aroused than those in another group. But, we do *not* know exactly how angry or how aroused they were in any absolute terms. We know that the direction of the difference between the effects subjects reported the manipulations had on them were in line with what the experimenter had intended. Of course, scaling difficulties often make it impractical in social psychological research to rely on anything other than ordinal measures (Mills, 1969). Although physiological measures of arousal could have been used, such elaborate manipulation checks are exceptional in social psychological research.

It is interesting to contrast this state of affairs with research in the field of physiological psychology, in which much more precise manipulation checks are possible. A good example may be seen in the classic work of Hetherington and Ranson (1940), who conducted experiments to determine whether a particular area of the brain was influential in regulating eating behavior. In a surgical procedure an electric current was used to destroy cells in the suspected eating control center of the brain, the ventromedial hypothalmus (VMH). After recovering from surgery, the eating behavior of these rats was compared to that of litter mates who also received surgical lesions, but whose VMH was not destroyed. Before concluding that any differences in eating behavior could be attributed to the lesions in the VMH, it first was necessary to conduct a manipulation check to ensure that the appropriate tissue was destroyed. To do this the rats were killed and their brains were examined to see if the lesions were placed precisely in the VMH region. Only those rats whose lesions were accurately placed qualified for inclusion in the treatment group. This type of precise post hoc procedure for determining eligibility for inclusion in experimental treatment groups is not typical—and usually not possible—in social psychological research.

Controversial Issues

Several issues regarding postexperimental inquiries have been raised in the last few decades. Our review of this literature reveals that theorists and researchers express discrepant opinions about several diverse matters, such as how to gather postexperimental information, the accuracy of subjects' self-reports about the experiment, the impact of demand awareness on the validity of the experimental results, and how to interpret the results of experiments in the light of apparently weak manipulations. Each of these issues are addressed in the following sections.

Methods of Conducting Postexperimental Assessments

Probably the most basic issue with respect to determining subjects' suspicions about experimental procedures concerns *how* this suspiciousness should be assessed. We have already noted that it is unusual for social psychological researchers to provide much, if any, detail about their subjects' suspicions about the experimental manipulations (Stricker, 1967). In studies in which suspiciousness is assessed, it is usually measured by "questionnaires or interviews of unknown validity" (Z. Rubin & Moore, 1971). From what few experimental reports have provided details on their suspiciousness-assessment procedures, it appears that *how* these suspicions are tapped may differentially influence the likelihood of subjects reporting their suspicions.

For example, Allen (1966) found that 7 out of 30 subjects who harbored suspicions about the manipulation used in a conformity study admitted these suspicions in a postexperimental discussion session, but not in a postexperimental questionnaire. In the context of a verbal conditioning study, Levin (1961) found that the proportion of subjects identified as "suspicious" jumped from only 5% when general interview questions were asked to about 33% when more specific and pointed questions were posed. In another study Z. Rubin and Moore (1971) assessed subjects' suspicions in the context of a study on the effects of status on social influence. Deception was assessed by analyzing subjects' responses to nine "strategic but nonleading" open-ended questionnaire items about the experimental procedure. When subjects were asked to respond by reporting their "impressions" they expressed greater suspiciousness than when they were asked to report their "recollections." In addition reports of "impressions" were more highly correlated with a criterion measure of suspiciousness obtained by engaging subjects in a lengthy nondirective interview. Taken together, these findings suggest that specific, but not leading, questionnaire items are most likely to elicit reports of suspiciousness.

Of course, the challenge for experimenters is to create assessment procedures that effectively minimize subjects' tendencies to supress the reporting of suspicions (Golding & Lichtenstein, 1970; Levy, 1967) without also encouraging them to report suspicions they actually did not feel but which they reported either to save face or to please the experimenter (Rubin & Moore, 1971). As such, it is not enough for experimenters to devise techniques for eliciting reports of suspiciousness from subjects; these reports must also be accurate if they are to provide a valid basis for identifying candidates for exclusion from experiments due to suspiciousness. In this regard two types of misclassification errors may be identified: *false-positives*, those subjects who are classified as being suspicious when they really are not, and *false-negatives*, those subjects who are classified as not being suspicious when they really are.

The major controversy with regard to assessing suspiciousness is based on the relative cost of making false-positive and false-negative errors in identifying suspicious subjects. Primarily, the controversy centers around Monte Page's (1969, 1971, 1973) assertion that false-negatives are much more serious than false-positives and that suspiciousness-checking procedures should be developed in appreciation of this. As Page (1971) put it, "it seems scientifically more rigorous and defensible to risk suggesting awareness to a few subjects who really are not [aware], than to risk not identifying subjects who really are aware" (p. 905). Making the point even more strongly, he adds that, "The purity of the actual data upon which our science depends is threatened by the possibility of false negatives remaining in the data" (M.M. Page, 1973, p. 306).

Operationally, the target of Page's criticism—and the alleged cause of many false-negative errors—is the brief, unstructured postexperimental interview consisting of a single question, which he calls "simply not valid" (M.M. Page, 1971, p. 903).

> The single question technique, while detecting some awareness, is not very accurate in its overall partitioning of awareness versus nonawareness. It would seem that the procedure of removing aware subjects and analyzing the remaining data would require an accurate measurement of awareness. With a single open-ended question this requirement is simply not met. (M.M. Page, 1971, p. 893)

The substantive context of M.M. Page's (1971) criticisms is work on the verbal conditioning of attitudes, following the work of Staats and Staats (A.W. Staats & Staats, 1958; C.K. Staats & Staats, 1957). In this paradigm subjects are repeatedly presented several written words. Immediately after seeing each of the words, subjects hear other words associated with each word that are consistently either positive, negative, or neutral in their evaluative meaning. Subjects' ratings of the meaning of the written words, after repeated association with the affect-laden spoken words, is taken as a measure of conditioning, following the classic conditioning paradigm. However, before data analysis, the Staats dropped subjects who expressed awareness of the relationship between the two lists, recognizing that subjects' awareness of the association between the two lists would potentially invalidate their classic conditing interpretation of the findings. The claim of conditioning effects requires that subjects are not aware of the associations (C.K. Staats & Staats, 1957).

Page's (1971) criticism of this procedure is that the single open-ended item used to check suspiciousness is too lenient and likely to allow the inclusion of false-negative subjects in the data pool, thereby providing a too-liberal test of the conditioning hypothesis. A question such as, "Did you feel as if you were supposed to rate the word in any particular way? If so, explain" is likely to lead subjects to say "no," allowing the responses of subjects who really were aware of the association between the words to remain in the pool of valid subjects. Carlsmith et al. (1976) also advocate the use of open-ended questions such as, "Do you think there may have been more to the experiment than meets the eye?" (p. 304). They claim that more specific prompts for suspiciousness overestimates the number of suspicious subjects. Single questions such as these, Page counters, are inadequate filters for subjects inasmuch as they do not allow the experimenter to get at whether or not the subject really was aware of the conditioning. Even one who was aware of the connection between the words and willing to admit it might not admit it in response to such a vague question. Single items that are scored for suspiciousness more stringently (e.g., Cohen, 1962) are also criticized on the same grounds. The problem with single open-ended items is that, "What is being measured. . .is clarity of expression rather than demand awareness" (M.M. Page, 1971, p. 894).

The argument made in favor of single open-ended items is that they give subjects an opportunity to express any awareness they might have without biasing them by forcing them to admit any suspicions they do not have. The belief that more extensive interviews could be too leading, has been expressed by A.W. Staats (1969) in rebutting a criticism from M.M. Page (1969). His point is that more extensive interviewing or questionnaire procedures may actually "*produce* varying levels of awareness as well as measure it" (A.W. Staats, 1969, p. 189, emphasis in original).[1] The same point has been made by Carlsmith et al. (1976).

Because this assumption is commonly held—but was untested in social psychology—M.M. Page (1969, 1971, 1973) conducted a series of experiments designed to test its validity and to compare the effects of a single general open-ended question to a more specific questionnaire.[2] Beginning this line of investigation, M.M. Page conducted several studies (1969, 1971) which showed that the C.K. Staats and Staats (1957) verbal conditioning effects were very strongly moderated by demand awareness, thereby casting doubt on the validity of the research on the classic conditioning of attitudes. The experimental paradigm closely paralleled the original C.K. Staats and Staats (1957) paradigm described earlier, but employed a much more elaborate postexperimental questionnaire. Specifically, a 17-item questionnaire was used "to enlist the honesty and cooperation of subjects while releasing them from the demand characteristics accompanying the experiment proper" (M.M. Page, 1969, p. 180). The questionnaire began with the typical open-ended question, "What was the purpose of this experiment and what were you supposed to do?" (p. 180) but contained progressively more specific questions, such as "What syllable was always or usually paired with words of unpleasant meaning?" (p. 180) Two independent judges assessed the responses to these questions with respect to the degree of subjects' *contingency awareness* (admissions of awareness of the interlist associations) and their *demand awareness* (admissions of awareness of what the experimenter expected him or her to rate). Finding that highly demand-aware subjects showed better conditioning than demand-unaware subjects (with a parallel, although weaker,

---

[1]Interestingly, a similar point has been made by Berkowitz (1971) in the context of the "weapons effect" in response to a criticism by M.M. Page and Scheidt (1971).

[2]Because some of this work deals with substantive issues germane to the classical conditioning of attitudes, it will be ignored in this discussion. Our presentation is limited to those aspects of the work comparing postexperimental demand awareness procedures.

effect with respect to contingency awareness), M.M. Page (1969) claimed that the "so-called conditioned attitudes are entirely artifacts of demand characteristics" (p. 185).

In subsequent research M.M. Page (1973) compared this extensive questionnaire procedure with two other types of postexperimental assessment techniques. Specifically, subjects were required to complete either (1) an "indirect" questionnaire (three general questions containing no specific information about the study); (2) a "direct" questionnaire (three questions identifying the word-association contingencies and the experimental hypotheses and asking subjects if they were aware of this); or (3) a "funnel" questionnaire, similar to that used in the previously mentioned studies (11 questions moving from the indirect ones through open-ended specific ones, to the most direct questions). On the basis of their conditioning resposes, subjects were identified as being either aware or unaware of the hypotheses.

M.M. Page (1973) found that the funnel and direct questionnaire methods more accurately identified demand-aware subjects than the indirect questionnaire method, which incorrectly classified 80% of the subjects (a false-negative error). It was also found that the funnel questionnaire did the best job of classifying demand-unaware subjects (it had the lowest rate of false-positive errors). Page takes these results as further evidence in support of the invalid and erroneous conclusions likely to be drawn from use of indirect questionnaires.

Following up on M.M. Page's (1973) efforts, Weber and Riddell (1975) compared the contingency awareness of subjects responding to a funnel questionnaire with those who responded to only a single critical item. No significant differences were found in awareness as a function of these techniques. These results are in line with M.M. Page's (1973) finding that some critical items were the most responsive to awareness in funnel questionnaires. It should be noted that only contingency awareness was assessed in this study instead of demand awareness, the more sensitive measure noted in Page's research. Nevertheless, these findings, together with Page's results suggest that direct probing for awareness may be a particularly conservative test of suspiciousness.

Before concluding this section it is important to note that the generalizability of these conclusions should be considered limited by the fact that they have used a single experimental domain—the verbal learning experiment. Although the issues with respect to probing for demand awareness *may* well generalize to other topics of social psychological inquiry, the paucity of analagous research in other domains makes it premature to generalize these conclusions at this time. This is not to say, however, that questions concerning the depth of questioning have not been addressed in other contexts. As a notable example, Hilgard and Loftus (1979) have noted in their review of 50 years of research on eyewitness testimony that the accuracy of testimony may be enhanced by allowing witnesses to report an incident freely before following up with specific questions.

Accuracy of Self-Reports

Having established that postexperimental information is usually obtained via self-reports, be they interview responses or questionnaire responses, questions may be raised about the accuracy of those self-reports. The issue of self-report accuracy, of course, is hardly unique to our interest in research methodology. General questions have been raised by Nisbett and Wilson (1977a, 1977b; T.D. Wilson & Nisbett, 1978) about the extent to which experimental subjects have introspective access to their own cognitive processes and are capable of accurately reporting these processes. Although Nisbett and Wilson's analyses have been challenged on many different grounds (e.g., Cotton, 1980; Rich, 1979; E.R. Smith & Miller, 1978; P. White, 1980), it is the implications of their ideas for verbal reports of experimental events (e.g., Adair & Spinner, 1981) that concern us here.

Nisbett and Wilson (1977a, 1977b) claim that subjects do not have direct access to the cognitive processes responsible for their behavior and that any statements made about their cognitive processes are based on causal connections between stimuli and responses. This conclusion is drawn from the results of seven studies—three in which subjects erroneously reported the influence of stimuli that actually had no effects, and four in which subjects failed to report the influence of effective stimuli. For example, in one of their studies, Nisbett and Wilson (1977b) manipulated the likability of teachers presented to subjects in the form of videotaped interviews. In one of the interviews, the teacher was made to appear likable (enthusiastic and respectful of students), and in the other the teacher was made to appear unlikable (rigid in style and cold and distrustful of students). The dependent variables were ratings of likability, as well as ratings of the teacher's physical attractiveness and other specific characteristics that were held constant. Subjects reported liking the "likable" teacher significantly more than the "not-likable" teacher and also gave more positive ratings on other, nonmanipulated dimensions, suggesting the influence of a "halo effect." Evidence for Nisbett and Wilson's (1977b) contention that subjects were unaware of the determinants of their ratings came in the form of their responses about the extent to which their overall liking had influenced their ratings of the individual dimensions. It was found that subjects believed their ratings of the teacher's likability were based on the teacher's characteristics, especially in the case of negative characteristics. Subjects responded that their overall negative evaluation was based on the fact that the teacher was presented as having specific negative attributes. Yet, Nisbett and Wilson contend that "subjects appear to have gotten the matter precisely backwards" (1977b, p. 255): Liking for the teacher was manipulated, which affected ratings of particular attributes. Postexperimental interviews confirmed that "most subjects persisted in their denial" (1977b, p. 255). Accordingly, Nisbett and Wilson take these results as "prima facie evidence that people lack awareness of the influence of one evaluation on another" (1977b, p. 256).

Adair and Spinner (1981) have challenged Nisbett and Wilson's (1977b) conclusions on the grounds that strong demand characteristics may have been responsible for the results. Drawing from Orne's (1973) work on demand characteristics, Adair and Spinner assume that the experiment as viewed by the subject may have been different from the experiment as viewed by the experimenter. In particular they claim that the instructions given Nisbett and Wilson's (1977b) subjects created an evaluative set that encouraged subjects to report the causal link as they did. Specifically, Nisbett and Wilson told their subjects that they were interested in seeing if their evaluations "at all resemble the evaluations of these teachers by students who were exposed to them for a whole semester" (1977b, p. 252). This, Adair and Spinner (1981) claim, made it likely for subjects to infer that the experimenter wanted to see if their ratings were "*as good as*" (p. 34) those of others. Accordingly, the specific attributes used in the rating scales "were legitimized in the instructions as the variables to be compared" (p. 34), and demand characteristics were responsible for subjects' denial of the influence of the overall ratings on their specific evaluations. Thus, Adair and Spinner claim that it *cannot* be concluded that subjects do not have introspective access and are incapable of accurately reporting their cognitions.

Although it is beyond the scope of this chapter to recount the details, Adair and Spinner (1981) reviewed several additional findings from Nisbett and Wilson's line of research (1977a; T.D. Wilson & Nisbett, 1978) and found them to be interpretable from a demand characteristics perspective as well. They criticize Nisbett and Wilson for ignoring the research on subjects' reports of suspiciousness (reviewed in the previous section of this chapter) which, they claim, has provided "considerable insight into the manner of asking questions so as to obtain accurate self-reports" (Adair & Spinner, 1981, p. 40). Two techniques in particular are identified—the *preinquiry quasi-control* technique, and the *sacrifice groups* technique (Orne, 1970).

In the preinquiry quasi-control technique, two groups of subjects are used—those who have been exposed to a treatment and those exposed to the same experimental setting but who received no treatment (see also Kidd, 1976). The idea is that subjects' expectations and past experiences may be responsible for their experimental behavior instead of the manipulation itself, and the use of a quasi-control group could tap this. If the verbal reports of quasi-control group subjects and treatment group subjects are identical, then it may be claimed that the causal links between cognitions and behaviors claimed by treatment group subjects may be of questionable validity. However, Adair and Spinner (1981) claim that any such similarity of verbal reports . . .

> does not necessarily mean that subjects are inaccurate or superficial in their reporting or that demand characteristics are present; rather, it may indicate that observers having experienced the same or similar stimuli in the past are able to articulate the stimulus–response link without re-experiencing it in the experiment. (p. 42)

The idea that such reports constitute valid sources of information about the rules governing behavior (Harré, 1974) has been elucidated previously in Chapter 3.

The accuracy of verbal reports also may be assessed via the use of "sacrifice groups" (Orne, 1970). This procedure requires the experimenter to run several additional groups of subjects who are stopped at various points in the experiment ("sacrificed") and interviewed. This procedure allows the experimenter the opportunity to assess subjects' reactions to the experiment at different phases of the experiment, although it is extremely costly with respect to the need for subjects (Adair & Spinner, 1981; Kidd, 1976).

Despite these problems, Adair and Spinner (1981) claim that retrospective verbal reports *can be* accurate under the proper conditions. Among these a plea is made for *more extended postexperimental questionnaires*. The basis for this claim rests in the successful use of "funnel" questionnaires by M.M. Page (1971, 1973) and the enhanced accuracy of eyewitness reports when free reports are followed up by more specific questions (Hilgard & Loftus, 1979).

They also claim that more accurate self-reports may result from *providing subjects the appropriate set*. Simply asking subjects to respond honestly (Bowers, 1967), accurately (T.D. Cook & Insko, 1968) or legitimizing their disclosure of cognitions (Golding & Lichtenstein, 1970) would be expected to enhance self-report accuracy. Similarly, asking subjects for their "impressions" as opposed to their "recollections" also has been shown to enhance the accuracy of verbal reports (Z. Rubin & Moore, 1971). Related to the idea of creating an appropriate set, Adair and Spinner (1981) also suggest that the *wording of experimental instructions* be designed to encourage honest experimental responding (Sutcliffe, 1972). Based on the important differences in claims made by legal witnesses to differences in questioning (Hilgard & Loftus, 1979), the wording of experimental instructions is identified as another potentially effective way of eliciting accurate verbal reports.

In addition to this set of revisions to existing procedures, Adair and Spinner (1981) have identified several alternative, and less commonly used, procedures for gathering introspective verbal reports. Most of these are drawn from the field of cognitive psychology. One such technique is *concurrent probing* (Ericsson & Simon, 1978), a technique in which subjects are asked to report their thoughts at several points throughout the study. It is like the "sacrifice groups" technique described earlier, except that no "sacrifice" is made, and the experiment continues. The approach is also similar to the *thought sampling* approach (Meichenbaum & Butler, 1979) in which, instead of being queried at various times during the study, subjects are encouraged to press buttons to indicate certain thoughts they are having. These *think aloud* or *talk aloud* techniques, as they are referred to collectively (Ericsson & Simon, 1978), are praised by Adair and Spinner (1981) on the grounds that they allow subjects' "thought processes to proceed unhindered by the need to self-observe or to analyze cognitions" (p. 46).

It would be misleading to conclude this section of the chapter without identifying another facet of the controversy over the accuracy of postexperimental self-reports that is equally central, but which has received less attention. We are speaking of the very basic question of whether accurate self-reports about experimental events are even necessary or to be expected. Kidd (1977) has raised this issue in his discussion of manipulation checks. In some experiments subjects may not be aware that there has been any change in their physical environment or psychological state, and yet there may be an impact. Complementing Nisbett and Wilson's (1977a) question of whether subjects are capable of accurate reflection (answered, "no"), Kidd's (1977) question is whether it even matters that subjects make accurate assessments of psychological states (answered, "not always").

As an example, Kidd (1977) notes that people who suffer a blow to their self-image may be completely unaware that their views of themselves are less positive. Of course, this does not necessarily mean that the change did not occur. Demonstrating awareness of a change (and one that can be accurately reported) may not be necessary to prove that a change has occurred and that it was responsible for behavior. A medical analogy may help emphasize this point: A person may be dying of a terminal illness but not know it, or admit it, until it is too late. Lack of awareness of a changed state in response to an experimental manipulation may not make the impact of the experiment any less effective or the manipulation any less real. Thus, to the extent possible, assessments of demand impact and manipulation effectiveness that are independent of self-reports may be desirable (Kidd, 1976, 1977). Such convergence of conceptual measures has long been considered desirable (Webb, Campbell, Schwartz, Sechrest & Grove, 1981).

Impact of Demand Awareness on Experimental Performance

One of the major reasons for assessing self-reports is the underlying belief that subjects who "saw through" the experimental manipulation would respond differently from those who did not, thereby biasing the results. Indeed, many studies have shown that subjects who are aware (or even think they are aware) of demand characteristics do, in fact, respond differently from those who are not—even if their beliefs are erroneous. Demand awareness biases experimental performance in many ways. These include attempting to conform to (Orne, 1962) or not conform to (Masling, 1966) the experimental hypotheses, scrupulously following instructions and not acting on their suspicions (Fillenbaum, 1966), and presenting oneself in a positive way (Rosenberg, 1969).

It is important to note that questions about the impact of demand awareness have been raised in the context of postexperimental inquiries. However, because these issues already have been thoroughly addressed in this book (primarily in Chapter 6), they will not be repeated here.

Interpreting Inconsistencies Between Treatment Effects and Manipulation Checks

The question of how to interpret subjects' postexperimental reports is one we have already introduced in this chapter. It may be recalled from our earlier discussion of techniques for conducting postexperimental inquities that one of M.M. Page's (1971, 1973) criticisms of the single global question technique is that response interpretation is difficult. Subjects who say "no" to a question asking them if they felt they were supposed to respond in any particular way may have misinterpreted the question, or may not actually be demand aware. Similarly, it may be difficult to interpret the meaning of an affirmative reply accompanied by an incorrect explanation (see M.M. Page, 1971). The difficulty of understanding subjects' responses to a single open-ended question is not the only problem of interpretation that investigators must face in dealing with postexperimental inquiries. There is also the problem of potential inconsistencies between the results of manipulation checks and treatment effects.

This issue has been raised in a dialogue between Kidd (1976, 1977) and Wetzel (1977). Kidd (1976) began by asking what conclusions can be drawn when the manipulation check reveals the manipulation to be successfully induced but the manipulation itself fails to produce differences between treatment groups on the dependent variable? Kidd identifies two possibilities. One is that the independent variable is not related (or only weakly related) to the dependent variable. Another possibility is that the manipulation check may have been a more sensitive measure of the independent variable than the dependent variable was as a measure of the behavior in question. Kidd also notes the interpretive problems raised when the independent variable successfully influences the dependent variable but the manipulation check reveals that the independent variable was not successfully manipulated. This situation may also result from the differential sensitivity of the dependent measures and the manipulation check measures. It may also be that the treatment variable influenced subjects in ways that were unknown to the experimenter and were thereby untapped by the manipulation checks. In other words the independent variable may have been multidetermined or confounded.

In commenting on these possibilities, Wetzel (1977) has agreed with Kidd's assessment that differential measurement sensitivity could account for either state. Accordingly, he cautions that experimenters should not necessarily take a lack of correspondence between the manipulation check and the dependent measure as grounds for disconfirming the hypothesis under consideration. Instead, he advises that such information is potentially valuable to the investigator, telling him or her that something is wrong in the conceptualization or operationalization of the variables. Specifically, Wetzel (1977) asserts that a lack of sensitivity in either the dependent measure or the manipulation check is, "a clear warning that the experimenter's notions of these constructs is probably too simplistic and that there is a need to re-evaluate the theoretical constructs or the operationalization of them" (p. 90). He adds that this information is particularly valuable during pilot testing, when procedural changes can be made.

In addition to the measurement problems and the confounding explanation identified by Kidd (1976), Wetzel (1977) has noted another explanation for finding unsuccessful manipulation checks accompanied by successful treatment effects. Namely, "the dependent variable assessment [may have] mitigated the effects of the independent variable manipulation" (p. 90). In other words, by the time a behavioral dependent measure is enacted (e.g., aggressive behavior), it is possible that the psychological state created by the manipulation (e.g., anger) that may have been responsible for the behavior may no longer be experienced. Accordingly, asking subjects how they feel "now" may not be a good indicator of the successfulness of a manipulation designed to induce certain psychological states earlier in an experiment.

Wetzel (1977) argues that such anomolies between dependent variables and manipulation checks may be useful (albeit in a negative sense) inasmuch as they force researchers to refine their theoretical constructs and experimental procedures—sending them "back to the drawing board," if you will. He further contends that it is precisely this potentially troublesome aspect of manipulation checks—revealing to experimenters something they'd rather not know—that has fostered resistance to manipulation checks (Stricker, 1967). Yet, not all researchers agree that unsuccessful manipulation checks should be interpreted as a caution signal. In particular, Hendrick and Jones (1972) note that unsuccessful manipulation checks are frequently ignored on the grounds that they are "secondary measures" and as such are "not as carefully designed or measured as the main dependent variable" (p. 27). If so, we would ask, then why were the measures taken in the first place? Given their imperfect status, what would it mean if they were found to be successful? Clearly, not all investigators would claim that manipulation checks should be ignored (Kidd, 1976).

It may be expected that most experimenters would be willing to admit the failure of their methods if their manipulations were found to be wholly inadequate. However, a question arises as to what should be done in the more typical case in which some subjects respond to the manipulation check as intended and some do not. Several investigators have advocated the practice of segregating subjects into groups on the basis of their responsiveness to the manipulations. Festinger (1955), for example, has argued that subjects on whom the independent variable had the greatest impact would be expected to show greater responsiveness to the dependent measures than those on whom the manipulation had a more modest impact. Similar arguments for such "internal analyses" have been echoed by Aronson and Carlsmith (1968). However, Kidd (1976) has questioned this practice on the grounds that it capitalizes on chance and also restricts the generalizability of the conclusions that can be drawn from the study. He also adds that such inconsistencies in the effectiveness of the manipulations should be made the topic of future research inquiries.

Current Status of the Controversy

It would appear that investigators' concerns about subjects' suspicions and the validity of their manipulations have stabilized. Not much has been written on these issues recently, and there seems to be an acceptance that subject suspiciousness *should* be assessed, especially in investigations in which this is expected to be a problem. Yet, there does not appear to be any increasingly widespread acceptance of reporting suspiciousness. Nor has there emerged any one accepted method for conducting postexperimental assessments. Both interviews and questionnaires tend to be used today.

Despite potential interpretive problems with manipulation checks, they continue to be an integral part of the modern social psychology experiment. Although some claim that manipulation checks may not be needed in areas of investigation (such as cognitive dissonance theory) in which well-controlled experimental inductions have become standardized (Gerard & Mathewson, 1966), the widespread treatment of manipulation checks in our methodology texts (e.g., Cherulnik, 1983; Kidder & Judd, 1986) suggests that investigators still recognize the need for independent checks on subjects' perceptions of and immediate reactions to experimental manipulations. In fact the need for manipulation checks was explicitly voiced in Greenwald's (1976a) editorial in the *Journal of Personality and Social Psychology*:

> Authors should not expect editors or readers to accept on faith the assertion that a given conceptual variable has been reliably and validly measured or manipulated by a given set of operations. Rather, the author should note relevant evidence, such as...data on subjects' perceptions of procedures. (p. 4)

Considering such specific admonishments from a journal editor, it is no wonder that the manipulation check remains alive and well in today's social psychology experiments.

Chapter 10

Meta-analysis Versus Traditional Integrations of Research

Scientists try to answer questions of theoretical interest by gathering relevant data. Controversies can arise from disagreements over the proper methods for gathering such evidence, and the preceding chapters have touched on controversial issues regarding various aspects of the data-gathering process. Procedures for collecting data, however, are not the only source of conflicting methodological viewpoints. The research process is not over once the data are in; indeed, it is clear that some of the liveliest debates concern how to interpret findings after they have been reported. Ideally, such interpretative squabbles will not be settled by a single study but on the basis of patterns emerging from evidence accumulated across numerous investigations. Thus, in the aftermath of research an additional problem often arises: What approaches should be used to summarize the results from a series of studies addressing the same issue?

The use of alternative approaches to summarizing data can become controversial when two different reviews of research findings reach conflicting conclusions. Reviews of the literature on self-serving attributional biases provide an example. On the one hand, Zuckerman (1979) conducted a traditional literature review and found little overall evidence that attributions are biased so as to enhance self-esteem. Arkin, Cooper, and Kolditz (1980), on the other hand, performed a meta-analysis—a quantitatively based literature review—and concluded that self-serving attributional bias is a highly reliable effect. T.D. Cook and Leviton's (1980) commentary on these divergent conclusions pointed out that interpretations of data summaries in such instances will inevitably hinge on assumptions underlying alternative approaches to the literature review process.

This chapter concentrates on issues regarding the use of meta-analysis. We address these controversies by contrasting meta-analysis with more traditional approaches to literature reviews; the latter are also known as "qualitative" or "narrative" reviews (Light & Pillemer, 1984). Before proceeding, however, we observe that differences of opinion on the topic of meta-analysis do not necessarily indicate the sharp cleavage of fiercely divided camps. For example, note the tone of the following remarks by Leviton and Cook (1981) that resulted from their exchange with Cooper and Arkin:

> The reader who follows the friendly debate we are having with Cooper and Arkin (1981) should not lose sight of one crucial fact: that everyone in the debate is an advocate of meta-analytic techniques to help summarize the literature on a particular topic. (Leviton & Cook, 1981, p. 231)

These remarks suggest that although disagreements exist regarding meta-analysis as it is sometimes used in practice, there is often little quarrel regarding its use in principle. As will become apparent from our examination of contrasting approaches or styles of review, however, differences in practice may also reflect differing purposes and alternative philosophical orientations.

Characterizing Alternative Types of Literature Reviews

The use of meta-analysis for literature reviews is becoming increasingly prevalent (R. Rosenthal & Rubin, 1986; Strube & Miller, 1986), but that set of analytical techniques was not commonly used for review purposes prior to the mid-1970s (e.g., R. Rosenthal, 1976b; M.L. Smith & Glass, 1977). Reviews without meta-analysis obviously have a much longer history. We first describe literature review practices as they existed prior to the advent of meta-analysis (and as they exist currently in reviews that do not contain meta-analyses). Following this examination of traditional approaches, we describe various types of meta-analytic techniques used for summarizing the data relevant to a given phenomenon under review. As will become apparent, these approaches differ along what Guzzo, Jackson, and Katzell (1987) refer to as a "continuum of quantification" (p. 409).

Traditional Literature Reviews

Reviews of research that appear in textbooks, monographs, and journals traditionally have taken the form of a narrative account—a descriptive summary that is relatively "informal and discursive" (Light & Pillemer, 1984). Such accounts offer a qualitative judgment regarding the evidence for (or against) some hypothesis of interest. That is, they typically attempt to reach an overall conclusion regarding the presence or absence of an effect under specified conditions. The simplest question that might be addressed, for example, is whether an effect is reliably produced by a standard experimental treatment, whereas no such effect appears when a standard control group is tested.

The attempt to reach an overall conclusion usually is guided by examining the statistical evidence from each independent study (i.e., evidence for or against rejecting the null hypothesis). In the two-group case, the evidence

from a given study can be classified as falling into one of the following mutual-
ly exclusive and exhaustive categories: (1) no significant difference between
conditions; (2) a significant difference in the predicted direction; or (3) a
significant difference, opposite from what was hypothesized. Thus, one way
of summarizing the results across several studies is to tally the number that
fall into each of those categories. This approach, which characterizes traditional reviews, has been called the "vote-counting" or "box-score" method
(Hedges & Olkin, 1980; Light & Smith, 1971).

The object of the vote-counting method is to determine a winner, namely
the category receiving the most votes. Some issues seem to be easily resolv-
able on that basis. Insko's (1967) review of the literature on counterattitudinal
role playing, for example, summarized the evidence simply by indicating that
five studies had concluded that the technique was effective in generating attitude change, whereas only one study had not. An example of a more ambiguous outcome comes from another source, one that had yielded highly
inconsistent findings at the time of Insko's textbook—namely, evidence concerning the dissonance prediction that compliance should produce more attitude change with small rewards than with large rewards. Insko concluded that
"some studies have found a positive relationship between reward and attitude
change...some studies have found a negative relationship...and some
studies have found no relationship" (1967, pp. 243–244).

Earlier, we mentioned an instance in which a traditional review and a meta-
analysis reached differing conclusions (Arkin et al., 1980; Zuckerman, 1979).
We must point out, however, that reviewers who rely on box-scores may also
disagree among themselves. For example, J.L. Freedman (1984) noted considerable disagreement among traditional reviews of research regarding the
effects of television violence on aggressiveness. Obviously, such disagreements will be more likely for mixed outcome cases than for instances in which
virtually all individual studies find similar effects. Given mixed outcomes,
there are at least three reasons why diverging conclusions might be reached
by separate research reviews based on vote-counting methods (cf. T.D. Cook
& Leviton, 1980).

First, box-scores will differ if the studies chosen for review are not the
same. For reasons that are discussed later, meta-analysts usually employ less
stringent criteria for excluding studies than do traditional reviewers. Deciding
on some rule for the exclusion or inclusion of studies, however, is a feature
shared by meta-analyses and traditional reviews alike.

Second, some traditional reviews further subclassify studies according to
the methodological adequacy of the research conducted (e.g., Crosby, 1976).
Thus, box-scores of the results from methodologically "adequate" studies
may vary, depending on subjective impressions of scientific merit (i.e., depending on which studies are considered sufficiently rigorous). An empirical
investigation of reviewing procedures (H.M. Cooper & Rosenthal, 1980)
illustrates this point. Cooper and Rosenthal asked 22 members of a psychology department (a sample of graduate students and professors) to review the

same seven articles by "whatever criteria you would use if this exercise were being undertaken for a class term paper or a manuscript for publication" (1980, p. 444). The articles all examined possible sex differences in persistence, and these traditional-review instructions produced the following distribution of conclusions regarding the hypothesis that females are more persistent than males: 16 reviewers said "definitely no" or "probably no," one said "probably yes," and five indicated that it was "impossible to say." These results might reflect differences in impressions of methodological adequacy, as suggested by free-response remarks in which "41% of the traditional reviewers noted that supporting studies used young children rather than adults" and "55% . . . bemoaned the lack of control in the studies or suggested that gender might interact with some unidentified variables" (p. 447).

A third possibility is that for a given level of significance reported as the test of an effect within any particular study, two different reviewers may not reach the same conclusion regarding rejection of the null hypothesis. For example, H.M. Cooper and Rosenthal (1980) reported that "Eleven of the 22 reviewers in the traditional condition (50%) reported that least one of the two studies with significant p levels did not support the hypothesis. . . [indicating] retrieval errors" (p. 446). Whatever the basis for such errors (e.g., clerical oversights, beliefs that the proper theoretical construct was not tested, subjective biases, insufficient attention to statistical evidence), it is clear that they could easily yield different outcomes by reviewers who use the vote-counting approach.

Meta-analytic Techniques

The development of meta-analysis can be regarded as a reaction against the shortcomings of traditional reviews in general and the vote-counting approach in particular (T.D. Cook & Leviton, 1980). Indeed, the reaction has been extreme, as meta-analytic techniques have surged in popularity in recent years. Guzzo et al. (1987), for example, found that "meta-analysis" was used as a key word in *Psychological Abstracts* fewer than five times in 1977, but estimated at just under 100 times in 1985.

The general criticism of traditional reviews is that they are inherently subjective; that is, they allow too much room for "art" and the "personal stamp" of the reviewer (Light & Pillemer, 1984, p. 105). For example, G.V. Glass (1976, 1977), one of the earliest proponents of meta-analysis, argued that conclusions from traditional reviews are too easily colored by the biases of the reviewer. The problem of subjectivity will be magnified when there are many studies to be reviewed and "cognitive overload" threatens to overwhelm the reviewer (Leviton & Cook, 1981). A related general criticism is that qualitative review procedures are "inefficient" by virtue of their dependence on detailed information from individual studies (Light & Pillemer, 1984, p. 4).

If detailed information is disregarded and only the probability values (p) of effects from each study are used for vote-counting purposes, however, additional problems are manifested. In particular, simply counting the number of significant and nonsignificant findings can lead to several statistical errors of a serious nature (Light & Pillemer, 1984). A major form of error consists of reaching a no-effect conclusion when the modal box-score category is failure to reject the null hypothesis—if the reviewer reaching such a conclusion ignores evidence that the remaining box-score categories (the two tails of the outcome distribution) get more votes than would be expected by chance. Light and Smith (1971), for example, describe a review of 189 studies in which the modal outcome (81 studies) was a null-effect finding. Yet significant effects of treatment (at the .05 level of significance) were found in one direction for 58 studies and in the opposite direction for the remaining 50 studies. These 108 significant findings far exceed the number that would be expected based on chance alone (fewer than 10, or 5% of 189), suggesting the influence of moderator variables—particular (unknown) levels of which apparently *did* make a difference of one form or another.

Simply counting the number of significant findings also contributes to another form of error, namely ignoring the influence of sample size (Light & Pillemer, 1984). The power of a statistical test to detect treatment effects depends on the size of the sample studied; the same effect reported "significant" when tested with adequate power will appear "nonsignificant" when the sample size is too small. Hedges and Olkin (1980), for example, demonstrated that studies with sample sizes less than 30 will fail to detect even reasonably substantial effects the majority of the time.

Indeed, vote counts of significance provide little or no information about the relative magnitude of effects (i.e., whether obtained effects ought to be considered miniscule, substantial, or whatever). The size of p values from a series of studies gives no clear indication concerning the strength of an effect unless all the studies have the same sample size and "a unimodal distribution reflecting one population" (Bangert-Drowns, 1986, p. 389)—two requirements that will rarely, if ever, be met in practice. Furthermore, the box-score tally may include in the "significant" category some studies whose effects were not substantial enough to be of any practical importance (Light & Pillemer, 1984). Hence, vote-counting methods are open to the charges of neglecting crucial information and weighting conclusions improperly (H.M. Cooper & Rosenthal, 1980).

Meta-analysis involves quantitative techniques that are more precise than vote-counting methods for integrating results from several studies addressing the same hypothesis. Essentially, such integration can be achieved in two major ways: by combining levels of significance and by combining effect sizes (Strube & Miller, 1986). There are, however, a variety of statistical approaches that can be adopted with respect to either of these forms of meta-analysis. For example, R. Rosenthal (1978) described six different formulas for combining significance levels across studies. Similarly, Light and Pillemer (1984) and Hedges (1982) have discussed several approaches to summarizing evidence about effect sizes.

In addition, reviewers who use these methods for integrating research studies typically opt for one of several meta-analytic "packages" or collections of techniques (T.D. Cook & Leviton, 1980). These packages vary in their guidelines concerning such issues as the criteria for inclusion or exclusion of studies, as well as in their purpose, unit of analysis, treatment of study variation, and outcomes of analysis (Bangert-Drowns, 1986). Three of the most currently popular packages, which we describe separately in the following sections, are attributable to the following advocates of meta-analysis and their colleagues (cf. Bangert-Drowns, 1986; T.D. Cook & Leviton, 1980): (1) G.V. Glass (e.g., 1976; Glass, McGaw, & Smith, 1981); (2) R. Rosenthal (e.g., 1976b, 1984); and (3) Hunter and Schmidt (1978; Hunter, Schmidt, & Jackson, 1982).[1]

Glass

G.V. Glass's approach to meta-analysis begins by collecting every available study relevant to the same research question, such as whether psychotherapy has a beneficial effect (M.L. Smith & Glass, 1977). As is the case for all three major approaches that we are examining, very liberal inclusion criteria are used. An attempt is made to locate unpublished studies and dissertations as well as published articles, and studies are not excluded on the basis of methodological quality.

The initial quantitative step in a Glassian meta-analysis is the conversion of outcomes from each study into a common metric, the effect size. Glass uses a variation of Cohen's (1962) *d* statistic for this purpose. Each estimate of effect size is calculated by subtracting the mean of the control group from the mean of the experimental group, then dividing this difference by the control group's standard deviation. Once every effect size has been calculated, it is possible to express the typical impact of treatment as the average value of all effect sizes. It is important to note that if one study reports its treatment results in terms of several dependent measures, each of these contributes one estimate of effect size. Thus, the more dependent measures a study uses, the more that single study influences the average effect size of a Glassian meta-analysis (Bangert-Drowns, 1986).

Glass also routinely looks for the influence of moderator variables, pri-

---

[1]Light and his associates (e.g., Light, 1979; Light & Smith, 1971) also have developed a related technique known as *cluster analysis*. Although it has been described as a major form of meta-analysis by T.D. Cook and Leviton (1980), we do not discuss cluster analysis because of its reliance on original data that may be unavailable (see Bangert-Drowns, 1986), and because Light has advocated a more eclectic approach that varies according to the purpose of a research summary (Light & Pillemer, 1984). Bangert-Drowns (1986) has provided a review of two other major approaches to meta-analysis (Hedges, 1982; Mansfield & Busse, 1977), but because these are intended as elaborations of G.V. Glass' (1977) approach, they are not covered separately.

marily by classifying studies on dimensions representing differences in ways they were conducted (e.g., by a categorical index of methodological quality, or by mode of treatment implementation). In this way it is possible to see whether different types of studies yield similar or dissimilar effect sizes. Regression analyses also can be used for determining the extent to which different features of studies account for variance in outcome measures (T.D. Cook & Leviton, 1980).

Rosenthal

R. Rosenthal's (1984) meta-analyses also involve calculations of the average effect size, typically based on Cohen's d. Only one effect size from each study, however, is used to compute the average across all studies. In addition Rosenthal adopts methods described by Stouffer (1949) and by Mosteller and Bush (1954) to determine an overall probability for rejecting the null hypothesis in favor of a theoretically predicted treatment effect. Presumably because of his interest in specific, directional hypotheses (cf. T.D. Cook & Leviton, 1980), Rosenthal bases his combined probability measure on a list of exact one-tailed p values and corresponding z-scores (Bangert-Drowns, 1986; R. Rosenthal, 1978).

Thus, Rosenthal (1984) normally presents both of the major types of meta-analytic statistics (a summary probability estimate and a summary effect-size estimate), whereas Glass (1976) is primarily more interested in effect sizes alone. Another indication of Rosenthal's interest in an overall probability estimate is attention to what he calls the "file drawer problem" (R. Rosenthal, 1979, 1980): Combining z-scores calculated from p-values in available studies could be misleading if null findings are chronically underreported (i.e., the data from failed studies lie forgotten in file drawers). For that reason Rosenthal also calculates a "fail-safe N" that provides an estimate of "the number of additional studies of no effect needed to reduce a significant combined probability to nonsignificance" (Bangert-Drowns, 1986, p. 394).

Finally, a recent innovation is the use of a table indicating how much the distributions of experimental and control groups overlap (based on Cohen, 1977). R. Rosenthal and Rubin (1982a) refer to this table as a Binomial Effect Size Display (BESD). The BESD represents one way of solving a problem endemic to the Glassian emphasis on effect sizes alone, namely that effect sizes are not very meaningful without some basis for comparison (Light & Pillemer, 1984; see also Cohen, 1977). Using a 2 × 2 table in which the strength of the relationship is determined by the size of the effect, for example, a BESD presentation would indicate the proportions of illnesses that are or are not cured by a treatment, versus the corresponding proportions for the presence or absence of spontaneous remissions among a control group. The use of such displays suggests that Rosenthal is equally as interested in practical importance as he is in statistical significance (e.g., R. Rosenthal, 1983).

Hunter and Schmidt

As with R. Rosenthal, the meta-analytic strategies recommended by Hunter, Schmidt, and their colleagues can be regarded as extensions and refinements of Glass's procedures. Hunter and Schmidt, however, seem far less interested than Rosenthal in combining probabilities from tests of significance across studies. This disinterest may stem partly from their disdain for the misuse of *p*-values in vote-counting traditional reviews:

> The use of significance tests within individual studies only clouded discussion in the review studies because narrative reviewers falsely believed that significance tests could be relied upon to give correct decisions about single studies. Sampling errors can never be detected or corrected in single studies. The only answer to the detection of sampling error is a cumulative analysis of results across studies in which the variance of results across studies is corrected for sampling error. (Schmidt & Hunter, 1981, pp. 1134–1135)

As this passage makes clear, the meta-analytic task to which Hunter and Schmidt address themselves is the detection and correction of error. Essentially, they are concerned that uncorrected error has led to the gross underestimation of effect sizes and hence to the underutilization of worthwhile treatments or tests. One of their most provocative conclusions, for example, is that the validity of employment selection tests is sufficiently high (although previously underestimated) as to have a potential $100 billion beneficial impact on national productivity (Hunter & Schmidt, 1978)!

Obviously, the more sources of error for which statistical corrections can be made, the greater the chances that treatments with true impact can be detected. Ordinary procedures for estimating effect sizes, however, correct only for sampling error (i.e., they take sample size into account). Hunter and Schmidt's major contribution has been in drawing attention to additional error components that are characteristically part of research findings. In particular, they have emphasized procedures for correcting error due to unreliability of measurement and restriction of range (e.g., Hunter & Schmidt, 1978; Schmidt & Hunter, 1981).

Thus, the first quantitative review procedure in a Hunter–Schmidt meta-analysis might be called a "statistical clean-up operation." Using information provided in the report of a study, for example, the effect size from that study would be corrected for measurement unreliability. The average unreliability reported could likewise be used to make corrections for measures whose reliability is not reported (Hunter, Schmidt, & Jackson, 1982).

Another feature of the Hunter–Schmidt meta-analysis is a set of guidelines for handling the variability of study outcomes. Estimated effect sizes constitute a sampling statistic whose variance can be calculated from a formula attributable to Snedecor and Cochran (1980; for generalized versions, see Hedges, 1982; Rosenthal & Rubin, 1982a). Hunter and Schmidt recommend calculating this variance and then determining the extent to which sampling error can account for it. If the total variability of the observed effect sizes is substantially greater than the amount estimated as due to sampling error, then Hunter and Schmidt proceed with analyses examining moderator variables in a fashion similar to that adopted by Glass.

Controversial Issues

Meta-analytic techniques, as we have seen, come in a variety of forms, all of which share some common controversial themes. Three problem areas are discussed in the following sections: (1) disagreements regarding criteria for the inclusion or exclusion of studies, (2) problems of nonindependence among effect sizes, and (3) issues concerning the breadth of categories for independent and dependent variables.

Inclusion/Exclusion Criteria

We have indicated that meta-analysts use liberal standards for including studies to be quantitatively summarized. It would be a mistake, however, to assume that every study addressing a given research topic always is included. For example, some reports may be difficult to retrieve even after considerable efforts have been made to locate them (G.V. Glass et al., 1981; Guzzo et al., 1987; Light & Pillemer, 1984). Other than the possible selection-artifact problem that might result from differential retrievability, there are primarily two types of inclusion/exclusion issues. The first pertains to selection based on the published versus unpublished status of a report, and the second concerns matters of methodological quality.

Publication Bias

Both Glass (e.g., G.V. Glass et al., 1981) and R. Rosenthal (e.g., 1978) favor including unpublished studies as a way of avoiding what has been termed *publication bias* (Light & Pillemer, 1984). This potential form of bias stems from a problem noted by Greenwald (1975a), namely that the editorial review process may contribute to an overrepresentation of significant findings in journals (e.g., via the tendency of reviewers to reject manuscripts reporting only null findings, as well as by virtue of the attendant tendency for researchers to refrain from submitting such manuscripts in the first place). A major advantage of seeking out unpublished findings is that if a sufficiently large number of reports fall into both the published and unpublished categories, publication status can itself be examined as a moderator variable. That is, it becomes possible to see whether effect sizes differ as a function of publication status. There is some evidence that journal articles are indeed likely to contain larger treatment effects (M.L. Smith, 1980) and higher correlations (K.R. White, 1982) than those appearing in unpublished reports.

R. Rosenthal's (1978) fail-safe N, which we mentioned earlier, was recommended by him as another form of protection against publication bias. There are, however, two criticisms that have been directed against that particular calculation. The first problem is that there is "no easy way to estimate *precisely* the impact of unpublished research on conclusions drawn from studies in hand" (Light & Pillemer, 1984, p. 79, emphasis added). Suppose, for example, the fail-safe N were 10,000; the problem is that it would still seem logical to be more alarmed if 9,000 null-effect findings existed than if only 10 such studies were lying in file drawers, even though both numbers are below the fail-safe value. The second point of concern is that the fail-safe N only guards against the possibility of null-effect findings (H.M. Cooper, 1979; R. Rosenthal, 1979). As Bangert-Drowns (1986) notes, "there may in fact be a smaller number of *negative* studies, studies favoring the control group, that would reduce the meta-analytic outcome to nonsignificance" (p. 394).

Methodological Quality

Publication bias is related to the larger issue of selectivity based on methodological grounds, in that inclusion of only published findings "may...enhance quality control" (Light & Pillemer, 1984, p. 35). Light and Pillemer go on to note that this *potential* advantage of restricting a research review to just the published literature has serious drawbacks outweighing the usefulness and relative ease of such a strategy. Specifically, simply excluding a particular category of studies—on methodological or any other grounds—makes it impossible to compare the nature of effects in excluded studies with those obtained from the studies included for review. This reasoning, which implies that possible differences between categories of studies should become a matter to be resolved *empirically* (G.V. Glass & Smith, 1978), is the basis for the decision by most meta-analysts to withhold initial judgment on methodological quality. Studies of whatever methodological variety are to be included (G.V. Glass et al., 1981) so that categorizations of methodological features can be examined as possible moderator variables.

Eysenck (1978) has offered some of the most strident criticisms of this empirical approach. Calling it "megasilliness," he has argued that it amounts to "advocacy of low standards of judgment" (p. 517). That these charges might have an *ad hominem* flavor (at least in the eyes of G.V. Glass & Smith, 1978) can be assessed from some of Eysenck's further remarks:

> A mass of reports—good, bad, and indifferent—are fed into the computer in the hope that people will cease caring about the quality of the material on which the conclusions are based. If...[this] abandonment of scholarship were to be taken seriously...it would mark the beginning of a passage into the dark age of scientific psychology. (1978, p. 517)

Eysenck (1978) also equates the Glassian approach with a failure to heed the "garbage in—garbage out" caveat sounded by computer scientists. Similar concerns have been expressed by Mansfield and Busse (1977). Bangert-Drowns (1986) has pointed out that such concerns about methodological quality have led some meta-analysts to adopt selection criteria that are considerably stricter than those used by Glass. J.A. Kulik and his colleagues (e.g., Bangert-Drowns, Kulik, & Kulik, 1983; Kulik, Kulik, & Cohen, 1979) are notable in this respect: "In Kulik's research...if any study suffers from flaws that may obscure treatment effects or if the study's method deviates too greatly from standard experimental practice, the study is rejected" (Bangert-Drowns, 1986, p. 393). Similarly, Wortman and Bryant (1985) performed a meta-analysis in which 33 criteria were used for excluding studies.

It is clear that a decision to exclude some studies on methodological or other grounds reintroduces a qualitative aspect characteristic of more traditional review practices, namely the exercise of subjective judgment. Cook and Leviton (1980) note that a priori exclusion by methodological criteria "would perhaps be a reasonable procedure if all issues of methodology were resolved and no debates about methods could be heard" but then go on to point out that "such is not the case" (p. 457). For this reason Glass and his colleagues (e.g., G.V. Glass et al. 1981) continue to insist that matters should be settled by the data. An alternative procedure is to have selection guided by a panel of experts (Light & Pillemer, 1984).

There is little question that the use of exclusion criteria can open the door to charges of subjectivity because it potentially offers "an undesirable opportunity for a reviewer's biases to creep into the review" (Bangert-Drowns, 1986, p. 393). Moreover, there seems to be no clear-cut pattern regarding the substantive form of bias that might thereby be introduced.

G.V. Glass and Smith (1978), for example, compared psychotherapy outcome studies of varying methodological quality and argued that these "show almost exactly the same results" regardless of quality (p. 518); a similar conclusion (i.e., no substantive bias due to quality) was reached in the case of randomized versus nonrandomized studies regarding the effect of classroom size on such nonachievement measures as attitudes (Smith & Glass, 1979). On the other hand G.V. Glass and Smith (1978) found that randomized class-size studies showed a much stronger impact on measures of achievement than did studies not involving random assignment. Light and Pillemer (1984) concluded that "research design matters" (p. 155) but that it is impossible to know in advance *how*—and how much—it will matter. Citing one review in which better controlled studies revealed stronger impact of treatment (Yin & Yates, 1974) and two in which research design made no difference (Stock, Okun, Haring, & Witter, 1982; Straw, 1983), they also indicated several in which higher quality designs actually yielded smaller effect sizes (Chalmers, 1982; DerSimonian & Laird, 1983; Wortman & Yeaton, 1983).

Nor is the precluding of empirical comparisons—with the possibility of introducing substantive bias—the only potential drawback of exclusion criteria. Bangert-Drowns (1986) suggests that applying strict methodological standards could conceivably reduce the number of studies to a size not meaningful for analysis. He recommends that reviewers "explicitly define and adhere to standards" (p. 394) and that such selection standards be used primarily when the research review has a specific focus warranted by substantive concerns.

Grounds for excluding some studies, indeed, will be found in almost all areas of review and will be seen as warranted even by liberal standards. As Light and Pillemer (1984) put it, "We do not believe that wrong information is better than no information" (p. 32). In responding to Eysenck's (1978) criticism that the M.L. Smith and Glass (1977) review of psychotherapy outcomes had ignored the problem of spontaneous remission rates, for example, G.V. Glass and Smith (1978) pointed out that rates of spontaneous remission are appropriately estimated through the use of control groups—and that for that reason, they had only examined studies whose designs included such a control. As this example should make clear, *all* forms of meta-analysis must at least implicitly involve inclusion/exclusion decisions. If such decisions are not based on methodological criteria, they nonetheless come into play in defining the nature of the problem to be reviewed in the first place.

Effect Size Nonindependence

One idiosyncracy of Glassian meta-analysis is that a given study can contribute more than one effect size toward the overall estimate. Indeed, Glass's approach involves calculating a separate effect size for each dependent variable that was measured in a given study. Where a given study uses several such measures, however, it is clear that there are not statistically independent data points. Landman and Dawes (1982) noted five distinct ways in which portions of the data from the M.L. Smith and Glass (1977) meta-analysis of psychotherapy outcomes, for example, violated the assumption of independence. As Bangert-Drowns (1986) has pointed out, the violation of independence makes statistical conclusions quite suspect. G.V. Glass et al. (1981) concur that this is a serious criticism.

Bangert-Drowns (1986) also has discussed how this same lack of independence can lead to a related interpretive problem, the problem of "inflated *N*s." As an example, he mentioned a meta-analysis by Burns (1981) in which 413 effect sizes were calculated from 33 reports; one study contributed 120 effect sizes by itself—almost 30% of the total! Clearly, the generalizability of conclusions is suspect when a single study could contribute so heavily to the overall effect size estimate.

Nonindependent findings from the same study "inflate" *N*s in the sense that conclusions might be reached with greater confidence than is warranted. This overconfidence would stem from a mistaken belief that sample sizes were adequate for reliable estimation of effects. Allowing each finding to contribute a separate effect size might yield cases in which it appeared that a very large number of effect sizes had been pooled to produce one overall estimate of treatment impact. However, if a substantial portion of these effect sizes came from only a handful of studies, then the sample of *independent* observations would actually be quite small. Deleterious consequences would be especially pronounced if the few studies contributing a disproportionate number of effect sizes were themselves, methodologically flawed. For these reasons Bangert-Drowns (1986) warns against combining nonindependent effect sizes (see also Kulik, 1984; Landman & Dawes, 1982), and Rosenthal, as well as most other meta-analysts, calculates only a single effect size from a given study. Rosenthal and Rubin (1986) have, in fact, presented a statistical procedure for deriving a single effect size from intercorrelated multiple dependent measures.

Category Breadth

Issues related to category breadth have been called the "apples-and-oranges" problem (Bangert-Drowns, 1986; T.D. Cook & Leviton, 1980). An analogous problem is encountered in developing summated attitude measures, such as those involved when Likert scale-construction procedures are used: If individual attitude items will be added together so that their total is said to represent an overall index of attitude, how can this index be meaningful unless there is a good indication that the items are all measuring the same thing (e.g., internal consistency is evidenced by an adequately high Cronbach's alpha)? By the same token, combining effect sizes from various studies is problematic as a way of estimating treatment impact, unless in some sense the studies all involved the "same" independent variable and the "same" dependent variable.

   Probably no two studies ever have exactly identical treatments and measures, of course, and so the issue becomes where to draw the line in classifying studies as similar enough for purposes of combining their effect sizes. Consider, for example, the dissimilarities among therapists and forms of therapy. Yet when M.L. Smith and Glass (1977) used meta-analysis to address the question of psychotherapy's effectiveness, studies were merely classified as involving either behavioral or nonbehavioral forms of treatment. Indeed, in some analyses even these two groups were averaged together in order to obtain a single estimate of psychotherapy effectiveness.

   Bangert-Drowns (1986) has indicated that there have been two kinds of responses to this particular case of wholesale aggregation. Critics such as Presby (1978) have argued that overly broad, all-encompassing categories such as behavioral/nonbehavioral can obscure important differences among the forms of therapy. Some have argued, however, that the appropriate breadth of categories varies according to the type of question being raised. Wortman (1983), for example, has pointed out that many broad policy issues—such as whether psychotherapists are entitled to reimbursement from insurance companies—call for data analyzed in broad categories (e.g., are therapists in general effective or not?).

   Light and Pillemer (1984) echo this theme—namely, that many practical matters call for only the most general of conclusions, whereas other purposes for reviewing a research literature may require highly specific answers. In analysis of variance terms, the person seeking to influence policy will be more interested in main effects, whereas the person seeking new directions for future investigation might be more interested in interactions. Thus, one resolution of the category breadth issue is to insist that no single degree of breadth is always appropriate; rather, the degree of breadth should vary with the nature of the question being asked.

T.D. Cook and Leviton (1980), on the other hand, suggest that although such an issue-contingent solution to the category-breadth problem makes sense in principle, it may overlook some difficulties that arise in practice. The major difficulty is that the greater the breadth of the categories used, the greater the tendency that important interactions may become impossible to detect and the greater the related tendency that too much confidence will be placed in main effect conclusions. The two possible types of main effect conclusions are that the treatment had an effect or that the treatment had no effect. Cook and Leviton provide examples of both types of conclusions being reached mistakenly because of interactions hidden by categories that were too broad.

The first illustration is an example of an undetected interaction contributing to a no-effect conclusion. T.D. Cook and Leviton (1980) suggest that before 1972, a meta-analytic review of the forced-compliance literature "would probably have concluded that the evidence for the dissonance effect was weak or inconsistent" (p. 461) because studies in a direction opposite to the dissonance prediction were as prevalent as supportive studies. The Collins and Hoyt (1972) review, however, specified an interaction based on choice and perceived responsibility. Subsequent research has shown that when the conditions necessary for dissonance are met by taking these mediating variables into account, the dissonance effect is quite robust.

T.D. Cook and Leviton (1980) also discuss an example of a significant main effect that might more properly be described in interaction terms. The illustrative meta-analysis is one conducted by H.M. Cooper (1979), an advocate of Rosenthal's general approach. Cooper's review reached the overall conclusion that women were more conforming than men. Stated in these main-effect terms, however, such a conclusion overlooks the possibility that significant gender differences might be specific to a single research paradigm. Fortunately, Cooper also provided separate meta-analyses for each research paradigm. T.D. Cook and Leviton claim these analyses show that gender effects were restricted virtually exclusively to studies involving face-to-face interaction, from which they draw the folllowing implications:

> Making statements about a main effect could be interpreted to mean that greater conformity by females is transsituational, whereas it is situation-specific. Moreover, had there been fewer face-to-face studies, the obtained effect would have been smaller and perhaps not even statistically reliable. It is not comforting to think that conclusions about the generality of a main effect depend on the accidental rate at which face-to-face situations happen to have been chosen over other situations in past research. (1980, p. 204)

These implications also translate into a general caution against overinterpreting main effect conclusions when extremely broad categories are used.

The necessity of making "either/or" policy decisions takes on a different character in the light of T.D. Cook and Leviton's (1980) arguments. In terms of our earlier example of the M.L. Smith and Glass (1977) psychotherapy outcome meta-analysis, suppose policy makers used that review as the basis for deciding whether or not to have psychotherapists reimbursed by insurance companies. A main effect conclusion that psychotherapy is effective would lead to reimbursement. Conceivably, many ineffective therapies could receive financial support from this policy, however, if outcome research happened to have been conducted primarily in connection with effective rather than ineffective therapies (i.e., if the set of all studies available for review happened to overrepresent effective forms of therapy, perhaps because those using ineffective therapies are less likely to allow outcome-research investigations).

The broad categorization of all therapies under one heading might be similarly misleading for no-effect conclusions. The absence of an overall main effect for therapy (vs. no therapy) could easily result from a situation in which some forms of therapy were highly effective and others were highly ineffective. Hence, one implication of T.D. Cook and Leviton's (1980) line of argument is that even in the context of broad policy issues, there may be unfortunate consequences of forcing the issue in terms of presence or absence of main effect by using broad categorizations.

Current Status of the Controversy

If the current interest in meta-analysis is any indication, then meta-analysis is here to stay. Clearly its popularity is growing (cf. Guzzo et al., 1987; Rosenthal & Rubin, 1986; Strube, 1986). Indeed, Cook and Leviton (1980) suggest that "pressure may arise in the near future to make meta-analysis obligatory for many kinds of dissertation, grant proposal, and research report, as well as for reviews in journals such as *Psychological Bulletin*" (p. 450). Use of meta-analysis is also likely to increase due to the availability of several excellent recent books regarding these techniques (e.g., H.M. Cooper, 1984; G.V. Glass et al., 1981; Hunter et al., 1982; Light & Pillemer, 1984; R. Rosenthal, 1984).

There are also several sources reviewing the current status of controversies about meta-analyses (e.g., Bangert-Drowns, 1986; Guzzo et al., 1987; Strube, Gardner, & Hartmann, 1985). Although each makes many valuable contributions, we find it useful to summarize issues in terms of conclusions from Light and Pillemer's (1984) book on "the science of reviewing research." Their conclusions were expressed as four themes developed throughout that book (as initially stated on pp. 9–10): (1) "Any reviewing strategy must come from the precise questions driving the review....Is an overall answer desirable, or is the purpose to identify setting-by-treatment interactions?" (2)

"Disagreements among findings are valuable and should be exploited." (3) "Both numerical and qualitative information play key roles in a good synthesis." (4) "Statistical precision cannot substitute for conceptual clarity."

The preceding statements reflect two underlying dimensions characterizing the current status of debates about meta-analysis. Statements 1 and 2 reflect a continuum of relative emphasis on main effects versus interactions, and those who disagree about meta-analysis typically find themselves at different points along this continuum. Statements 3 and 4 play a similar role in identifying a second dimension, namely the relative emphasis to be placed on mathematical calculations versus subjective judgment.

Controversy is likely to surround meta-analysis for at least a brief period in the future, despite its widespread acceptance and increasing prevalence, because its users are sometimes perceived as taking positions that are extreme on these dimensions. With respect to the first dimension, for example, T.D. Cook and Leviton (1980) claim that "Glass and Rosenthal focus primarily on global summary statements rather than interactions" (p. 463). After cautioning against an emphasis on a main effect when it is qualified by an interaction, Cook and Leviton continue as follows:

> Our guess is that, with their stress on broad generalization, meta-analysts are even more prone than qualitative reviewers to overlook or to down play the importance of contingency-specifying interactions that in most situations have an inferential precedence over statements about main effects. (1980, p. 464)

We further note that although Light and Pillemer's (1984) first thematic statement implies that searching for an "overall answer" (main effect) is sometimes justified by a review's basic purpose, their second statement suggests that the search for interactions is perhaps more fruitful (or "exploitable," in their terms).

We must hasten to add, however, that the controversial status of meta-analysis may be due less to reality than to the *perception* of extremity on this first dimension. H.M. Cooper and Arkin (1981), for example, claim that "the common practice of disaggregating studies according to various potentially interactive factors reflects a sensitivity among meta-analysts to the issue of interactive variables" (p. 229). It is easy to imagine how meta-analytic reviews that make striking claims about nonqualified main effects might receive more publicity, as has been true of Hunter and Schmidt's (1978) position regarding the "billions" to be gained for the gross national product by an across-the-board use of cognitive tests for selection purposes. But as Cooper and Arkin point out, "if an interest in main effects does presently predominate in the meta-analysis literature, it is probably the main effect interest that led to the use of the method and not vice versa" (1981, p. 228).

The second dimension on which extreme stands will continue to evoke controversy, the qualitative/quantitative, may also be a difficult one for separating reality from perception. True, the meta-analytic literature contains many instances of claims such as H.M. Cooper's (1979; see also H.M. Cooper & Arkin, 1981) that reviews are generally bound to benefit from increased quantification. But Light and Pillemer (1982)—staunch advocates of meta-analysis—appear quite balanced in their initial thematic statement on this issue ("both...play key roles"), and their final statement's emphasis on "conceptual clarity" seems, if anything, to give precedence to qualitative understanding. What makes meta-analysis controversial probably is not its quantitative nature per se but what some critics see as a tendency toward the misuse of numbers because of a failure to question how they were obtained in the first place (the source of the original data points that are aggregated in a meta-analysis).

T.D. Cook and Leviton (1980) have been among those speaking out most sharply against this alleged failure to note that "the descriptive accuracy of a point estimate in meta-analysis can have mischievous consequences because of its apparent 'objectivity,' 'precision,' and 'scientism'... [collectively amounting to] misplaced specificity" (p. 455). Quantitative precision, as they point out, can be especially misleading in the case of an effect size aggregated from a large number of studies that all happen to share the same methodological or theoretical flaw. This problem echoes the "garbage in—garbage out" charge raised by Eysenck (1978).

Again, however, we must stress that this problem is not unique to meta-analysis nor inherent to its use; abuses are "caused by reviewer practices and not the method itself" (H.M. Cooper & Arkin, 1981, p. 229). There inevitably will be some need for qualitative judgment no matter how quantitatively oriented the review (T.D. Cook & Leviton, 1980; Leviton & Cook, 1981; Light & Pillemer, 1984). The necessity of "conceptual clarity" is not something that will vanish with the development of new methodologies, but is instead a constant across *all* techniques.

What the future holds for meta-analytic techniques will depend, no doubt, on the extent to which they are recognized as improving qualitative literature reviews. Of course, such techniques should, at the very least, assist scholars in the integration of research findings. But how? If the benefits do not derive from doing what traditional, narrative reviews do, only better, then they will likely stem from offering new dimensions of improvement. Although time will tell whether meta-analytic techniques will aid social scientists in identifying gaps in current knowledge and helping to test (as opposed to generating) theoretical propositions—two particularly promising domains—it is clear that meta-analyses will, at least, help shape the nature and choice of future research questions (cf. Guzzo et al., 1987).

We may conclude by noting general acceptance of the idea that, despite its benefits, meta-analysis is not a panacea for the ills of narrative literature reviews. Indeed, although meta-analysis has provided a powerful new set of procedures for summarizing research literatures, it has not done away with the need to exercise certain judgmental skills that are also required in traditional reviews (McGrath, 1982; Wanous, Sullivan, & Malinak, 1987).

Judgment often may entail the willingness to ignore, or at least accept only provisionally, a given statistically derived conclusion. In this vein, Guzzo et al., concluding that "there is no clear advantage of meta-analysis over narrative reviews or vice versa" (1987, p. 439), caution against "allowing the mere use of a statistical technique in a review paper to influence our perception of the type of contribution made..." (p. 435). These sentiments bode well for a forthcoming rapprochement of both traditional and meta-analytic skills in a truly complementary fashion.

References

Abelson, R.P. (1968). Simulation of social behavior. In G. Lindzey & E. Aronson (Eds.), *Handbook of social psychology* (2nd ed., vol. 2, pp. 274–356). Reading, MA: Addison-Wesley.

Abrahams, D. (1967). *The effect of concern on debriefing following a deception experiment.* Unpublished Master's thesis, University of Minnesota, Minneapolis.

Abramson, P.R. (1977). Ethical requirements for research on human sexual behavior: From the perspective of the participating subjects. *Journal of Social Issues, 33*, 184–192.

Ad Hoc Committee on Ethical Standards in Psychological Research. (1973). *Ethical principles in the conduct of research with human participants.* Washington, DC: American Psychological Association.

Adair, J.G. (1973). *The human subject: The social psychology of the psychological experiment.* Boston: Little, Brown.

Adair, J.G. (1982). Meaning of the situation to subjects. *American Psychologist, 37*, 1406–1408.

Adair, J.G., Dushenko, T.W., & Lindsay, R.C.L. (1985). Ethical regulations and their impact on research practice. *American Psychologist, 40*, 59–72.

Adair, J.G., & Epstein, J. (1967, May). *Verbal cues in the mediation of experimenter bias.* Paper presented at the meeting of the Midwestern Psychological Association, Chicago, IL.

Adair, J.G., Lindsay, R.C.L., & Carlopio, J. (1983). Social artifact research and ethical regulations: Their impact on the teaching of experimental methods in psychology. *Teaching of Psychology, 10*, 159–162.

Adair, J.G., & Schachter, B.S. (1972). To cooperate or to look good: Subjects' and experimenters' perceptions of each other's intentions. *Journal of Experimental Social Psychology, 8*, 74–85.

Adair, J.G., & Spinner, B. (1981). Subjects' access to cognitive processes: Demand characteristics and verbal report. *Journal for the Theory of Social Behavior, 11*, 31–52.

Agency for International Development. (1972). *Evaluation handbook.* Washington, DC: Author.

Alegre, C., & Murray, E.J. (1974). Locus of control, behavioral intention and verbal conditioning. *Journal of Personality, 42*, 668–681.

Alexander, C.N., Jr., & Scriven, G.D. (1977). Role playing: An essential component of experimentation. *Personality and Social Psychology Bulletin, 3*, 455–466.

Allen, V. (1966). Effects of knowledge of deception on conformity. *Journal of Social*

Psychology, 69, 101–106.

Allport, G.W. (1968). The historical background of modern psychology. In G. Lindzey, & E. Aronson (Eds.), *The handbook of social psychology* (2nd ed., Vol. 1,
pp. 1–80). Reading, MA: Addison-Wesley.

Anderson, J.R., & Bower, G. (1973). *Human associative memory.* Washington, DC:
Winston.

Annas, G.J. (1978). Informed consent. *Annual Review of Medicine, 29,* 9–33.

Annas, G.J., Glantz, L.H., & Katz, B.F. (1977). *Informed consent to human experimentation: The subject's dilemma.* Cambridge, MA: Ballinger Publishing.

Argyris, C. (1968). Some unintended consequences of rigorous research. *Psychological Bulletin, 70,* 185–197.

Arkin, R., Cooper, H., & Kolditz, T. (1980). A statistical review of literature concerning the self-serving bias in interpersonal influence situations. *Journal of Personality, 48,* 435–448.

Aronson, E. (1966). Avoidance of inter-subject communication. *Psychological
Reports, 19,* 238.

Aronson, E., Brewer, M., & Carlsmith, J.M. (1985). Experimentation in social psychology. In G. Lindzey, & E. Aronson (Eds.), *Handbook of social psychology* (3rd
ed., Vol. 1, pp. 441–486). New York: Random House.

Aronson, E., & Carlsmith, J.M. (1968). Experimentation in social psychology. In G.
Lindzey & E. Aronson, (Eds.), *The handbook of social psychology* (2nd ed., Vol. 2,
pp. 1–79). Reading, MA: Addison-Wesley.

Aronson, E., & Mills, J. (1959). The effect of severity of initiation on liking for a
group. *Journal of Abnormal and Social Psychology, 59,* 177–181.

Asch, S.E. (1951). Effects of group pressure upon the modification and distortion of
judgments. In H. Guetzkow (Ed.), *Groups, leadership, and men* (pp. 177–190).
Pittsburgh: Carnegie Press.

Asch, S.E. (1956). Studies of independence and conformity: I. A minority of one
against a unanimous majority. *Psychological Monographs, 70* (9, Whole No. 416).

Atkinson, R.C. (1974). Teaching children to read using a computer. *American
Psychologist, 29,* 169–178.

Babbie, E.R. (1975). *The practice of social research.* Belmont, CA: Wadsworth.

Bandura, A. (1969). *Principles of behavior modification.* New York: Holt, Rinehart,
and Winston.

Bandura, A. (1986). *Social foundations of thought and action: A social cognitive
theory.* Englewood Cliffs, NJ: Prentice-Hall.

Bangert-Drowns, R.L. (1986). Review of developments in meta-analytical method.
Psychological Bulletin, 99, 388–399.

Bangert-Drowns, R.L., Kulik, J.A., & Kulik, C.-L.C. (1983). Effects of coaching
programs on achievement test performance. *Review of Educational Research, 53,*
571–585.

Bannister, D. (1966). Psychology as an exercise in paradox. *Bulletin of the British
Psychological Society, 19,* 21–26.

Banuazizi, A., & Movahedi, S. (1975). Interpersonal dynamics in a simulated prison:
A methodological analysis. *American Psychologist, 30,* 152–160.

Barber, T.X. (1976). *Pitfalls in human research.* New York: Pergamon Press.

Barber, T.X., Calverly, D.S., Forgione, A., McPeake, J.D., Chaves, J.F., & Bowen,
B. (1969). Five attempts to replicate the experimenter bias effect. *Journal of
Consulting and Clinical Psychology, 33,* 1–6.

Barber, T.X., & Silver, M.J. (1968a). Fact, fiction and the experimenter bias effect.
Psychological Bulletin (Monograph Supplement), *70,* 1–29.

Barber, T.X., & Silver, M.J. (1968b). Pitfalls in data analysis and interpretation: A
reply to Rosenthal. *Psychological Bulletin* (Monograph Supplement), *70,* 48–62.

Barker, R.G. (1968). *Ecological psychology.* Stanford, CA: Stanford University
Press.

Baron, R.A. (1974). Sexual arousal and physical aggression: The inhibiting influence of "cheesecake" and nudes. *Bulletin of the Psychonomic Society*, *3*, 337–339.

Baron, R.A. (1977). *Human aggression*. New York: Plenum Press.

Baron, R.A. (1981). The "costs of deception" revisited: An openly optimistic rejoinder. *IRB: A Review of Human Subjects Research*, *3*(1), 8–10.

Baron, R.M. (1977). Role playing and experimental research: The identification of appropriate domains of power. *Personality and Social Psychology Bulletin*, *3*, 505–513.

Bass, A.R., & Firestone, I.J. (1980). Implications of representativeness for generalizability of field and laboratory research findings. *American Psychologist*, *35*, 463–464.

Baumrind, D. (1964). Some thoughts on the ethics of research: After reading Milgram's "Behavioral study of obedience." *American Psychologist*, *19*, 421–423.

Baumrind, D. (1971). Principles of ethical conduct in the treatment of subjects: Reactions to the draft report of the Committee on Ethical Standards in Psychological Research. *American Psychologist*, *26*, 887–896.

Baumrind, D. (1985). Research using intentional deception: Ethical issues revisited. *American Psychologist*, *40*, 165–174.

Beaman, A.L., Barnes, J., Klentz, B., & McQuirk, B. (1978). Increasing helping rates through information dissemination: Teaching pays. *Personality and Social Psychology Bulletin*, *4*, 406–411.

Beecher, H.K. (1962). Some fallacies and errors in the application of the principle of consent in human experimentation. *Clinical Pharmacology and Therapeutics*, *3*, 141–145.

Beecher, H.K. (1959). Generalization from pain of various types and diverse origins. *Science*, *130*, 267–268.

Beecher, H.K. (1966). Ethics and clinical research. *New England Journal of Medicine*, *274*, 1354–1360.

Belmont Report. (1978). *Ethical principles and guidelines for the protection of human subjects of research* (Vol. 1). (DHEW Publication No. OS 78-0012). Washington, DC: U.S. Government Printing Office.

Bem, D.J. (1967). Self-perception: An alternative interpretation of cognitive dissonance phenomena. *Psychological Review*, *74*, 183–200.

Bem, D.J. (1968). Epistemological status of interpersonal simulations: A reply to Jones, Linder, Kiesler, Zanna, and Brehm. *Journal of Experimental Social Psychology*, *4*, 270–274.

Bem, D.J. (1972). Self-perception theory. In L. Berkowitz (Ed.), *Advances in experimental social psychology* (Vol. 6, pp. 89–122). Orlando, FL: Academic Press.

Bennett, D.H., & Holmes, D.S. (1975). Influence of denial (situation redefinition) and projection on anxiety associated with threat to self-esteem. *Journal of Personality and Social Psychology*, *32*, 915–921.

Berkowitz, L. (1971). The "weapons effect," demand characteristics and the myth of the compliant subject. *Journal of Personality and Social Psychology*, *20*, 332–338.

Berkowitz, L., & Donnerstein, E. (1982). External validity is more than skin deep: Some answers to criticisms of laboratory experiments. *American Psychologist*, *37*, 245–257.

Berscheid, E., Baron, R.S., Dermer, M., & Libman, M. (1973). Anticipating informed consent: An empirical approach. *American Psychologist*, *28*, 913–925.

Bickman, L., & Henchy, T. (Eds.) (1972). *Beyond the laboratory: Field research in social psychology*. New York; McGraw-Hill.

Black, A.H., & Cott, A. (1976). Biofeedback: A useful tool in basic research, but its therapeutic value is still unproven. *Science Forum*, *9*, 11–15.

Blake, B.F., & Heslin, R. (1971). Evaluation apprehension and subject bias in experiments. *Journal of Experimental Research in Personality*, *5*, 57–63.

Blanchard, F.A., & Cook, S.W. (1976). Effects of helping a less competent member of a cooperating interracial group on the development of interpersonal attraction. *Journal of Personality and Social Psychology, 34,* 1245–1255.

Bok, S. (1974, November). The ethics of giving placebos. *Scientific American, 231,* 17–23.

Borgatta, E.F., & Bohrnstedt, G.W. (1974). Some limitations on generalizability from social psychological experiments. *Sociological Methods and Research, 3,* 111–120.

Boring, E.G. (1953). A history of introspection. *Psychological Bulletin, 50,* 169–189.

Boruch, R.F. (1975). On common contentions about randomized field experiments. In R.F. Boruch & H.W. Riecken (Eds.), *Experimental testing of public policy: The proceedings of the 1974 Social Science Research Council Conference on Social Experiments* (pp. 107–142). Boulder, CO: Westview Press.

Boruch, R.F., & Rindskopf, D. (1977). On randomized experiments, approximations to experiments, and data analysis. In L. Rutman (Ed.), *Evaluation research methods: A basic guide.* Beverly Hills, CA: Sage.

Boruch, R.F., Rindskopf, D., Anderson, P.S., Amidjaya, I.R., & Jansson, D.M. (1979). Randomized experiments for evaluating and planning local programs: A summary on appropriateness and feasibility. *Public Administration Review, 18,* 36–40.

Bouchard, T.J., Jr., (1976). Field research methods: Interviewing, questionnaires, participant observation, systematic observation, unobtrusive measures. In M.D. Dunnette (Ed.), *Handbook of industrial and organizational psychology* (pp. 363–413). Chicago: Rand McNally.

Bowerman, W. (1976). The effectiveness of debriefing: Lingering doubts. *Psychological Reports, 30,* 8–14.

Bowers, K.S. (1967). The effects of demands for honesty on reports of visual and auditory hallucinations. *International Journal of Clinical and Experimental Hypnosis, 15,* 31–36.

Bradley, G.W. (1978). Self-serving bias in the attribution process: A reexamination of the fact or fiction question. *Journal of Personality and Social Psychology, 36,* 56–71.

Brady, J.V. (1979). A consent form does not informed consent make. *IRB: Review of Human Subjects Research, 1*(7), 6–7.

Bramel, D., & Friend, R. (1981). Hawthorne, the myth of the docile worker, and class bias in psychology. *American Psychologist, 36,* 867–878.

Bramel, D., & Friend, R. (1982). Is industrial psychology none of Marxism's business? *American Psychologist, 37,* 860–862.

Brehm, J.W., & Cohen, A.R. (1962). *Explorations in cognitive dissonance.* New York: Wiley.

Brock, T.C. (1965). Communicator–recipient similarity and decision change. *Journal of Personality and Social Psychology, 2,* 650–654.

Brock, T.C., & Becker, L.A. (1966). "Debriefing" and susceptibility to subsequent experimental manipulations. *Journal of Experimental Social Psychology, 2,* 314–323.

Bronfenbrenner, U. (1976, September). Ecological validity in research on human development. In *External validity in the study of human development.* Symposium presented at the meeting of the American Psychological Association, Washington, DC.

Brophy, J.E., & Good, T.L. (1974). *Teacher–student relationships.* New York: Holt, Rinehart & Winston.

Brown, R. (1962). Modes of attitude change. In R. Brown, E. Galanter, E.H. Hess, & G. Mandler (Eds.), *New directions in psychology* (Vol 1., pp. 44–66). New York: Holt, Rinehart & Winston.

Brown, R. (1965). *Social psychology.* New York: Free Press.

Brush, S.G. (1974). Should history of science be rated X? *Science, 183,* 1164–1172.

Burkart, B.R. (1975). Apprehension about evaluation, paralanguage cues, and the experimenter-bias effect. *Psychological Reports*, *39*, 15–23.

Burns, P.K. (1981). A quantitative synthesis of research findings relative to the pedagogical effectiveness of computer-assisted mathematics instruction in elementary and secondary schools. *Dissertation Abstracts International*, *42*, 2946A. (University Microfilms No. 81–28, 378)

Buss, A.R. (1975). The emerging field of the sociology of psychological knowledge. *American Psychologist*, *30*, 988–1002.

Calder, B.J., Phillips, L.W., & Tybout, A.M. (1981). Designing research for application. *Journal of Consumer Research*, *8*, 197–207.

Calder, B.J., Phillips, L.W., & Tybout, A.M. (1982). The concept of external validity. *Journal of Consumer Research*, *9*, 240–244.

Calder, B.J., Phillips, L.W., & Tybout, A.M. (1983). Beyond external validity. *Journal of Consumer Research*, *10*, 112–114.

Campbell, D.T. (1957). Factors relevant to the validity of experiments in social settings. *Psychological Bulletin*, *54*, 297–312.

Campbell, D.T. (1969). Prospective: Artifact and control. In R. Rosenthal & R.L. Rosnow (Eds.), *Artifact in behavioral research* (pp. 351–382). Orlando, FL: Academic Press.

Campbell, D.T., & Boruch, R.F. (1975). Making the case for randomized assignment to treatments by considering the alternatives: Six ways in which quasi-experimental evaluations in compensatory education tend to underestimate effects. In C.A. Bennett, & A.A. Lumsdaine (Eds.), *Evaluation and experiment: Some critical issues in assessing social programs* (pp. 67–84). Orlando, FL: Academic Press.

Campbell, D.T., & Stanley, J.C. (1963). Experimental and quasi-experimental designs for research on teaching. In N.L. Gage (Ed.), *Handbook of research on teaching* (pp. 171–246). Chicago: Rand McNally.

Campbell, D.T., & Stanley, J.C. (1967). *Experimental and quasi-experimental designs for research*. Chicago: Rand McNally.

Campbell, J.P. (1986). Labs, fields, and straw issues. In E.A. Locke (Ed.), *Generalizing from laboratory to field settings* (pp. 270–279). Lexington, MA: Lexington Books.

Carey, A. (1967). The Hawthorne studies: A radical criticism. *American Sociological Review*, *32*, 403–416.

Carlsmith, J.M., Ellsworth, P.C., & Aronson, E. (1976). *Methods of research in social psychology*. Reading MA: Addison-Wesley.

Carlston, D.C., & Cohen, J.L. (1980). A closer examination of subject roles. *Journal of Personality and Social Psychology*, *38*, 857–870.

Cason, H. (1934). Organic psychology II: The psychological organism. *Psychological Review*, *41*, 356–367.

Chalmers, T.C. (1982). The randomized controlled trial as a basis for therapeutic decisions. In J.M. Lachin, N. Tygstrup, & E. Juhl (Eds.), *The randomized clinical trial and therapeutic decisions* (pp. 68–88). New York: Marcel Dekker.

Chapanis, N., & Chapanis, A. (1964). Cognitive dissonance: Five years later. *Psychology Bulletin*, *61*, 1–22.

Cherulnik, P.D. (1983). *Behavioral research*. New York: Harper & Row.

Chevalier-Skolnikoff, S. (1981). The Clever Hans phenomenon, cuing, and ape signing: A Piagetian analysis of methods for instructing animals. *Annals of the New York Academy of Sciences*, *364*, 60–93.

Christensen, L. (1977). The negative subject: Myth, reality, or a prior experience effect. *Journal of Personality and Social Psychology*, *35*, 392–400.

Christensen, L. (1981). Positive self-presentation: A parsimonious explanation of subject motives. *Psychological Record*, *31*, 553–571.

Christensen, L. (1982). Examination of subject roles: A critique of Carlston and Cohen. *Personality and Social Psychology Bulletin*, *8*, 579–583.

Clark, R.D., & Word, L.E. (1974). Where is the apathetic bystander? Situational characteristics of the emergency. *Journal of Personality and Social Psychology, 29,* 279–287.

Clore, G.L., & Jeffrey, K.M. (1972). Emotional role playing, attitude change, and attraction toward a disabled person. *Journal of Personality and Social Psychology, 23,* 105–111.

Coch, L., & French, J.R.P., Jr. (1948). Overcoming resistance to change. *Human Relations, 1,* 512–532.

Cohen, J.W. (1962). The statistical power of abnormal-social psychological research: A review. *Journal of Abnormal and Social Psychology, 65,* 145–153.

Cohen, J.W. (1977). *Statistical power analysis for the behavioral sciences* (rev. ed.). Orlando, FL: Academic Press.

Collins, B.E., & Hoyt, M.F. (1972). Personal responsibility-for-consequences: An integration and extension of the "forced compliance" literature. *Journal of Experimental Social Psychology, 8,* 448–593.

Committee for the Protection of Human Participants in Research. (1982). *Ethical principles in the conduct of research with human participants.* Washington, DC: American Psychological Association.

Cook, S., Kimble, G., Hicks, L., McGuire, W., Schoggen, P., & Smith, M. (1971, July). Ethical standards for psychological research. *APA Monitor,* pp. 9–28.

Cook, T.D., Bean, J., Calder, B., Frey, R., Krovetz, M., & Reisman, S. (1970). Demand characteristics and three conceptions of the frequently deceived subject. *Journal of Personality and Social Psychology, 14,* 185–194.

Cook, T.D., & Campbell, D.T. (1976). The design and conduct of quasi-experiments and true experiments in field settings. In M.D. Dunnette (Ed.), *Handbook of industrial and organizational psychology* (pp. 223–326). Chicago: Rand McNally.

Cook, T.D., & Campbell, D.T. (1979). *Quasi-experimentation: Design and analysis issues for field settings.* Chicago: Rand McNally.

Cook, T.D., & Flay, B.R. (1978). The persistence of experimentally induced attitude change. In L. Berkowitz (Ed.), *Advances in experimental social psychology* (Vol. 11, pp. 1–57). Orlando, FL: Academic Press.

Cook, T.D., & Insko, C.A. (1968). Persistence of attitude change as a function of conclusion re-exposure: A laboratory-field experiment. *Journal of Personality and Social Psychology, 9,* 322–328.

Cook, T.D., & Leviton, B.F. (1980). Effects of suspiciousness of deception and perceived legitimacy of deception on task performance in an attitude change experiment. *Journal of Personality, 39,* 204.

Cook, T.D., Leviton, L.C., & Shadish, W.R. (1985). Program evaluation. In G. Lindzey & E. Aronson (Eds.), *Handbook of social psychology* (3rd ed., Vol. 1, pp. 699–777). New York: Random House.

Cook, T.D., & Perrin, B.F. (1971). The effects of suspiciousness of deception and the perceived legitimacy of deception on task performance in an attitude change experiment. *Journal of Personality, 39,* 204–224.

Cooper, H.M. (1979). Statistically combining independent studies: A meta-analysis of sex differences in conformity research. *Journal of Personality and Social Psychology, 37,* 131–146.

Cooper, H.M. (1984). *The integrative research review: A social science approach.* Beverly Hills, CA: Sage.

Cooper, H.M., & Arkin, R.M. (1981). On quantitative reviewing. *Journal of Personality, 49,* 225–230.

Cooper, H.M., & Rosenthal, R. (1980). Statistical versus traditional procedures for summarizing research findings. *Psychological Bulletin, 87,* 442–449.

Cooper, J. (1976). Deception and role playing: On telling the good buys from the bad guys. *American Psychologist, 31,* 605–610.

Cotton, J.L. (1980). Verbal reports on mental processes: Ignoring data for the sake of theory. *Personality and Social Psychology Bulletin, 6*, 278–281.

Coutu, W. (1951). Role-playing vs. role-taking: An appeal for clarification. *American Sociological Review, 16*, 180–187.

Cox, D.E., & Sipprelle, C.N. (1971). Coercion in participation as a research subject. *American Psychologist, 26*, 726–728.

Crespi, L.P. (1948). The interview effect in polling. *Public Opinion Quarterly, 12*, 99–111.

Cronbach, L.J. (1975). Beyond the two disciplines of scientific psychology. American Psychologist, *30*, 116–127.

Cronbach, L.J. (1982). *Designing evaluations of educational and social programs.* San Francisco: Jossey-Bass.

Cronbach, L.J., Ambron, S.R., Dornbusch, S.M., Hess, R.D., Hornik, R.C., Phillips, D.C., Walker, D.P., & Weiner, S.S. (1981). *Toward reform of program evaluation.* San Francisco: Jossey-Bass.

Crosby, F. (1976). A model of egoistical relative deprivation. *Psychological Review, 83*, 85–113.

Crowne, D.P., & Marlowe, D. (1964). *The approval motive.* New York: Wiley.

Dabbs, J.M., & Helmreich, R.L. (1972). Fear, anxiety, and affiliation following a role played accident. *Journal of Social Psychology, 86*, 269–278.

Dane, F.C. (1975). *On participants' willingness to admit to prior experimental knowledge.* Unpublished manuscript, University of Wisconsin—Milwaukee.

Darley, J.M., & Batson, C.D. (1973). "From Jerusalem to Jericho": A study of situational and dispositional variables in helping behavior. *Journal of Personality and Social Psychology, 27*, 100–108.

Darroch, R.K., & Steiner, I.D. (1970). Role playing: An alternative to laboratory research? *Journal of Personality, 38*, 302–311.

Davis, J.H., Bray, R.M., & Holt, R.W. (1977). The empirical study of decision processes in juries: A critical review. In J.L. Tapp, & F.J. Levine (Eds.), *Law, justice, and the individual in society* (pp. 326–361). New York: Holt, Rinehart & Winston.

Davis, J.R., & Fernald, P.S. (1975). Laboratory experience versus subject pool. *American Psychologist, 30*, 523–524.

Department of Health, Education, and Welfare. (1975, March 13). Protection of human subjects. *Federal Register, 40*(50), Part II.

DerSimonian, R., & Laird, N.M. (1983). Evaluating the effect of coaching on SAT scores: A meta-analysis. *Harvard Educational Review, 53*, 1–15.

Derwing, B.L. (1973). *Transformational grammar as a theory of language acquisition.* New York: Cambridge University Press.

Diener, E., & Crandall, R. (1978). *Ethics in social and behavioral research.* Chicago: University of Chicago Press.

Dill, C.A., Gilden, E.R., Hill, P.C., & Hanselka, L.L. (1982). Federal Human subjects regulations: A methodological artifact? *Personality and Social Psychology Bulletin, 8*, 417–425.

Dipboye, R.L., & Flanagan, M.F. (1979). Research settings in industrial and organizational psychology: Are findings in the field more generalizable than in the laboratory? *American Psychologist, 34*, 141–150.

Dipboye, R.L., & Flanagan, M.F. (1980). Reply to Willems and Howard. *American Psychologist, 35*, 388–390.

Dresser, R.S. (1981). Deception research and the HHS final regulations. *IRB: A Review of Human Subjects Research, 3*(4), 3–4.

Dreyfus, H. (1972). *What computers can't do.* New York: Harper & Row.

Duhem, P. (1954). *The aim and structure of physical theory* (P.L. DeBroglie, Trans.). Princeton, NJ: Princeton University Press. (Original work published 1906)

Duncan, S.D., & Rosenthal, R. (1968). Vocal emphasis in experimenters' instruction reading as unintended determinant of subjects' responses. *Language and Speech*, *11*, (Part 1), 20–26.

Duncan, S.D., Jr., Rosenberg, M.J., & Finkelstein, J. (1969). The paralanguage of experimenter bias. *Sociometry*, *32*, 207–219.

Dunnette, M.D. (Ed.). (1976). *Handbook of industrial and organizational psychology*. Chicago: Rand McNally.

Edlund, M.J., Craig, T.J., & Richardson, M.A. (1985). Informed consent as a form of volunteer bias. *American Journal of Psychiatry*, *142*, 624–627.

Edwards, A.L. (1957). *The social desirability variable in personality assessment and research*. New York: Dryden.

Edwards, W., & Guttentag, M. (1975). Experiments and evaluations: A reexamination. In C.A. Bennett & A.A. Lumsdaine (Eds.), *Evaluation and experiment: Some critical issues in assessig social programs* (pp. 9–30). Orlando, FL: Academic Press.

Elashoff, J.D., & Snow, R.E. (1971). *Pygmalion reconsidered*. Worthington, OH: Charles A. Jones.

Ellis, R.S. (1946). Validity of personality questionnaires. *Psychological Bulletin*, *43*, 385–440.

Elms, A.C. (1975). The crisis of confidence in social psychology. *American Psychologist*, *30*, 967–976.

Elms, A.C., & Janis, I.L. (1965). Counter-norm attitudes induced by consonant vs. dissonant conditions of role-playing. *Journal of Experimental Research in Personality*, *1*, 50–60.

Enis, B.M., Cox, K.K., & Stafford, J.E. (1972). Students as subjects in consumer behavior experiments. *Journal of Marketing Research*, *9*, 72–74.

Epstein, L.C., & Lasagna, L. (1969). Obtaining informed consent: Form or substance. *Archives of Internal Medicine*, *123*, 682–688.

Epstein, Y.M., Suedfeld, P., & Silverstein, S.J. (1973). The experimental contract: Subjects' expectations of and reactions to behaviors and experimenters. *American Psychologist*, *28*, 212–221.

Ericsson, K.A., & Simon, H.A. (1978). *Retrospective verbal reports as data*. CIP Working Paper No. 388, Carnegie-Mellon University.

Errera, P. (1972). Statement based on interviews with four "worst cases" in the Milgram obedience experiments. In J. Katz (Ed.), *Experimentation with human beings* (pp. 42–56). New York: Russel Sage Foundation.

Evans, M.E. (1982). Legal background of the institutional review board. In R.A. Greenwald, M.K. Ryan, & J.E. Mulvihill (Eds.), *Human subjects research: A handbook for institutional review boards* (pp. 19–27). New York: Plenum Press.

Eysenck, H.J. (1978). An exercise in mega-silliness. *American Psychologist*, *33*, 517.

Farrow, J.M., Lohss, W.E., Farrow, B.J., & Taub, S.I. (1975). Intersubject communication as a contaminating factor in verbal conditioning. *Perceptual and Motor Skills*, *40*, 975–982.

Fast, J. (1970). *Body language*. New York: M. Evans.

Fazio, R.H., Zanna, M.P., & Cooper, J. (1979). The relationship of data to theory: A reply to Ronis & Greenwald *Journal of Experimental Social Psychology*, *15*, 70–76.

Feldman, J. (1982). Ideology without data. *American Psychologist*, *37*, 857–858.

Ferber, R. (1977). Research by convenience. *Journal of Consumer Research*, *4*, 57–58.

Fernberger, S.W. (1914). The effect of the attitude of the subject upon the measure of sensitivity. *American Journal of Psychology*, *25*, 538–543.

Festinger, L. (1955). Laboratory experiments. In L. Festinger, & D. Katz (Eds.), *Research methods in the behavioral sciences* (pp. 54–67). New York: Holt, Rinehart & Winston.

Festinger, L., & Carlsmith, J.M. (1959). Cognitive consequence of forced compliance.

Journal of Abnormal and Social Psychology, *58*, 203–210.

Fillenbaum, S. (1966). Prior deception and subsequent experimental performance: The "faithful" subject. *Journal of Personality and Social Psychology*, *4*, 532–537.

Fillenbaum, S., & Fry, R. (1970). More on the "faithful" behavior of suspicious subjects. *Journal of Personality*, *38*, 43–51.

Fishbein, M., & Ajzen, I. (1974). Attitudes toward objects as predictive of single and multiple behavioral criteria. *Psychological Review*, *81*, 59–74.

Fisher, C.D. (1984). Laboratory experimentation. In T.S. Bateman, & G.R. Ferris (Eds.), *Method and analysis in organizational research* (pp. 169–185). Reston, VA: Reston Publishing.

Flanagan, M.F., & Dipboye, R.L. (1980). Implications of representativeness for the generalizability of laboratory and field research findings. *American Psychologist*, *35*, 464–467.

Fletcher, J. (1973). Realities of patient consent to medical research. *Hastings Center Studies*. *1*(1), 39–49.

Folger, R., & Belew, J. (1985). Nonreactive measurements: A focus for research on absenteeism and occupational stress. In L.L. Cummings & B.M. Staw (Eds.), *Research in organizational behavior* (Vol. 7, pp. 129–170). Greenwich, CT: JAI Press.

Forsyth, D.R. (1976). Crucial experiments and social psychological inquiry. *Personality and Social Psychology Bulletin*, *2*, 454–459.

Forward, J., Canter, R., & Kirsch, N. (1976). Role-enactment and deception methodologies: Alternative paradigms. *American Psychologist*, *31*, 595–604.

Fost, N.C. (1975). A surrogate system for informed consent. *Journal of the American Medical Association*, *233*, 800–803.

Franke, R.H. (1980). Worker productivity at Hawthorne (Reply to Schlaifer). *American Sociological Review*, *45*, 1006–1027.

Franke, R.H., & Kaul, J.D. (1978). The Hawthorne experiments: First statistical interpretation. *American Sociological Review*, *43*, 623–648.

Freedman, B. (1975). A moral theory of informed consent. *Hastings Center Report*, *5*(4), 32–39.

Freedman, J.L. (1969). Role playing: Psychology by consensus. *Journal of Personality and Social Psychology*, *13*, 107–114.

Freedman, J.L. (1984). Effect of television violence on aggressiveness. *Psychological Bulletin*, *96*, 227–246.

Fried, S.B., Gumpper, D.C., & Allen, J.C. (1973). Ten years of social psychology: Is there a growing commitment to field research? *American Psychologist*, *28*, 155–156.

Friend, R., & Bramel, D. (1982). More Harvard humbug. *American Psychologist*, *37*, 1399–1401.

Fromkin, H.L., & Streufert, S. (1976). Laboratory experimentation. In M.D. Dunnette (Ed.), *Handbook of industrial and organizational psychology* (pp. 415–465). Chicago: Rand McNally.

Gallo, P.S., Jr., Smith, S., & Mumford, S. (1973). Effects of deceiving subjects upon experimental results. *Journal of Social Psychology*, *89*, 99–107.

Gardner, G.T. (1978). Effects of federal human subjects regulations on data obtained in environmental stressor research. *Journal of Personality and Social Psychology*, *36*, 628–634.

Gay, C. (1973, November 30). A man collapsed outside a UW building. Others ignore him. What would you do? *University of Washington Daily*, pp. 14–15.

Gerard, H.B., & Mathewson, G.C. (1966). The effects of severity of initiation on liking for a group: A replication. *Journal of Experimental Social Psychology*, *2*, 278–287.

Gerdes, E.P. (1979). College students' reactions to social psychological experiments involving deception. *Journal of Social Psychology*, *107*, 99–110.

Gergen, K.J. (1965). The effects of interaction goals and personalistic feedback on presentation of self. *Journal of Personality and Social Psychology, 1*, 413–425.

Gergen, K.J. (1973). Social psychology as history. *Journal of Personality and Social Psychology, 26*, 309–320.

Gergen, K.J. (1976). Social psychology, science and history. *Personality and Social Psychology Bulletin, 2*, 373–383.

Gergen, K.J. (1977). Stability, change and chance in understanding human development. In N. Datan & H. Reese (Eds.), *Life-span developmental psychology: Dialectical perspectives on experimental research* (pp. 119–141). Orlando, FL: Academic Press.

Gergen, K.J. (1978a). Experimentation in social psychology: A reappraisal. *European Journal of Social Psychology, 8*, 507–527.

Gergen, K.J. (1978b). Toward generative theory. *Journal of Personality and Social Psychology, 36*, 1344–1360.

Gergen, K.J. (1979). The positivist image in social psychological theory. In A.R. Buss (Ed.), *Psychology in social context* (pp. 86–102). New York: Irvington.

Gergen, K.J. (1980a). Toward intellectual audacity in social psychology. In R. Gilmore & S. Duck (Eds.), *The development of social psychology* (pp. 212–249). London: Academic Press.

Gergen, K.J. (1980b). The emerging crisis in life-span developmental theory. In P. Baltes & O. Brim (Eds.), *Life-span development and behavior* (Vol. 3, pp. 201–218). New York: Academic Press.

Gergen, K.J. (1982). *Toward transformation in social knowledge.* New York: Springer-Verlag.

Gergen, K.J., & Bassechs, M. (1980). The potentiation of social knowledge. In R.F. Kidd & M. Saks (Eds.), *Advances in applied social psychology* (Vol. 1, pp. 25–46). Hillsdale, NJ: Lawrence Erlbaum Associates.

Gergen, K.J., & Benack, S. (1984). Metatheoretical influences on conceptions of human development. In M. Lewin (Ed.), *Woman, man and child as seen by psychology: A critical history.* New York: Columbia University Press.

Gergen, K.J., & Gergen, M.M. (1983). Narratives of the self. In K. Scheibe & T. Sarbin (Eds.), *Studies in social identity* (pp. 66–84). New York: Praeger.

Gergen, K.J., & Morawski, J. (1980). An alternative metatheory for social psychology. In L. Wheeler (Ed.), *Review of personality and social psychology* (Vol. 1, pp. 326–352). Beverly Hills, CA: Sage.

Ghiselli, E.E. (1974). Some perspectives for industrial psychology. *American Psychologist, 29*, 80–87.

Gibson, J.J. (1966). *The senses considered as perceptual systems.* London: Allen & Unwin.

Gilbert, J.P., Light, R.J., & Mosteller, F. (1975). Assessing social innovation: An empirical base for policy. In C.A. Bennett, & A.A. Lumsdaine (Eds.), *Evaluation and experiment: Some critical issues in assessing social programs* (pp. 222–244). Orlando, FL: Academic Press.

Ginsburg, G.P. (1979). The effective use of role-playing in social psychological research. In G.P. Ginsburg (Ed.), *Emerging strategies in social psychological research* (pp. 4–16). London: Wiley.

Glass, D.C., & Singer, J.E. (1972). *Urban stress: Experiments on noise and social stressors.* Orlando, FL: Academic Press.

Glass, G.V. (1976). Primary, secondary, and meta-analysis research. *Educational Researcher, 5*, 3–8.

Glass, G.V. (1977). Integrating findings: The meta-analysis of research. *Review of Research in Education, 5*, 351–379.

Glass, G.V., McGaw, B., & Smith, M.L. (1981). *Meta-analysis in social research.* Beverly Hills, CA: Sage.

Glass, G.V., & Smith, M.L. (1978). Exercise in mega-silliness: A reply. *American*

Psychologist, 33, 517–519.

Godow, R.A., Jr. (1976). Social psychology as both science and history. *Personality and Social Psychology Bulletin, 2*, 420–426.

Goldberg, P.A. (1965). Expectancy, choice, and the other person. *Journal of Personality and Social Psychology, 2*, 685–691.

Golden, J.S., & Johnston, G.D. (1970). Problems of communication in doctor-patient communications. *Psychiatry in Medicine, 1*, 127–149.

Golding, S.L., & Lichtenstein, E. (1970). Confession of awareness and prior knowledge of deceptions as a function of interview set and approval motivation. *Journal of Personality and Social Psychology, 14*, 213–223.

Goldstein, A.P., & Simonson, N.R. (1971). Social psychological approaches to psychotherapy research. In A.E. Bergin & S.L. Garfield (Eds.), *Handbook of psychotherapy and behavior change*. New York: Wiley.

Goldstein, J.H., Davis, R.W., & Herman, D. (1975). Escalation of aggression: Experimental studies. *Journal of Personality and Social Psychology, 31*, 162–170.

Goldstein, R. (1981). On deceptive rejoinders about deceptive research: A reply to Baron. *IRB: A Review of Human Subjects Research, 3*(8), 5–6.

Gordon, M.E., Slade, L.A., & Schmitt, N. (1986). The "science of the sophomore" revisited: From conjecture to empiricism. *Academy of Management Review, 11*, 191–207.

Gordon, M.E., Slade, L.A., & Schmitt, N. (1987). Student guinea pigs: Porcine predictors and particularistic phenomena. *Academy of Management Review, 12*, 160–163.

Gough, H.G. (1947). Simulated patterns on the MMPI. *Journal of Abnormal and Social Psychology, 42*, 215–225.

Gray, B. (1975). *Human subjects in medical experimentation*. New York: Wiley.

Gray, B., & Cooke, R.A. (1980). The impact of institutional review boards on research. *Hastings Center Report, 10*(2), 36–41.

Gray, B., Cooke, R.A., & Tannenbaum, A.S. (1978). Research involving human subjects. *Science, 201*, 1094–1101.

Greenberg, J. (1987). The college sophomore as guinea pig: Setting the record straight. *Academy of Management Review, 12*, 157–159.

Greenberg, J., Pyszczynski, T., & Solomon, S. (1982). The self-serving attributional bias: Beyond self-presentation. *Journal of Experimental Social Psychology, 18*, 56–67.

Greenberg, M.S. (1967). Role playing: An alternative to deception? *Journal of Personality and Social Psychology, 7*, 152–157.

Greenspoon, J., & Brownstein, A.J. (1967). Psychotherapy from the standpoint of a behaviorist. *Psychological Record, 17*, 401–416.

Greenwald, A.G. (1975a). Consequences of prejudice against the null hypothesis. *Psychological Bulletin, 82*, 1–20.

Greenwald, A.G. (1975b). On the inconclusiveness of "crucial" cognitive tests of dissonance versus self-perception theories. *Journal of Experimental Social Psychology, 11*, 490–499.

Greenwald, A.G. (1976a). An editorial. *Journal of Personality and Social Psychology, 33*, 1–7.

Greenwald, A.G. (1976b). Transhistorical lawfulness of behavior: A comment on two papers. *Personality and Social Psychology Bulletin, 2*, 391.

Greenwald, R.A. (1982). Informed consent. In R.A. Greenwald, M.K. Ryan, & J.E. Mulvihill (Eds.), *Human subjects research: A handbook for institutional review boards* (pp. 79–90). New York: Plenum Press.

Greenwald, R.A., Ryan, M.K., & Mulvihill, J.E. (1982). *Human subjects research: A handbook for institutional review boards*. New York: Plenum Press.

Gross, A.E., & Fleming, I. (1982). Twenty years of deception in social psychology.

Personality and Social Psychology Bulletin, 8, 402–408.

Gruder, C.L., Stumpfhauser, A., & Wyer, R.S. (1977). Improvement in experimental performance as a result of debriefing about deception. *Personality and Social Psychology Bulletin, 3*, 434–437.

Grunder, T.M. (1980). On the readability of surgical consent forms. *New England Journal of Medicine, 302*, 900–902.

Guba, E.G. (1965, August). *Methodological strategies for educational change.* Conference on strategies for educational change. Washington, DC.

Guetzkow, H., Alger, C.F., Brody, R.A., Noel, R.C., & Snyder, R.C. (1963). *Simulation in international relations.* Englewood Cliffs, NJ: Prentice-Hall.

Guzzo, R.A., Jackson, S.E., & Katzell, R.A. (1987). Meta-analysis analysis. In B.M. Staw & L.L. Cummings (Eds.), *Research in organizational behavior* (Vol. 9, pp. 407–442). Greenwich, CT: JAI Press.

Hall, E.T. (1959). *The silent language.* New York: Doubleday.

Hamilton, D.L. (Ed.) (1981). *Cognitive processes in stereotyping and intergroup behavior.* Hillsdale, NJ: Lawrence Erlbaum Associates.

Hamilton, V.L. (1976). Role play and deception: A reexamination of the controversy. *Journal for the Theory of Social Behaviour, 6*, 233–250.

Haney, C., Banks, W.C., & Zimbardo, P.G. (1973). International dynamics in a simulated prison. *International Journal of Criminology and Penology, 1*, 69–97.

Hardy, A. (1965). *The living stream: A restatement of evolution theory and its relation to the spirit of man.* London: Collins.

Harré, R. (1974). Some remarks on "rule" as a scientific concept. In T. Mischel (Ed.), *Understanding other persons* (pp. 140–177). Oxford, England: Blackwell Scientific.

Harré, R. (1977a). Automatisms and autonomies: In reply to Professor Schlenker. In L. Berkowitz (Ed.), *Advances in experimental social psychology* (Vol. 10, pp. 331–334). New York: Academic Press.

Harré, R. (1977b). The ethogenic approach: Theory and practice. In L. Berkowitz (Ed.), *Advances in experimental social psychology* (Vol. 10, pp. 283–314). New York: Academic Press.

Harré, R., & Secord, P.F. (1972). *The explanation of social behaviour.* Oxford, England: Blackwell Scientific.

Harrington, G.M. (1967). Psychology of the scientist: XXVII. Experimenter bias: Occam's razor versus Pascal's wager. *Psychological Reports, 21*, 527–528.

Harrington, G.M., & Ingraham, L.H. (1967). Psychology of the scientist: XXV. Experimenter bias and tails of Pascal. *Psychological Reports, 21*, 513–516.

Harris, R.J. (1976). Two factors contributing to the perception of the theoretical intractability of social psychology. *Personality and Social Psychology Bulletin, 2*, 411–417.

Hedges, L.V. (1982). Estimation of effect size from a series of independent experiments. *Psychological Bulletin, 92*, 490–499.

Hedges, L.V., & Olkin, I. (1980). Vote counting methods in research sythesis. *Psychological Bulletin, 88*, 359–369.

Heidiger, H.K.P. (1981). The Clever Hans phenomenon from an animal psychologists's point of view. *Annals of the New York Academy of Sciences, 364*, 1–17.

Helmer, O., & Rescher, N. (1959). On the epistemology of the inexact sciences. *Management Science, 6*, 25–52.

Hempel, C.G., & Oppenheim, P. (1948). A definition of "degree of confirmation." *Philosophy of Science, 12*, 98–115.

Henchy, T., & Glass, D.C. (1968). Evaluation apprehension and social facilitation of dominant and subordinate responses. *Journal of Personality and Social Psychology, 10*, 446–454.

Hendrick, C. (1976). Social psychology as history and as traditional science: An appraisal. *Personality and Social Psychology Bulletin, 2*, 392–402.

Hendrick, C. (1977). Role-taking, role-playing, and the laboratory experiment. *Personality and Social Psychology Bulletin, 3*, 467–478.

Hendrick, C., & Jones, R.A. (1972). *The nature of theory and research in social psychology.* Orlando, FL: Academic Press.

Henshel, R.L. (1980). The purposes of laboratory experimentation and the virtues of deliberate artificiality. *Journal of Experimental Social Psychology, 16*, 466–478.

Hetherington, A.W., & Ranson, S.W. (1940). The spontaneous activity and food intake of rats with hypothalmic lesions. *American Journal of Physiology, 136*, 609–617.

Higbee, K.L., Lott, W.J., & Graves, J.P. (1976). Experimentation and college students in social psychology research. *Personality and Social Psychology Bulletin, 2*, 239–241.

Higbee, K.L., Millard, R.J., & Folkman, J.R. (1982). Social psychology research during the 1970's: Predominance of experimentation and college students. *Personality and Social Psychology Bulletin, 8*, 180–183.

Hilgard, E.R., & Loftus, E.F. (1979). Effective interrogation of the eyewitness. *International Journal of Clinical and Experimental Hypnosis, 27*, 342–355.

Holmes, D.S. (1967). Amount of experience in experiments as a determinant of performance in later experiments. *Journal of Personality and Social Psychology, 7*, 403–407.

Holmes, D.S. (1973). Effectiveness of debriefing after a stress-producing deception. *Journal of Research in Personality, 7*, 127–138.

Holmes, D.S. (1974). Investigations of repression: Differential recall of material experimentally or naturally associated with ego threat. *Psychological Bulletin, 81*, 632–653.

Holmes, D.S. (1976a). Debriefing after psychological experiments: I. Effectiveness of postdeception dehoaxing, *American Psychologist, 31*, 858–867.

Holmes, D.S. (1976b). Debriefing after psychological experiments: II. Effectiveness of postdeception desensitizing. *American Psychologist, 31*, 868–875.

Holmes, D.S. (1976c). *Effects of debriefing: A two-month follow-up.* Unpublished manuscript, University of Kansas.

Holmes, D.S. (1976d). *The effectiveness of debriefing after a personally stressful obedience experiment.* Unpublished manuscript, University of Kansas, Lawrence.

Holmes, D.S., & Appelbaum, A.S. (1970). Nature of prior experimental experience as a determinant of performance in a subsequent experiment. *Journal of Personality and Social Psychology, 14*, 195–202.

Holmes, D.S., & Bennett, D.H. (1974). Experiments used to answer questions raised by the use of deception in psychological research. *Journal of Personality and Social Psychology, 29*, 358–367.

Horka, S.T., & Farrow, B.J. (1970). Methodological note on intersubject communication as a contaminating factor in psychological experiments. *Journal of Experimental Child Psychology, 10*, 363–366.

Horowitz, I.A., & Rothschild, B.H. (1970). Conformity as a function of deception and role playing. *Journal of Personality and Social Psychology, 14*, 224–226.

Houston, B.K., & Holmes, D.S. (1975). Role playing versus deception: The ability of subjects to simulate self-report and physiological responses. *Journal of Social Psychology, 96*, 91–98.

Hovland, C.I. (1959). Reconciling conflicting results derived from experimental and survey studies of attitude change. *American Psychologist, 14*, 8–17.

Hovland, C.I., Lumsdaine, A.A., & Sheffield, F.D. (1949). *Studies in social psychology in World War II. Vol. 3: Experiments on mass communication.* Princeton, NJ: Princeton University Press.

Hultsch, D.F., & Hickey, T. (1978). External validity in the study of human development: Theoretical and methodological issues. *Human Development, 21*, 76–91.

Hunt, M. (1982, September 12). Research through deception. *New York Times Magazine*, pp. 66–67, 138, 140–143.

Hunter, J.E., & Schmidt, F.L. (1978). Differential and single-group validity of employment test by race: A critical analysis of three recent studies. *Journal of Applied Psychology*, *63*, 1–11.

Hunter, J.E., Schmidt, F.L., & Jackson, G.B. (1982). *Meta-analysis: Cumulating research findings across studies.* Beverly Hills, CA: Sage.

Ilgen, D.R. (1986). Laboratory research: A question of when, not if. In E.A. Locke (Ed.), *Generalizing from laboratory to field settings* (pp. 257–267). Lexington, MA: Lexington Books.

Ingraham, L.H., & Harrington, G.M. (1966). Experience of *E* as a variable in reducing experimenter bias. *Psychological Reports*, *19*, 455–461.

Innes, J.M., & Young, R.F. (1975). The effect of presence of an audience, evaluation apprehension, and objective self-awareness on learning. *Journal of Experimental Social Psychology*, *11*, 35–42.

Insko, C.A. (1967). *Theories of attitude change.* New York: Appleton-Century-Crofts.

Jenkins, J. (1974). Remember that old theory of memory? Well forget it! *American Psychologist*, *29*, 785–795.

Jensen, A.R. (1969). How much can we boost IQ and scholastic achievement? *Harvard Educational Review*, *39*, 1–123.

Johnson, R.W. (1967). *Subject performance as affected by experimenter expectancy, sex of experimenter, and verbal reinforcement.* Unpublished master's thesis, University of New Brunswick, Fredericton, New Brunswick, Canada.

Johnson, R.W. (1970). *Inducement of expectancy and set of subjects as determinants of subjects' responses in experimenter expectancy research.* Unpublished doctoral dissertation, University of Manitoba, Winnipeg, Manitoba, Canada.

Johnson, R.W., & Adair, J.G. (1970). The effects of systematic recording error vs. experimenter bias on latency of word association. *Journal of Experimental Research in Personality*, *4*, 270–275.

Johnson, R.W., & Adair, J.G. (1972). Experimenter expectancy vs. systematic recording error under automated and nonautomated stimulus presentation. *Journal of Experimental Research in Personality*, *6*, 88–94.

Jones, E.E. (1964). *Ingratiation.* New York: Appleton-Century-Crofts.

Jones, E.E. (1985). Major developments in social psychology during the past five decades. In G. Lindzey & E. Aronson (Eds.), *Handbook of social psychology* (3rd ed., Vol. 1, pp. 47–107). New York: Random House.

Jones, E.E., & Wortman, C. (1973). *Ingratiation: An attributional approach.* Morristown, NJ: General Learning Press.

Jones, R.A. (1985). *Research methods in the social and behavioral sciences.* Sunderland, MD: Sinauer Associates.

Jones, R.A., & Cooper, J. (1971). Mediation of experimenter effects. *Journal of Personality and Social Psychology*, *20*, 70–74.

Jones, R.A., Linder, D.E., Kiesler, C.A., Zanna, M., & Brehm, J.W. (1968). Internal states or external stimuli: Observers' attitude judgments and the dissonance theory—self-perception theory controversy. *Journal of Experimental Social Psychology*, *4*, 247–269.

Jourard, S.M. (1968). *Disclosing man to himself.* Princeton, NJ: Van Nostrand Reinhold.

Jung, J. (1969). Current practices and problems in the use of college students for psychological research. *Canadian Psychologist*, *10*, 280–290.

Jung, J. (1975). Snoopology. *Human Behavior*, *4*(10), 56–59.

Jung, J. (1981). Is it possible to measure generalizability from laboratory to life and is it really that important? In I. Silverman (Ed.), *New directions for methodology of social and behavioral science: Generalizing from laboratory to life* (pp. 39–49). San

Francisco: Jossey-Bass.

Jung, J. (1982). *The experimenter's challenge: Methods and issues in psychological research*. New York: Macmillan.

Katz, D. (1937). *Animals and men: Studies in comparative psychology*. London: Longman, Green.

Katz, D. (1953). Field studies. In L. Festinger, & D. Katz (Eds.), *Research methods in the behavioral sciences*, (pp. 75–89). New York: Holt, Rinehart & Winston.

Katz, J. (1969). The education of the physician-investigator. *Daedalus, 98*, 480–451.

Katz, J. (1972). *Experimentation with human beings*. New York: Russel Sage Foundation.

Katz, J. (1977), Informed consent—a fairy tale? *University of Pittsburgh Law Review, 39*, 138–158.

Katz, J., & Capron, A.M. (1975). *Catastrophic diseases: Who decides what?* New York: Russell Sage Foundation.

Kelly, E.L., Miles, C.C., & Terman, L. (1936). Ability to influence one's score on a typical paper and pencil test of personality. *Character and Personality, 4*, 206–215.

Kelman, H.C. (1967). Human use of human subjects: The problem of deception in social psychological experiments. *Psychological Bulletin, 67*, 1–11.

Kelman, H.C. (1968). *A time to speak: On human values and social research*. San Francisco: Jossey-Bass.

Kenny, D.A. (1985). Quantitative methods for social psychology. In G. Lindzey & E. Aronson (Eds.), *Handbook of social psychology* (3rd ed., Vol. 1, pp. 487–508). New York: Random House.

Kerlinger, F.N. (1964). *Foundations of behavioral research*. New York: Holt, Rinehart and Winston.

Kidd, R.F. (1976). Manipulation checks: Advantage or disadvantage? *Representative Research in Social Psychology, 7*, 160–165.

Kerr, W.A. (1945). Experiments on the effect of music on factory production. *Applied Psychological Monographs* (No. 5).

Kidd, R.F. (1977). Manipulation checks: Some further considerations. *Representative Research in Social Psychology, 8*, 94–97.

Kidder, L.H. (1981). *Seltiz, Wrightsman, and Cook's Research methods in social relations* (4th ed.). New York: Holt, Rinehart & Winston.

Kidder, L.H., & Judd, C. (1986). *Research methods in social relations* (5th ed.). New York: Holt, Rinehart & Winston.

Koestler, A. (1971). *The case of the midwife toad*. New York: Random House.

Kruglanski, A.W. (1975). The human subject in the psychology experiment: Fact and artifact. In L. Berkowitz (Ed.), *Advances in experimental social psychology* (Vol. 8, pp. 101–147). Orlando, FL: Academic Press.

Kruglanski, A.W., & Kroy, M. (1976). Outcome validity in experimental research: A re-conceptualization. *Representative Research in Social Psychology, 7*, 166–178.

Krupat, E. (1977). A re-assessment of role playing as a technique in social psychology. *Personality and Social Psychology Bulletin, 3*, 498–504.

Kulik, J.A. (1984, April). *The uses and misuses of meta-analysis*. Paper presented at the meeting of the American Educational Research Association, New Orleans.

Kulik, J.A., Kulik, C.L.C., & Cohen, P.A. (1979). A meta-analysis of outcome studies of Keller's personalized system of instruction. *American Psychologist, 34*, 307–318.

Laforet, E.G. (1976). The fiction of informed consent. *Journal of the American Medical Association, 235*, 1579–1585.

Landman, J., & Dawes, R.M. (1982). Psychotherapy outcome. *American Psychologies, 37*, 504–516.

Landsberger, H.A. (1958). *Hawthorne revisited, management and the worker: Its critics and developments in human relations and industry*. Ithaca, NY: Cornell

University Press.

Langer, E.J. (1975). The illusion of control. *Journal of Personality and Social Psychology, 32*, 311–328.

Latané, B., & Bidwell, L.D. (1977). Sex and affiliation in college cafeterias. *Personality and Social Psychology Bulletin, 3*, 571–574.

Latané, B., & Darley, J.M. (1970). *The unresponsive bystander: Why doesn't he help?* New York: Appleton-Century-Crofts.

Latané, B., & Rodin, J. (1969). A lady in distress: Inhibiting effects of friends and strangers on bystander intervention. *Journal of Experimental Social Psychology, 5*, 189–202.

Lazarsfeld, P.F. (1948). *Training guide on the controlled experiment in social research.* New York: Columbia University, Bureau of Applied Social Research.

Leak, G.K. (1981). Debriefing and gratuitous procedures. [Comment] *American Psychologist, 36*, 317.

Lebacquez, K., & Levine, R.J. (1977). Respect for persons and informed consent to participate in research. *Clinical Research, 25*, 101–107.

Levin, S.M. (1961). The effects of awareness on verbal conditioning. *Journal of Experimental Psychology, 61*, 67–75.

Levine, R.J. (1975). *The nature and definition of informed consent in various research settings.* Paper prepared for the National Commission for the Protection of Human Subjects of Biomedical and Behavioral Research, U.S. Department of Health, Education, and Welfare, Bethesda, MD.

Levine, R.J. (1978). The role of assessment of risk–benefit criteria in the determination of the appropriateness of research involving human subjects. Appendix to *The Belmont Report: Ethical Principles and Guidelines for the Protection of Human Subjects.* Vol. 1. (DHEW Publication No. OS 78-0013). Washington, DC: U.S. Government Printing Office.

Leviton, L.C., & Cook, T.D. (1981). What differentiates meta-analysis from other forms of review? *Journal of Personality, 49*, 231–236.

Levitt, E.E. (1959). Problems of experimental design and methodology in psychopharmacology research. In R.H. Branson (Ed.), *Report of the conference on mental health research.* Indianapolis, IN: Association for Advances in Mental Health Research Education.

Levy, L.H. (1967). Awareness, learning, and the beneficient subject as expert witness. *Journal of Personality and Social Psychology, 6*, 365–370.

Lewin, K. (1951). Problems of research in social psychology: 1941. In K. Lewin (Ed.), *Field theory in social science: Selected theoretical papers* (pp. 18–36). New York: Harper & Row.

Lichtenstein, E. (1970). "Please don't talk to anyone about this experiment": Disclosure of deception by debriefed subjects. *Psychological Reports, 26*, 485–486.

Lidz, C.W., Meisel, A., Zerubavel, E., Carter, M., Sestak, R.M., & Roth, L.H. (1984). *Informed consent: A study of decisionmaking in psychiatry.* New York: Guilford Press.

Lidz, C.W., & Roth, L.H. (1983). The signed form—informed consent? In R.F. Boruch & J.S. Cecil (Eds.), *Solutions to ethical and legal problems in social research* (pp. 145–157). Orlando, FL: Academic Press.

Light, R.J. (1979). Capitalizing on variation: How conflicting research findings can be helpful for policy. *Educational Researcher, 8*, 3–11.

Light, R.J., & Pillemer, D.B. (1982). Numbers and narrative: Combining their strengths in research reviews. *Harvard Educational Review, 41*, 429–471.

Light, R.J., & Pillemer, D.B. (1984). *Summing up: The science of reviewing research.* Cambridge, MA: Harvard University Press.

Light, R.J., & Smith, P.V. (1971). Accumulating evidence: Procedures for resolving contradictions among different research studies. *Harvard Educational Review, 41*,

429–471.

Linder, D.E., Cooper, J., & Jones, E.E. (1967). Decision freedom as a determinant of the role of incentive magnitude in attitude change. *Journal of Personality and Social Psychology, 6,* 244–254.

Lindzey, G., & Aronson, E. (1968). *The handbook of social psychology* (2nd ed., Vol. 5). Reading MA: Addison-Wesley.

Lindzey, G., & Aronson, E. (Eds.) (1985). *Handbook of social psychology* (3rd ed., Vol. 1). New York: Random House.

Littman, R.A. (1961). Psychology: The "socially indifferent" science. *American Psychologist, 16,* 232–236.

Locke, E.A. (1982). Critique of Bramel and Friend. *American Psychologist, 37,* 858–859.

Locke, E.A. (Ed.). (1986a). *Generalizing from laboratory to field settings.* Lexington, MA: Lexington Books.

Locke, E.A. (1986b). Generalizing from laboratory to field: Ecological validity or abstraction of essential elements? In E.A. Locke (Ed.), *Generalizing from laboratory to field settings* (pp. 3–9). Lexington, MA: Lexington Books.

Loftus, E.F., & Fries, J.F. (1979). Informed consent may be hazardous to health. *Science, 204,* 11.

London, P. (1977, November). Experiments on humans: Where to draw the line? *Psychology Today,* pp. 20, 23.

Ludlam, J.E. (1978). *Informed consent.* Chicago: American Hospital Association.

Lueptow, L., Mueller, S.A., Hammes, R.A., & Master, L.S. (1977). The impact of informed consent regulations on response rate and response bias. *Sociological Methods and Research, 6,* 183–204.

Lumsdaine, A.A., & Bennett, C.A. (1975). Assessment alternative conceptions of evaluation. In C.A. Bennett, & A.A. Lumsdaine (Eds.), *Evaluation and experiment: Some critical issues in assessing social programs* (pp. 99–129). Orlando, FL: Academic Press.

Lynch, J.G., Jr. (1982). On the external validity of experiments in consumer research. *Journal of Consumer Research, 9,* 225–239.

Lynch, J.G., Jr. (1983). The role of external validity in theoretical research. *Journal of Consumer Research, 10,* 109–111.

Lyons, J. (1964). On the psychology of the psychological experiment. In C. Scheerer (Ed.), *Cognitions: Theory, research, promise.* New York: Harper & Row.

MacCoun, R.J., & Kerr, N.L. (1987). Suspicion in the psychological laboratory: Kelman's prophecy revisited. *American Psychologist, 42,* 199.

MacKinney, A.C. (1955). Deceiving experimental subjects. *American Psychologist, 10,* 133.

Maloney, D.M. (1984). *Protection of human research subjects.* New York: Plenum Press.

Manis, M. (1975). Comment on Gergen's social psychology as history. *Personality and Social Psychology Bulletin, 1,* 450–455

Manis, M. (1976). Is social psychology really different? *Personality and Social Psychology Bulletin, 2,* 427–436.

Mann, L., & Janis, I.L. (1968). A follow-up study of the long-term effects of emotional role playing. *Journal of Personality and Social Psychology, 8,* 339–342.

Mansfield, R.S., & Busse, T.V. (1977). Meta-analysis of research: A rejoinder to Glass. *Educational Researcher, 6,* 3.

Mark, M.M. (1986). Validity typologies and the logic and practice of quasi-experimentation. In W.M.K. Trochim (Ed.), *New directions for program evaluation: Advances in quasi-experimental design and analysis* (No. 31, pp. 47–66). San Francisco: Jossey-Bass.

Mark, M.M., & Cook, T.D. (1984). Design of randomized experiments and quasi-experiments. In L. Rutman (Ed.). *Evaluation research methods: A basic guide* (2nd ed., pp. 65–120). Beverly Hills, CA: Sage.

Marwit, S.J. (1969). Communication of tester bias by means of modeling. *Journal of Projective Techniques and Personality Assessment*, *33*, 345–352.

Masling, J. (1960). The influence of situational and interpersonal variables in projective testing. *Psychological Bulletin*, *57*, 65–85.

Masling, J. (1966). Role-related behavior of the subject and psychologist and it effects upon psychological data. In D. Levine (Ed.), *Nebraska symposium on motivation* (pp. 67–103). Lincoln: University of Nebraska Press.

Mawhinney, T.C. (1986). Reinforcement schedule stretching effects. In E.A. Locke (Ed.), *Generalizing from laboratory to field settings* (pp. 181–186). Lexington, MA: Lexington Books.

Mayo, E. (1933). *The human problems of an industrial civilization*. New York: Macmillan.

Mayo, E. (1945). *The social problems of an industrial civilization*. Cambridge, MA: Harvard University, Graduate School of Business Administration.

McCarthy, C.R. (1981). The development of federal regulations for social science research. In A.J. Kimmel (Ed.) *Ethics of human subject research* (pp. 31–39). San Francisco: Jossey-Bass.

McFall, R.M., & Schenkein, D. (1970). Experimenter expectancy effects, need for achievement, and field dependence. *Journal of Experimental Research in Personality*, *4*, 122–128.

McGrath, J.E. (1982). Dilemmatics: The study of research choices and dilemmas. In J.E. McGrath, J. Martin, & R.A. Kulka (Eds.), *Judgment calls in research* (pp. 69–102). Beverly Hills, CA: Sage.

McGuire, W.J. (1967). Some impending reorientations in social psychology: Some thoughts provoked by Kenneth Ring. *Journal of Experimental Social Psychology*, *3*, 124–139.

McGuire, W.J. (1969). Suspiciousness of experimenter's intent. In R. Rosenthal, & R.L. Rosnow (Eds.), *Artifact in behavioral research* (pp. 13–57). Orlando, FL: Academic Press.

McNamara, J.R., & Woods, K.M. (1977). Ethical considerations in psychological research: A comparative view. *Behavior Therapy*, *8*, 703–708.

McNemar, Q. (1946). Opinion-attitude methodology. *Psychological Bulletin*, *43*, 289–374.

Meehl, P.E., & Hathaway, S.R. (1946). The K-factor. *Journal of Applied Psychology*, *30*, 525–564.

Meichenbaum, D., & Butler, L. (1979). Cognitive ethology: Assessing the streams of cognition and emotion. In K. Blankstein, P. Pilner, & J. Polivy (Eds.). *Advances in the study of communication and affect: Assessment and modification of emotional behavior* (Vol. 6, pp. 121–146). New York: Plenum Press.

Melton, C.B., Koocher, G.P., & Saks, M.J. (1983). *Children's competence to consent*. New York: Plenum Press.

Menges, R.J. (1973). Openness and honesty versus coercion and deception in psychological research. *American Psychologist*, *28*, 1030–1034.

Merton, R.K. (1948). The self-fulfilling prophecy. *Antioch Review*, *8*, 193–210.

Merton, R.K. (1957). *Social theory and social structure*. New York: Free Press.

Michaels, T.F., & Oetting, E.R. (1979). The informed consent dilemma: An empirical approach. *Journal of Social Psychology*, *109*, 223–230.

Milgram, S. (1963). Behavioral study of obedience. *Journal of Abnormal and Social Psychology*, *67*, 371–378.

Milgram, S. (1964). Issues in the study of obedience: A reply to Baumrind. *American Psychologist*, *19*, 848–852.

Milgram, S. (1974). *Obedience to authority*. New York: Harper & Row.

Miller, A.G. (1972). Role playing: An alternative to deception? A review of the evidence. *American Psychologist, 27*, 623–636.

Miller, D.B. (1977). Roles of naturalistic observation in comparative psychology. *American Psychologist, 32*, 211–219.

Miller, K.A. (1970). *A study of "experimenter bias" and "subject awareness" as demand characteristic artifacts in attitude change experiments.* Unpublished doctoral dissertation. Bowling Green State University, Bowling Green, OH.

Mills, J. (1969). The experimental method. In J. Mills (Ed.), *Experimental social psychology* (pp. 407–448). New York: Macmillan.

Mills, J. (1976). A procedure for explaining experiments involving deception. *Personality and Social Psychology Bulletin, 2*, 3–13.

Minor, M.W. (1970). Experimenter-expectancy effect as a function of evauation apprehension. *Journal of Personality and Social Psychology, 15*, 326–332.

Minton, J.F. (1984). J.F. Brown's social psychology of the 1930's: A historical antecedent to the contemporary crisis in social psychology. *Personality and Social Psychology Bulletin, 10*, 31–42.

Mitchell, E.V. (1975). *Role playing as alternative to deception in psychological experiments.* Unpublished Master's Thesis, Ohio State University, Columbus, OH.

Mitchell, E.V., Kaul, T.J., & Pepinsky, H.B. (1977). The limited role of psychology in the role playing controversy. *Personality and Social Psychology Bulletin, 3*, 514–518.

Mixon, D. (1971). Behaviour analysis treating subjects as actors rather than organisms. *Journal for the Theory of Social Behavior, 1*, 19–32.

Mixon, D. (1972). Instead of deception. *Journal for the Theory of Social Behavior, 2*, 145–174.

Mixon, D. (1974). If you won't deceive, what can you do? In N. Armistead (Ed.), *Reconstructing social psychology* (pp. 79–90). Baltimore, MD: Penguin Books.

Mixon, D. (1976). Studying feignable behaviour. *Representative Research in Social Psychology, 7*, 89–104.

Mixon, D. (1977). Temporary false belief. *Personality and Social Psychology Bulletin, 3*, 479–488.

Mixon, D. (1979). Understanding shocking and puzzling conduct. In G. Ginzburg (Ed.), *Emerging strategies in social psychological research* (pp. 99–115). London: Wiley.

Moll, A. (1898). *Hypnotism* (4th ed.). New York: Scribner's.

Mook, D.G. (1983). In defense of external invalidity. *American Psychologist, 38*, 379–387.

Morrow, G.R. (1980). How readable are subject consent forms? *Journal of the American Medical Association, 244*, 56–58.

Moscovici, S. (1972). Society and theory in social psychology. In J. Israel & H. Tajfel (Eds.), *The context of social psychology: A critical assessment* (pp. 17–68). New York: Academic Press.

Mosteller, F. & Bush, R.R. (1954). Selected quantitative techniques. In G. Lindzey (Ed.), *Handbook of social psychology* (Vol. 1, pp. 289–334). Reading, MA: Addison-Wesley.

Movahedi, S. (1977). Role playing: An alternative to what? *Personality and Social Psychology Bulletin, 3*, 489–497.

Munn, N.L. (1933). *An introduction to animal psychology.* New York: Houghton Mifflin.

Murray, T.H. (1982). Ethics, power, and applied social psychology. In L. Bickman (Ed.), *Applied social psychology annual* (Vol. 3, pp. 75–95). Beverly Hills, CA: Sage.

National Commission for the Protection of Human Subjects of Biomedical and Behavioral Research. (1978). *Protection of human subjects.* Washington, DC: U.S.

Government Printing Office.

Newberry, B.H. (1973). Truth telling in subjects with information about experiments: Who is being deceived? *Journal of Personality and Social Psychology*, *25*, 369–374.

Newell, A., & Simon, H.A. (1972). *Human problem solving*. Englewood Cliffs, NJ: Prentice-Hall.

Nickel, T. (1974). The attribution intervention as a critical factor in the relation between frustration and aggression. *Journal of Personality*, *42*, 482–492.

NIE Task Force on Research Planning. (1974). *Building capacity for renewal and reform*. Washington, DC: NIE Office of R & D Resources.

Nisbett, R.E., & Ross, L. (1980). *Human inference: Strategies and shortcomings of social judgment*. Englewood Cliffs, NJ: Prentice-Hall.

Nisbett, R.E., & Wilson, T.D. (1977a). Telling more than we can know: Verbal reports on mental processes. *Psychological Review*, *84*, 231–259.

Nisbett, R.E., & Wilson, T.D. (1977b). The halo effect: Evidence for unconscious alteration of judgments. *Journal of Personality and Social Psychology*, *35*, 250–256.

Oakes, W. (1972). External validity and the use of real people as subjects. *American Psychologist*, *27*, 959–962.

Olian, J.D. (1986). Staffing. In E.A. Locke (Ed.), *Generalizing from laboratory to field settings* (pp. 13–42). Lexington, MA: Lexington Books.

Orne, M.T. (1959). The nature of hypnosis: Artifact and essence. *Journal of Abnormal and Social Psychology*, *58*, 277–299.

Orne, M.T. (1962). On the social psychology experiment: With particular reference to demand characteristics and their implications. *American Psychologist*, *17*, 776–783.

Orne, M.T. (1969). Demand characteristics and the concept of quasi-controls. In R. Rosenthal & R.L. Rosnow (Eds.), *Artifact in behavioral research* (pp. 143–179). New York: Academic Press.

Orne, M.T. (1970). Hypnosis, motivation, and the ecological validity of the psychological experiment. *Nebraska Symposium on Motivation*, *18*, 187–265.

Orne, M.T. (1973). Communication by the total experimental situation: Why it is important, how it is evaluated, and its significance for the ecological validity of findings. In P. Pliner, L. Krames, & T. Alloway (Eds.), *Communication and affect* (pp. 157–191). Orlando, FL: Academic Press.

Orne, M.T., & Evans, F.J. (1965). Social control in the psychological experiment: Antisocial behavior and hypnosis. *Journal of Personality and Social Psychology*, *1*, 189–200.

Orne, M.T., & Evans, F.J. (1966). Inadvertent termination of hypnosis with hypnotized and simulating subjects. *International Journal of Clinical and Experimental Hypnosis*, *14*, 61–78.

Ozar, D.T. (1983). An alternative rationale for informed consent by human subjects. *American Psychologist*, *38*, 230–232.

Page, J.S. (1970). *Experimenter-subject interaction in the verbal conditioning experiment*. Unpublished doctoral dissertation, University of Toronto.

Page, M.M. (1968). Modification of figure-ground perception as a function of awareness of demand characteristics. *Journal of Personality and Social Psychology*, *9*, 59–66.

Page, M.M. (1969). Social psychology of a classical conditioning of attitudes experiment. *Journal of Personality and Social Psychology*, *11*, 177–186.

Page, M.M. (1970). Demand characteristics, subject sophistication, and the effectiveness of a verbal "reinforcement." *Journal of Personality*, *38*, 287–301.

Page, M.M. (1971). Postexperimental assessment of awareness in attitude conditioning. *Educational and Psychological Measurement 31*, 891–906.

Page, M.M. (1972). Demand characteristics and the verbal operant conditioning experiment. *Journal of Personality and Social Psychology*, *23*, 372–378.

Page, M.M. (1973). On detecting, demand awareness by postexperimental questionnaire. *Journal of Social Psychology*, *91*, 305–323.

Page, M.M., & Lumia, A.R. (1968). Cooperating with demand characteristics and the bimodal distribution of verbal conditioning data. *Psychonomic Science*, *12*, 243–244.

Page, M.M., & Scheidt, R.H. (1971). The elusive weapons effect: Demand awareness, evaluation apprehension, and slightly sophisticated subjects. *Journal of Personality and Social Psychology*, *20*, 304–318.

Parsons, H.M. (1974). What happened at Hawthorne? *Science*, *183*, 922–932.

Parsons, H.M. (1978). What caused the Hawthorne effect? A scientific detective story. *Administration and Society*, *10*, 259–283.

Parsons, H.M. (1982). More on the Hawthorne effect. *American Psychologist*, *37*, 856–857.

Patterson, F. (1978). Conversations with a gorilla. *National Geographic*, *154*, 438–466.

Pavlov, I.P. (1927). *Conditioned reflexes*. (Translated by G.V. Anrep). London: Oxford.

Pendleton, M.G., & Batson, C.D. (1979). Self-presentation and the door-in-the-face technique for inducing compliance. *Personality and Social Psychology Bulletin*, *5*, 77–81.

Pepitone, A. (1976). Toward a normative and comparative biocultural social psychology. *Journal of Personality and Social Psychology*, *34*, 641–653.

Perry, L.B., & Abramson, P.R. (1980). Debriefing: A gratuitous procedure? [Comment] *American Psychologist*, *35*, 298–299.

Pfungst, O. (1965). *Clever Hans (the horse of Mr. von Osten)*. New York: Holt, Rinehart & Winston. (Original work published 1904)

Piliavin, I.M., Rodin, J., & Piliavin, J.A. (1969). Good Samaratinism: An underground phenomenon? *Journal of Personality and Social Psychology*, *13*, 289–299.

Popper, K.R. (1959). *The logic of scientific discovery*. New York: Basic Books.

Postman, L., & Bruner, J.S. (1948). Perception under stress. *Psychological Review*, *55*, 314–322.

Presby, S. (1978). Overly broad categories obscure important differences between therapies. *American Psychologist*, *33*, 514–515.

Pritchard, R.D., Dunnette, M.D., & Jorgenson, D.O. (1972). Effects of perceptions of equity and inequity on worker performance and satisfaction. *Journal of Applied Psychology*, *56*, 75–94.

Proshansky, H.M. (1976). Environmental psychology and the real world. *American Psychologist*, *31*, 303–310.

Quimby, F.H., McKensie, S.R., & Chapman, C.B. (1975). *Federal regulation of human experimentation: 1975*. Washington, DC: U.S. Government Printing Office.

Rankin, R.E., & Campbell, D.T. (1955). Galvanic skin response to Negro and white experimenters. *Journal of Abnormal and Social Psychology*, *51*, 30–33.

Reis, H.T., & Gruzen, J. (1976). On mediating equity, equality, and self-interest: The role of self-presentation in social exchange. *Journal of Experimental Social Psychology*, *12*, 287–303.

Resnick, J.H., & Schwartz, T. (1973). Ethical standards as an independent variable in psychological research. *American Psychologist*, *28*, 134–139.

Reynolds, P.D. (1979). *Ethical dilemmas and social science research*. San Francisco: Jossey-Bass.

Rice, S.A. (1929). Contagious bias in the interview: A methodological note. *American Journal of Sociology*, *8*, 433–438.

Rich, M.C. (1979). Verbal reports on mental processes: Issues of accuracy and awareness. *Journal for the Theory of Social Behavior*, *9*, 29–37.

Riecken, H.W. (1962). A program for research on experiments in social psychology. In N.F. Washburne (Ed.), *Decisions, values and groups* (Vol. 2, pp. 25–41). Elmsford, NY: Pergamon Press.

Riecken, H.W., & Boruch, R.F. (Eds.). (1974). *Social experimentation*. Orlando, FL: Academic Press.

Ring, K. (1967). Experimental social psychology: Some sober questions about some frivolous values. *Journal of Experimental Social Psychology, 3*, 113–123.

Ring, K., Wallston, K., & Corey, M. (1970). Mode of debriefing as a factor affecting subjective reaction to a Milgram-type obedience experiment: An ethical inquiry. *Representative Research in Social Psychology, 1*, 67–88.

Robinson, R., & Greenberg, C.I. (1980, September). Informed consent: An artifact in human crowding. In J.R. Aiello (Chair), *Crowding and human population density*. Symposium presented at the meeting of the American Psychological Association, Montreal.

Roethlisberger, F.J. (1941). *Management and morale*. Cambridge, MA: Harvard University Press.

Roethlisberger, F.J., & Dickson, W.J. (1939). *Management and the worker*. Cambridge, MA: Harvard University Press.

Roethlisberger, F.J., & Dickson, W.J. (1966). *Counseling in an organization: A sequel to the Hawthorne researchers*. Cambridge, MA: Harvard University, Graduate School of Business Administration.

Rokeach, M. (1973). *The nature of human values*. New York: Free Press.

Ronis, D.L., & Greenwald, A.G. (1979). Dissonance theory revised again: A comment on the paper by Fazio, Zanna, and Cooper. *Journal of Experimental Social Psychology, 15*, 62–69.

Rosen, B., & Jerdee, T.H. (1973). The influence of sex-role stereotypes on the evaluation of male and female supervisory behavior. *Journal of Applied Psychology, 57*, 44–48.

Rosen, B., & Jerdee, T.H. (1974). Effects of applicant's sex and difficulty of job on evaluations of candidates for managerial positions. *Journal of Applied Psychology, 59*, 511–512.

Rosenberg, M.J. (1965). When dissonance fails: On eliminating evaluation apprehension from attitude measurement. *Journal of Personality and Social Psychology, 1*, 28–42.

Rosenberg, M.J. (1969). The conditions and consequences of evaluation apprehension. In R. Rosenthal & R. Rosnow (Eds.), *Artifact in behavioral research* (pp. 280–349). Orlando, FL: Academic Press.

Rosenberg, M.J., & Abelson, R.P. (1960). An analysis of cognitive balancing. In M.J. Rosenberg, C.I. Hovland, W.J. McGuire, R.P. Abelson, & J.W. Brehm (Eds.), *Attitude organization and change: An analysis of consistency among attitude components* (pp. 123–145). New Haven, CT: Yale University Press.

Rosenthal, R. (1963). On the social psychology of the psychological experiment: The experimenter's hypothesis as unintended determinant of experimental results. *American Scientist, 51*, 268–283.

Rosenthal, R. (1964a). Experimenter outcome-orientation and the results of the psychological experiment. *Psychological Bulletin, 61*, 405–412.

Rosenthal, R. (1964b). The effect of the experimenter on the results of psychological research. In B.A. Maher (Ed.), *Progress in experimental personality research* (Vol. 1, pp. 79–114). Orlando, FL: Academic Press.

Rosenthal, R. (1966). *Experimenter effects in behavioral research*. New York: Appleton-Century-Crofts.

Rosenthal, R. (1967a). Covert communication in the psychological experiment. *Psychological Bulletin, 67*, 356–367.

Rosenthal, R. (1967b). Experimenter expectancy, experimenter experience, and Pascal's Wagner. *Psychological Reports, 20*, 619–622.

Rosenthal, R. (1967c). Experimenter expectancy, on tale of Pascal, and the distribution of three tails. *Psychological Reports, 21,* 517–520.

Rosenthal, R. (1967d). *The eternal triangle: Investigators, data, and the hypotheses called null.* Unpublished manuscript, Harvard University, Cambridge, MA.

Rosenthal, R. (1968). Experimenter expectancy and the reassuring nature of the null hypothesis decision procedure. *Psychological Bulletin, 70,* 30–47.

Rosenthal, R. (1969). Interpersonal expectations: Effects of the experimenter's hypothesis. In R. Rosenthal & R.L. Rosnow (Eds.), *Artifact in behavioral research* (pp. 689–691). Orlando, FL: Academic Press.

Rosenthal, R. (1976a). Interpersonal expectancy effects: A follow-up. In R. Rosenthal (Ed.), *Experimenter effects in behavioral research* (pp. 440–471). New York: Irvington.

Rosenthal, R. (1976b). *Experimenter effects in behavioral research* (2nd ed.). New York: Irvington.

Rosenthal, R. (1978). Combining results of independent studies. *Psychological Bulletin, 85,* 185–193.

Rosenthal, R. (1979). The "file drawer problem" and tolerance for null results. *Psychological Bulletin, 86,* 638–641.

Rosenthal, R. (1980). On telling tales when combining results of independent studies. *Psychological Bulletin, 88,* 496–497.

Rosenthal, R. (1981). Pavlov's mice, Pfungst's horse, and Pygmalion's PONS: Some models for the study of interpersonal expectancy effects. *Annals of the New York Academy of Science, 364,* 182–198.

Rosenthal, R. (1983). Assessing the statistical and social importance of the effects of psychotherapy. *Journal of Consulting and Clinical Psychology, 51,* 4–13.

Rosenthal, R. (1984). Meta-analytic procedures for social research. Beverly Hills, CA: Sage.

Rosenthal, R., & Fode, K. (1963). Psychology of the scientist. V: Three experiments in experimenter bias. *Psychological Reports, 12,* 491–511.

Rosenthal, D., & Frank, J.O. (1956). Psychotherapy and the placebo effect. *Psychological Bulletin, 53,* 294–302.

Rosenthal, R., & Jackson, L. (1966). Teachers' expectancies: Determinants of pupils' I.Q. gains. *Psychological Reports, 19,* 115–118.

Rosenthal, R., & Jacobsen, L. (1968). *Pygmalion in the classroom.* New York: Holt, Rinehart & Winston.

Rosenthal, R., Persinger, G.W., Mulry, R.C., Vikan-Kline, L., & Grothe, M. (1964). Emphasis on experimental procedure, sex of subjects, and the biasing effects of experimental hypotheses. *Journal of Projective Techniques and Personality Assessment, 28,* 465–469.

Rosenthal, R., Persinger, G.W., Vikan-Kline, L., & Mulry, R.C. (1963). The role of the research assistant in the mediation of experimenter bias. *Journal of Personality, 31,* 313–335.

Rosenthal, R., & Rosnow, R.L. (1969). The volunteer subject. In R. Rosenthal, & R.L. Rosnow (Eds.), *Artifact in behavioral research* (pp. 59–118). Orlando, FL: Academic Press.

Rosenthal, R., & Rubin, D.B. (1971). Pygmalion reaffirmed. In J.D. Elashoff & R.E. Snow (Eds.), *Pygmalion reconsidered* (pp. 139–155). Worthington, OH: Clarles A. Jones.

Rosenthal, R., & Rubin, D.B. (1978). Comparing significance levels of independent studies. *Psychological Bulletin, 86,* 1165–1168.

Rosenthal, R., & Rubin, D.B. (1980). Summarizing 345 studies of interpersonal expectancy effects. *New Directions for Methodology of Social and Behavioral Science, 5,* 79–95.

Rosenthal, R., & Rubin, D.B. (1982a). Comparing effect sizes of independent studies. *Psychological Bulletin, 92,* 500–504.

Rosenthal, R., & Rubin, D.B. (1982b). Further meta-analytical procedures for assessing cognitive gender differences. *Journal of Educational Psychology*, *74*, 708–712.

Rosenthal, R., & Rubin, D.B. (1986), Meta-analytic procedures for combining studies with multiple effect sizes. *Psychological Bulletin*, *99*, 400–406.

Rosenzweig, S. (1933). The experimental situation as a psychological problem. *Psychological Review*, *40*, 337–354.

Rosnow, R.L. (1981). *Paradigms in transition: The methodology of social inquiry.* New York: Oxford University Press.

Rosnow, R.L., & Aiken, L.S. (1973). Mediation of artifacts in behavioral research. *Journal of Experimental Social Psychology*, *9*, 181–201.

Ross, J., & Smith, P. (1968). Orthodox experimental design. In H.M. Blalock, & A.B. Blalock (Eds.), *Methodology in social research* (pp. 333–389). New York: McGraw-Hill.

Ross, L., Lepper, M.R., Hubbard, M. (1975). Perspectives in self-perception and social perception: Biased attributional processes in the debriefing paradigm. *Journal of Personality and Social Psychology*, *32*, 880–892.

Rossi, P.H., Freeman, H.E., & Wright, S.R. (1979). *Evaluation: A systematic approach.* Beverly Hills, CA: Sage.

Rozelle, R.M., & Druckman, D. (1971). Role playing versus laboratory deception: A comparison of methods in the study of compromising behavior. *Psychonomic Science*, *25*, 241–243.

Rubin, J.Z., & Brown, B.R. (1975). *The social psychology of bargaining and negotiation.* Orlando, FL: Academic Press.

Rubin, Z. (1970, December). Jokers wild in the lab. *Psychology Today*, pp. 18, 20, 22–24, 79.

Rubin, Z., & Moore, J.C. (1971). Assessment of subjects' suspicions. *Journal of Personality and Social Psychology*, *17*, 163–170.

Rugg, E.A. (1975). Ethical judgments of social research involving experimental deception. *Dissertation Abstracts International*, 4–B.

Sampson, E.E. (1978). Scientific paradigms and social values: Wanted—a scientific revolution. *Journal of Personality and Social Psychology*, *36*, 1332–1343.

Sarbin, T.R., & Allen, V.R. (1968). Role theory. In G. Lindzey & E. Aronson (Eds.), *Handbook of social psychology* (2nd ed., Vol. 1, pp. 488–567). Reading, MA: Addison-Wesley.

Sawyer, A.G. (1975). Demand artifacts in laboratory experiments in consumer research. *Journal of Consumer Research*, *1*, 20–30.

Schachter, S. (1959). *The psychology of affiliation.* Stanford, CA: Stanford University Press.

Schank, R.L., & Goodman, C. (1939). Reactions to propaganda on both sides of a controversial issue. *Public Opinion Quarterly*, *3*, 107–112.

Schaps, E. (1972). Cost, dependency, and helping. *Journal of Personality and Social Psychology*, *21*, 74–78.

Scheffler, I. (1963). *The anatomy of inquiry: Philosophical studies in the theory of science.* New York: Alfred A. Knopf.

Scherer, K.R., Rosenthal, R., & Koivumaku, J. (1972). Mediating interpersonal expectancies via vocal cues: Differential speech intensity as a means of social influence. *European Journal of Social Psychology*, *2*, 163–176.

Schlaifer, R. (1980). The relay assembly test room: An alternative statistical interpretation. *American Sociological Review*, *45*, 995–1005.

Schlenker, B.R. (1974). Social psychology as a science. *Journal of Personality and Social Psychology*, *29*, 1–15.

Schlenker, B.R. (1976). Social psychology and science: Another look. *Personality and Social Psychology Bulletin*, *2*, 384–390.

Schlenker, B.R. (1977). On the ethogenic approach: Etiquette and revolution. In L. Berkowitz (Ed.), *Advances in experimental social psychology* (Vol. 10, pp. 315–330). Orlando, FL: Academic Press.

Schlenker, B.R., Forsyth, D.R., Leary, M.R., & Miller, R.S. (1980). Self-presentational analysis of the effects of incentives on attitude change following counterattitudinal behavior. *Journal of Personality and Social Psychology, 39,* 553–577.

Schmidt, F.L., & Hunter, J.E. (1981). Employment testing: Old theories and new research findings. *American Psychologist, 36,* 1128–1137.

Schulman, A.D., & Berman, H.J. (1975). Role expectations about subjects and experimenters in psychological research. *Journal of Personality and Social Psychology, 32,* 368–380.

Schultz, D.P. (1969). The human subject in psychological research. *Psychological Bulletin, 72,* 214–228.

Schwitzgebel, R.K. (1969). Ethical problems in research with offenders. *American Journal of Orthopsychiatry, 38,* 738–748.

Scott, R.A., & Shore, A.R. (1979). *Why sociology does not apply.* New York: Elsevier.

Scriven, M. (1959). Explanations and prediction in evolutionary theory. *Science, 130,* 477–482.

Scriven, M. (1962). Explanations, predictions and laws. In H. Feigl & G. Maxwell (Eds.), *Minnesota studies in the philosophy of science* (Vol. 3, pp. 170–230). Minneapolis, MN: University of Minnesota Press.

Scriven, M. (1964). Views of human nature. In T.W. Wann (Ed.), *Behaviorism and phenomenology* (pp. 160–180). Chicago: University of Chicago Press.

Scriven, M. (1974). The exact role of value judgments in science. In K. Scheffner & R. Cohen (Eds.), *Proceedings of the 1972 biennial meetings of the Philosophy of Science Association* (pp. 229–235). Boston, MA: Reidel.

Sebeok, T.A. (1979). *The sign and its masters.* Austin: University of Texas Press.

Sebeok, T.A., & Rosenthal, R. (Eds.). (1981). The Clever Hans phenomenon: Communication with horses, whales, apes, and people. *Annals of the New York Academy of Sciences, 234,* 145–166.

Secord, P.F. (1976). Transhistorical and transcultural theory. *Personality and Social Psychology Bulletin, 2,* 418–420.

Seeman, J. (1969). Deception in psychological research. *American Psychologist, 24,* 1025–1028.

Shepard, J.M., (1971). On Alex Carey's radical criticism of the Hawthorne studies. *Academy of Management Journal, 14,* 23–32.

Sherif, M. (1937). An experimental approach to the study of attitudes. *Sociometry, 1,* 90–98.

Sherif, M., Harvey, O.J., White, B.J., Hood, W.R., & Sherif, C.W. (1961). *Intergroup cooperation and competition: The Robber's Cave experiment.* Norman, OK: University Book Exchange.

Shulman, A.D., & Berman, A.J. (1975). Expectations about subjects and experimenters in psychological research. *Journal of Personality and Social Psychology, 32,* 368–380.

Shulman, A.D., & Silverman, I. (1972). The experimenter as a source of variation in psychological research: Modeling and sex effects. *Journal of Personality and Social Psychology, 21,* 219–227.

Shuptrine, F.K. (1975). On the validity of using students as subjects in consumer behavior investigations. *Journal of Business, 48,* 383–390.

Sidis, B. (1906). Are there hypnotic hallucinations? *Psychological Review, 13,* 239–257.

Siebere, J. (1979, January). Working on ethics. *APA Monitor,* p. 3.

Sieber, J. (1983). Deception in social research III: The nature and limits of debriefing.

IRB: A Review of Human Subjects Research, 5(3), 1–4.

Siegel, A.E., & Siegel, S. (1957). Reference groups, membership groups, and attitude change. *Journal of Abnormal and Social Psychology*, 55, 360–364.

Sigall, H., Aronson, E., & Van Hoose, T. (1970). The cooperative subject: Myth or reality? *Journal of Experimental Social Psychology*, 6, 1–10.

Silverman, I. (1971). Crisis in social psychology: The relevance of relevance. *American Psychologist*, 22, 583–584.

Silverman, I. (1977). Why social psychology fails. *Canadian Psychological Review*, 18, 16–25.

Silverman, I., Shulman, A.D., & Wiesenthal, D.L. (1970). Effects of deceiving and debriefing psychological subjects on performance in later experiments. *Journal of Personality and Social Psychology*, 14, 203–212.

Singer, E. (1978a). Informed consent: Consequences for response rate and response quality in social surveys. *American Sociological Review*, 43, 144–162.

Singer, E. (1978b). The effects of informed consent procedures on respondents' reactions to surveys. *Journal of Consumer Research*, 5, 49–57.

Singer, E. (1983). Informed consent procedures in surveys: Some reasons for minimal effects on response. In R.F. Boruch & J.S. Cecil (Eds.), *Solutions to ethical and legal problems in social research* (pp. 183–211). Orlando, FL: Academic Press.

Sirgy, M.J. (1983). *Social cognition and consumer behavior*. New York: Praeger.

Smart, R. (1966). Subject selection bias in psychological research. *Canadian Psychologist*, 7, 115–121.

Smith, C.P. (1981). How (un)acceptable is research involving deception? *IRB: A Review of Human Subjects Research*, 3, 1–4

Smith, C.P. (1983). Ethical issues: Research on deception, informed consent, and debriefing. In L. Wheeler & P. Shaver (Eds.), *Review of personality and social psychology* (Vol. 4, pp. 297–328). Beverly Hills, CA: Sage.

Smith, C.P., & Bernard, S.P. (1982). Why are human subjects less concerned about ethically problematic research than human subjects committees? *Journal of Applied Social Psychology*, 12, 209–221.

Smith, C.P., Bernard, S., & Malinowski, C. (1980). Ethical issues in research: How harmful is deception? [Abstract] *Resources in Education*, 15, 42.

Smith, E.R., & Miller, F.D. (1978). Limits on perception of cognitive processes: A reply to Nisbett and Wilson. *Psychological Review*, 85, 355–362.

Smith, M.B. (1972). Is experimental social psychology advancing? *Journal of Experimental Social Psychology*, 8, 86–96.

Smith, M.B. (1976a). Social psychology, science and history: So what? *Personality and Social Psychology Bulletin*, 2, 438–444.

Smith, M.B. (1976b). Some perspectives on ethical/political issues in social science research. *Personality and Social Psychology Bulletin*, 2, 445–453.

Smith, M.L. (1980). Publication bias and meta-analysis. *Evaluation in Education*, 4, 22–24.

Smith, M.L., & Glass, G.V. (1977). Meta-analysis of psychotherapy outcome studies. *American Psychologist*, 32, 752–760.

Smith, M.L., & Glass G.V. (1979). *Class size and its relationship to attitude and instruction*. San Francisco: Far West Laboratory.

Smith, S.S., & Richardson, D. (1983). Amelioration of deception and harm in psychological research: The important role of debriefing. *Journal of Personality and Social Psychology*, 44, 1075–1082.

Snedecor, G.W., & Cochran, W.G. (1980). *Statistical methods* (7th ed.). Ames, IA: Iowa State University Press.

Snow, C.P. (1962). The moral un-neutrality of science. In P. Obler & H. Estrin (Eds.), *The new scientist: Essays on methods and values of modern science* (pp. 199–212). Garden City, NY: Doubleday.

Snow, R.E. (1974). Representative and quasi-representative designs for research on teaching. *Review of Educational Research*, *44*, 265–291.

Snyder, M., & Swann, W.B., Jr. (1976). When actions reflect attitudes: The politics of impression management. *Journal of Personality and Social Psychology*, *34*, 1034–1042.

Snyder, M., Tanke, E.D., & Berscheid, E. (1977). Social perception and interpersonal behavior: On the self-fulfilling nature of social stereotypes. *Journal of Personality and Social Psychology*, *35*, 656–666.

Sobal, J. (1984). The content of survey introductions and the provision of informed consent. *Public Opinion Quarterly*, *48*, 788–793.

Soble, A. (1978, October). Deception in social science research: Is informed consent possible? *Hastings Center Report*, *8*, 40–46.

Sommer, R. (1969). *Personal space*. Englewood Cliffs, NJ: Prentice-Hall.

Sonnefeld, J. (1982). Clarifying critical confusion in the Hawthorne hysteria. *American Psychologist*, *37*, 1397–1399.

Speilberger, C.D., Gorsuch, R.L., & Lushene, R.E. (1970). *STAI Manual*. Palo Alto, CA: Consulting Psychologists Press.

Spencer, C.D. (1978). Two types of role playing: Threats to internal and external validity. *American Psychologist*, *33*, 265–268.

Spinner, B., Adair, J., & Barnes, G.E. (1977). A reexamination of the faithful subject role. *Journal of Experimental Social Psychology*, *13*, 543–551.

Spohn, H.E., & Fitzpatrick, T. (1980). Informed consent and bias in samples of schizophrenic subjects at risk for drug withdrawal. *Journal of Abnormal Psychology*, *89*, 79–92.

Staats, A.W. (1969). Experimental demand characteristics and the classical conditioning of attitudes. *Journal of Personality and Social Psychology*, *11*, 187–192.

Staats, A.W., & Staats, C.K. (1958). Attitudes established by classical conditioning. *Journal of Abnormal and Social Psychology*, *57*, 37–40.

Staats, C.K., & Staats, A.W. (1957). Meaning established by classical conditioning. *Journal of Experimental Psychology*, *54*, 74–80.

Stagner, R. (1982). The importance of historical context. *American Psychologist*, *37*, 856.

Stanley, B., Sieber, J.E. & Melton, G.E. (1987). Empirical studies of ethical issues in research: A research agenda. *American Psychologist*, *42*, 735–741.

Stanton, F., & Baker, K.H. (1942). Interviewer-bias and the recall of incompletely learned materials. *Sociometry*, *5*, 123–134.

Staw, B.M. (1974). Attitudinal and behavioral consequences of changing a major organizational reward: A natural field experiment. *Journal of Personality and Social Psychology*, *29*, 742–751.

Steinmetz, H.C. (1932). Measuring ability to fake occupational interest. *Journal of Applied Psychology*, *16*, 123–130.

Stock, W.A., Okun, M., Haring, M., & Witter, R. (1982, May). *Health and subjective well-being: A meta-analysis*. Paper presented at the annual meeting of the American Gerontological Association, Boston.

Stouffer, S.A. (1949). *Studies in social psychology in World War II*. Princeton, NJ: Princeton University Press.

Straw, R.B. (1983). Deinstitutionalization in mental health: A meta-analysis. In R.J. Light (Ed.), *Evaluation studies review annual* (Vol. 8, pp. 56–78). Beverly Hills, CA: Sage.

Stricker, L.J. (1967). The true deceiver. *Psychological Bulletin*, *68*, 13–20.

Stricker, L.J., Messick, S., & Jackson, D.N. (1967). Suspicion of deception: Implications for conformity research. *Journal of Personality and Social Psychology*, *5*, 379–389.

Strube, M.J., Gardner, W., & Hartman, D.P. (1985). Limitations, liabilities and obstacles in reviews of the literature: The current status of meta-analysis. *Clinical Psychology, 5*, 63–78.

Strube, M.J., & Miller, R.H. (1986). Comparison of power rates for combined probability procedures: A simulation study. *Psychological Bulletin, 99*, 407–415.

Stufflebaum, D.L. (1969). Evaluation as enlightenment for decision making. In *Improving educational assessment and an inventory of effective behavior*. Washington, DC: Association for Supervision and Curriculum Development, National Educational Association.

Sullivan, D.S., & Deiker, T.A. (1973). Subject–experimenter perceptions of ethical issues in human research. *American Psychologist, 28*, 587–591.

Suls, J.M., & Rosnow, R.L. (1981). The delicate balance between ethics and artifacts in behavioral research. In A.J. Kimmel (Ed.), *New directions for methodology of social and behavioral science: Ethics of human subject research* (No. 10, pp. 55–68). San Francisco: Jossey-Bass.

Sutcliffe, J.P. (1972). On the role of "instructions to the subject" in psychological experiments. *American Psychologist, 27*, 755–758.

Tanke, E.D., & Tanke, T.J. (1982). Regulation and education: The role of institutional review boards in social science research. In J.E. Sieber (Ed.), *The ethics of social research: Fieldwork, regulation, and publication* (pp. 131–149). New York: Springer-Verlag.

Tedeschi, J.T., & Rosenfeld, P. (1981). The experimental research controversy at SUNYA: A case study. In A.J. Kimmel (Ed.), *New directions for methodology of social and behavioral science: Ethics of human subject research* (No. 10, pp. 5–18). San Francisco: Jossey-Bass.

Tedeschi, J.T., Schlenker, B.R., & Bonoma, T.V. (1971). Cognitive dissonance: Private ratiocination or public spectacle. *American Psychologist, 26*, 685–695.

Tesch, F.E. (1977). Debriefing research participants: Though this be method there is madness to it. *Journal of Personality and Social Psychology, 35*, 217–224.

Thorndike, R.L. (1968). Review of Pygmalion in the classroom. *American Educational Research Journal, 5*, 708–711.

Thorngate, W. (1975). Process invaiance: Another red herring. *Personality and Social Psychology Bulletin, 1*, 485–487.

Thorngate, W. (1976). "In general" vs. "It depends": Some comments on the Gergen-Schlenker debate. *Personality and Social Psychology Bulletin, 2*, 403–409.

Titchener, E.B. (1895). Simple reactions. *Minds, 4*, 74–81.

Toch, H. (1982). Sed qui dicit, non qui negat? *American Psychologist, 37*, 855.

Triplett, N. (1897–1898). The dynamogenic factors in pacemaking and competition. *American Journal of Psychology, 9*, 507–533.

Trower, P., Bryant, B., & Argyle, M. (1977). *Social skills and mental health*. London: Methuen.

Tunnell, G.B. (1977). Three dimensions of naturalness: An expanded definition of field research. *Psychological Bulletin, 84*, 426–437.

Turner, C.W., & Simons, L.S. (1974). Effects of subject sophistication and evaluation apprehension on aggressive responses to weapons. *Journal of Personality and Social Psychology, 30*, 341–348.

United States Public Health Service. (1969). *Protection of the individual as a research subject*. Washington, DC: U.S. Government Printing Office.

Valins, S. (1966). Cognitive effects of false heart-rate feedback. *Journal of Personality and Social Psychology, 4*, 400–408.

Veatch, R.M. (1978). Three theories of informed consent: Philosophical foundations and policy implications. Appendix to *The Belmont Report: Ethical principles and guidelines for the protection of human subjects* (Vol. 2) (DHEW Publication No. OS 78-0014). Washington, DC: U.S. Government Printing Office.

Vernon, P.E. (1934). The attitude of the subject in personality testing. *Journal of*

Applied Psychology, *18*, 165–177.

Vinacke, W.E. (1954). Deceiving experimental subjects. *American Psychologist*, *9*, 155.

Vogel, W. (1982). A Judeo-Christian rejoinder to Bramel and Friend's Marxist critique of the capitalist "Hawthorne effect." *American Psychologist*, *37*, 859–860.

Wachtel, P.L. (1980). Investigation and its discontents: Some constraints on progress in psychological research. *American Psychologist*, *35*, 399–408.

Walsh, W.B., & Stillman, S.M. (1974). Disclosure of deception by debriefed subjects. *Journal of Consulting Psychology*, *21*, 315–319.

Walster, E. (1965). The effects of self-esteem on romantic liking. *Journal of Experimental Social Psychology*, *1*, 184–197.

Walster, E., Berscheid, E., Abrahams, D., & Aronson, V. (1967). Effectiveness of debriefing following deception experiments. *Journal of Personality and Social Psychology*, *6*, 371–380.

Wanous, J.P., Sullivan, S.E., & Malinak, J. (1987). *The role of judgment calls in meta-analysis*. Working Paper no. 87–76, College of Business, Ohio State University, Columbus.

Warwick, D. (1975, October). Deceptive research: Social scientists ought to stop lying. *Psychology Today*, pp. 38–40.

Wax, M.L. (1982). Research reciprocity rather than informed consent in fieldwork. In J.E. Sieber (Ed.), *The ethics of social research: Fieldwork, regulation, and publication* (pp. 33–48). New York: Springer-Verlag.

Webb, E.J., Campbell, D., Schwartz, R., & Sechrest, L. (1966). *Unobtrusive measures: Nonreactive research in the social sciences*. Chicago: Rand McNally.

Webb, E.J., Campbell, D.T., Schwartz, R.D., Sechrest, L., & Grove, J.B. (1981). *Nonreactive measures in the social sciences* (2nd ed.). Dallas: Houghton Mifflin.

Weber, S.J., & Cook, T.D. (1972). Subject effects in laboratory research: An examination of subject roles, demand characteristics, and valid inference. *Psychological Bulletin*, *77*, 273–295.

Weber, S.J., & Riddell, J.C. (1975). An examination of postexperimental questionnaires used to assess awareness. *Representational Research in Social Psychology*, *6*, 1–6.

Webster, M., Jr., & Kervin, J.B. (1971). Artificiality in experimental sociology. *Canadian Review of Sociology and Anthropology*, *8*, 263–272.

Weick, K.E. (1965). Laboratory experiments with organizations. In J.G. March (Ed.), *Handbook of organizations* (pp. 194–260). Chicago: Rand McNally.

Weick, K.E. (1985). Systematic observational methods. In G. Lindzey & E. Aronson (Eds.), *Handbook of social psychology* (3rd ed., Vol. 1, pp. 567–634). New York: Random House.

Weinberger, C.W. (1975, 13 March). Protection of human subjects: Technical amendments. *Federal Register*, *40*(50), 11854–11858.

Weithorn, L.A., & Campbell, S.B. (1982). The competency of children and adolescents to make informed treatment decisions. *Child Development*, *53*, 1589–1598.

West, S.G., Gunn, S.P., & Chernicky, P. (1975). Ubiquitous Watergate: An attributional analysis. *Journal of Personality and Social Psychology*, *32*, 55–65.

Westfall, R.S. (1973). Newton and the fudge factor. *Science*, *179*, 751–758.

Wetzel, C.G. (1977). Manipulation checks: A reply to Kidd. *Representative Research in Social Psychology*, *8*, 88–93.

White, K.R. (1982). The relation between socioeconomic status and academic achievement. *Psychological Bulletin*, *91*, 461–481.

White, P. (1980). Limitations on verbal reports of internal events: A refutation of Nisbett and Wilson and of Bem. *Psychological Review*, *87*, 105–112.

Whitehead, T.N. (1938). *The industrial worker* (Vols. 1 & 2). Cambridge, MA: Harvard University Press.

Willems, E.P., & Howard, G.S. (1980). The external validity of papers on external validity. *American Psychologist, 35*, 387–388.

Willems, E.P., & Raush, H.L. (Eds.) (1969). *Naturalistic viewpoints in psychological research*. New York: Holt, Rinehart & Winston.

Willis, R.H., & Willis, Y.A. (1970). Role playing versus deception: An experimental comparison. *Journal of Personality and Social Psychology, 16*, 472–477.

Wilson, E.B. (1952). *An introduction to scientific research*. New York: McGraw-Hill.

Wilson, D.W., & Donnerstein, E. (1976). Legal and ethical aspects of nonreactive social psychological research: An excursion into the public mind. *American Psychologist, 31*, 765–773.

Wilson, T.D., & Nisbett, R.E. (1978). The accuracy of verbal reports about the effects of stimuli on evaluations and behavior. *Social Psychology, 41*, 118–131.

Winch, R.F., & Campbell, D.T. (1969). Proof? No! Evidence? Yes! The significance of tests of significance. *American Sociologist, 4*, 140–143.

Woodward, W. (1979). Informed consent of volunteers: A direct measurement of comprehension and retention of information. *Clinical Research, 27*, 248–258.

Word, C.O., Zanna, M.P., & Cooper, J. (1974). The nonverbal mediation of self-fulfilling prophecies in interracial interaction. *Journal of Experimental Social Psychology, 10*, 109–120.

Wortman, P.M. (1983). Evaluation research: A methodological perspective. *Annual Review of Psychology, 34*, 223–260.

Wortman, P.M., & Bryant, F.B. (1985). School desegregation and black achievement: An integrative review. *Social Methods and Research, 13*, 289–324.

Wortman, P.M., & Yeaton, W.H. (1983). Synthesis of results in controlled trials of coronary artery bypass graft surgery. In R.J. Light (Ed.), *Evaluation studies review annual* (Vol. 8, pp. 22–55). Beverly Hills, CA: Sage.

Wuebben, P.L. (1967). Honesty of subjects and birth order. *Journal of Personality and Social Psychology, 5*, 350–352.

Yin, R.K., & Yates, D. (1974). *Street-level governments: Assessing decentralization and urban services*. Santa Monica, CA: Rand Corporation.

Zajonc, R.B. (1980). Compresence. In P.B. Paulus (Ed.), *Psychology of group influence* (pp. 35–60). Hillsdale, NJ: Lawrence Erlbaum Associates.

Zelditch, M., Jr. (1968). Can you really study an army in the laboratory? In A. Etzioni (Ed.), *A sociological reader on complex organizations* (pp. 123–145). New York: Holt, Rinehart & Winston.

Zobel, E.J., & Lehman, R.S. (1969). Interaction of subject and experimenter expectancy effects in a tone length discrimination task. *Behavioral Science, 14*, 357–363.

Zuckerman, M. (1979). Attribution of success and failure revisited, or: The motivational bias is alive and well in attribution theory. *Journal of Personality, 47*, 245–287.

Author Index

Subject Index

Springer Series in Social Psychology

Attention and Self-Regulation: A Control-Theory Approach to Human Behavior
Charles S. Carver/Michael F. Scheier

Gender and Nonverbal Behavior
Clara Mayo/Nancy M. Henley (Editors)

Personality, Roles, and Social Behavior
William Ickes/Eric S. Knowles (Editors)

Toward Transformation in Social Knowledge
Kenneth J. Gergen

The Ethics of Social Research: Surveys and Experiments
Joan E. Sieber (Editor)

The Ethics of Social Research: Fieldwork, Regulation, and Publication
Joan E. Sieber (Editor)

Anger and Aggression: An Essay of Emotion
James R. Averill

The Social Psychology of Creativity
Teresa M. Amabile

Sports Violence
Jeffrey H. Goldstein (Editor)

Nonverbal Behavior: A Functional Perspective
Miles L. Patterson

Basic Group Processes
Paul B. Paulus (Editor)

Attitudinal Judgment
J. Richard Eiser (Editor)

Social Psychology of Aggression: From Individual Behavior to Social Interaction
Amélie Mummendey (Editor)

Directions in Soviet Social Psychology
Lloyd H. Strickland (Editor)

Sociophysiology
William M. Waid (Editor)

Compatible and Incompatible Relationships
William Ickes (Editor)

Facet Theory: Approaches to Social Research
David Canter (Editor)

Action Control: From Cognition to Behavior
Julius Kuhl/Jürgen Beckmann (Editors)

Springer Series in Social Psychology